Advance praise for
MC5: An Oral Biography of Rock's Most Revolutionary Band

"Our band moved to Detroit because we saw that MC5 and the Stooges were part of an incredible rock & roll scene with plenty of places to play and a community of real rock & roll fans, radio, and press. There was nothing like it anywhere else in the USA. MC5 would just explode onto the stage, amps and energy dialed up way beyond 11. A tight rhythm section supporting the two-guitar attack of Wayne Kramer and Fred Smith and then frontman Rob Tyner, who was a force of nature onstage. MC5 were synonymous with Detroit rock, and always will be. And this book is a true testimonial to that." —Alice Cooper

"The MC5 were a revelation when I first saw them in 1969, kicking out jams with a commitment I hadn't seen from any of the other peace-and-love bands of the day. The future of rock personified! Fuck, they were great, and so is *MC5: An Oral Biography of Rock's Most Revolutionary Band*." —Billy Idol

"With *MC5*, Tolinski, Uhelszki, and from his writing desk in the great beyond, Edmonds, have created the definitive work on a band that more than a half-century after its dissolution is still undeniably—and perhaps terrifyingly—relevant."
—Tom Beaujour, *New York Times* bestselling author of *Nöthin' But a Good Time*

"An unruly jumble of Detroit proto-punk, radical politics, censorship, hard drugs, and music business machinations, the sadly short-lived saga of the MC5 was among the wildest and most intense in rock history. *MC5: An Oral Biography of Rock's Most Revolutionary Band* captures their careening story with a candor and blunt force worthy of the band's legacy."
—David Browne, *Rolling Stone*, author of *Fire and Rain* and *Crosby, Stills, Nash & Young*

"A loving but unflinching account of how the magnificent beast that was the MC5 was laid low by its two conflicting imperatives: to be the greatest rock band in the world, and to righteously serve and further a counterculture revolution against the American Ruse. Like the Clash almost a decade later, they fought the biz and the biz won."
—Charles Shaar Murray, author of *Crosstown Traffic: Jimi Hendrix and Post-War Pop*, Ralph Gleason Music Book Award winner

"The story of the MC5 has been told before, but never like this: an almost real-time oral history of the legendary group's history as told by the band members themselves, as well as crucial associates like manager John Sinclair, Detroit artist Gary Grimshaw, and their far-too-often-overlooked girlfriends and wives. Culled from dozens of hours of interviews conducted by writer Ben Edmonds, who was there at the time, and edited by Brad Tolinski and another who was there, Jaan Uhelzski, the book is a fascinating and endlessly revealing firsthand account filled with previously unpublished words, mostly from people who are no longer with us. *MC5: An Oral Biography of Rock's Most Revolutionary Band* is the final, definitive word on one of the twentieth century's greatest, most influential, and perennially under-recognized groups. It brings to life the words of singer Rob Tyner, written just before his death in the liner notes to a 1991 reissue of *Kick Out the Jams*, their debut album: 'People of tomorrow: From the deep past, we salute you! Thunder in the night forever!'"
—Jem Aswad, executive music editor, *Variety*

"I'm afraid the world has no idea and will never know the full musical authority, integrity, and force of nature that the mighty MC5 boys were at their peak 67–69! No recording ever came anywhere close to accurately representing their sheer musical power. Certainly, they deserve adulation for their critical thinking, revolutionary defiant stands, and posturing, but as a musical entity they ranked right up there with Little Richard, James Brown, and all the greatest soul music masters of all time. Wayne, Fred, Michael, Dennis, and Rob put their heart and soul into every song, every

gig, every lick, every night unleashing a ferocity of tightness and musicality second to none. Sharing the stage with them with my Amboy Dukes and witnessing hundreds of their concerts, we all stood in awe of their unique and dangerous energy. Their performances pummeled the senses with outrageous, sophisticated yet raw, and primal virtuosity that forced every other band to practice harder and dig deeper. Those motherfuckers were something to behold!"
—Ted Nugent

"The MC5 were the Rosetta Stone of revolutionary rock and roll, bringing together the freest of jazz with the highest energy impact of the music's insurrectionary power to empower and enflame. Their political idealism matched their moment in time, when all seemed possible amid intense confrontation. If their tale went aground too soon, their influence and dedication will ever provide a beacon of liberation through the power of rama-lama-fa-fa-fa. This intimate and detailed eyewitness and ear-witness account, from those who were memorably there, is the closest we will get to what it was like to feel the wind from the amps as the music poured off the stage and into one's spiritual awakening."
—Lenny Kaye, guitarist, author of *Lightning Striking: Ten Transformative Moments in Rock and Roll*

"There are two epic stories at work here—the glorious dysfunction of the MC5 and the book itself, a grand and ambitious project thankfully rescued from incompletion. Brad Tolinski and Jaan Uhelszki have kicked out the proverbial jams in bringing what the late Ben Edmonds started to life, driven by their own Motor City roots and their years of writing at the upper echelon of music journalism to confront and make sense of the complexities and contradictions that make the MC5's tale so compelling—and entertaining. The words of the group members and those around them leave us mourning for what might have been, but more often celebrating, and perhaps even testifying about, what was achieved."
—Gary Graff, veteran Detroit music journalist, cofounder of the Detroit Music Awards

"Mostly overlooked and underappreciated, the MC5 certainly knew how to bring the ruckus. They were one of the best live acts to perform on this planet and their inspiring but often calamitous career has always cried out to be detailed in book form. Now—with this fine tome—that story is available for all to read."
—Nick Kent, author of *The Dark Stuff* and *Apathy for the Devil*

"*MC5: An Oral Biography of Rock's Most Revolutionary Band* is the book that Brothers Wayne/Rob/Mike/Sonic/Machine Gun have deserved forever. Only fellow Detroit-born-and-bred-ites such as Brad Tolinski, Jaan Uhelzski, and the late Ben Edmonds could have crafted this volume, out of Edmonds's extensive archive of interviews with all the principals. It's the closest we will get to an MC5 autobiography, with Rob Tyner's voice taking center stage, as he did all those late '60s nights at the Grande Ballroom. Now, as then, Tyner is the spiritual heart of the Five, a fount of calm, sweet wisdom. Be there as these guys invent punk, refine heavy rock, and embody Lester Bangs's vision of a band combining the Yardbirds' sonic science with free jazz's wild ambition. Thrill, as they forevermore demonstrate that any rock 'n' roll which doesn't deal with gritty, real-life issues is just so much pathetic, pandering nonsense. Children of the future, we bring you a testimonial—THE MC5!!!"
—Tim Stegall, editor at The Tim "Napalm" Stegall Substack and author of *Anarchy in the Studio: Punk Music 1970–1979, The Rise of Punk Rock*

MC5

Also by Brad Tolinski

Eruption: Conversations with Eddie Van Halen
(with Chris Gill)

Play It Loud: An Epic History of the Style, Sound, and Revolution of the Electric Guitar (with Alan di Perna)

Light and Shade: Conversations with Jimmy Page

Classic Hendrix: The Ultimate Hendrix Experience
(with Ross Halfin)

Also by Ben Edmonds

Marvin Gaye: What's Going On and the Last Days of the Motown Sound

Copyright © 2024 by Brad Tolinski, Jaan Uhelszki and Ben Edmonds
This edition copyright © 2024 Omnibus Press
(A Division of Wise Music Limited)

This edition published by arrangement with Hachette Books,
an imprint of Perseus Books, LLC, a subsidiary of Hachette Book Group, Inc.,
New York, New York, USA. All rights reserved.

Jacket photograph © Michael Ochs Archives/Getty Images
Jacket design by Terri Sirma and Ruth Keating
Jacket copyright © 2024 by Hachette Book Group, Inc.
Print book interior design by Amy Quinn

HB ISBN: 978-1-9158-4158-2

Brad Tolinski, Jaan Uhelszki and Ben Edmonds hereby asserts their right to
be identified as the authors of this work in accordance with Sections 77 to 78
of the Copyright, Designs and Patents Act 1988.

All rights reserved. No part of this book may be reproduced in any form or
by any electronic or mechanical means, including information storage or
retrieval systems, without permission in writing from the publisher, except
by a reviewer who may quote brief passages.

Every effort has been made to trace the copyright holders of the photographs
in this book but one or two were unreachable. We would be grateful if the
photographers concerned would contact us.

A catalogue record for this book is available from the British Library.

Printed in Poland

www.omnibuspress.com

For Ben Edmonds

CONTENTS

Introduction	**ix**
Preface by Rob Tyner	**xvii**
Cast of Characters	**xix**
CHAPTER I: Come Together	**1**
CHAPTER II: Ballroom Blitz	**35**
Part 2. Motor City Is Burning	**59**
Part 3. Rama Lama Fa Fa Fa!	**73**
CHAPTER III: Kick Out the Jams!	**111**
Part 2. Rise, Panther, Rise	**141**
CHAPTER IV: Motherfuckers!	**159**
CHAPTER V: Full-On Destructo	**187**
Part 2. Free John Now!	**223**
Part 3. End Times	**235**
Epilogue	**259**
Acknowledgments	**269**
Index	**271**

INTRODUCTION

"KICK OUT THE JAMS, MOTHERFUCKERS!!!"

What people know about the MC5 is contained in those five little words. The first four have become a permanent part of the culture. That fifth word can still get you in as much trouble as it did the MC5 back in 1968, but trouble was also what this band was known for. Although, through a modern lens, much of it was what we would now call "good trouble."

Managed by legendary '60s radical and hippie spokesperson John Sinclair, the MC5 preached the gospel of police reform and cannabis legalization fifty years before those topics became part of the mainstream conversation. And for their efforts, the rabble-rousing musical arm of the White Panther Party, the scourge of J. Edgar Hoover's FBI and other defenders of public decency, were often beaten with clubs, threatened at gunpoint, and tossed into jail.

Police raided MC5 shows, record stores were busted for selling their albums, and the group was unceremoniously dumped by its record company even as their record was storming up the charts—all of this transpiring while the Sex Pistols were still on training wheels.

What has been lost in this proto-punk notoriety is the MC5 itself—vocalist Robin Tyner, guitarists Wayne Kramer and Fred "Sonic" Smith, bassist Michael Davis, and drummer Dennis Thompson. Though they never quite got the hang of making records, turned loose on a stage the group could be among the most awesome and awe-inspiring noise machines rock 'n' roll has ever produced. The Five are worth remembering not because they were bad boys but because they were so *damn good*.

Becoming the house band at Detroit's Grande Ballroom—one of the first hippie music palaces outside San Francisco—gave them a personal laboratory in which to hone their skills. When the Ballroom began to bring in "name" acts from both coasts and England the following year, the MC5 were ready. This local band quickly acquired a reputation for blowing the headliners like Janis Joplin and Cream off the stage, such that some of these music hotshots specifically requested that the Five not open for them. Their mettle had been tempered on Motor City's intense Battle of the Bands circuit, but competition was only part of it. It had as much to do with the performer's basic responsibility to give their audience everything, to hold back nothing. Eventually they came up with a catchphrase that expressed this philosophy, and a song to go with it.

This made the MC5 hometown heroes. But only a few miles outside Detroit's city limits, the ambassadors of weirdness could get a very different reaction.

"We weren't just a rock-'n'-roll band that came in to play some songs," said guitarist Wayne Kramer. "We brought a whole new way of life with us. We were there to convince people to run away and join us in this wonderful, free alternative lifestyle! We were the first longhairs they'd seen in some of these little farm towns, and the hostility could get intense."

As the Five's visibility increased, so did law enforcement scrutiny. "We began to get hassled constantly," said Sinclair. "We'd show up at a job and the authorities would already be waiting, looking for any excuse to fuck with us. The promoters would be trying to tell us what we could and couldn't do—one even had it written into the contract that the band were not to move onstage, fearing that our salacious undulations would corrupt the young girls in the audience! Club owners regularly pulled the plug on us, saying we were too loud. Or they'd beat us out of our money and call in the cops to beat us up if we complained. These were the frustrations being felt by forward-thinking young people all over—with the government, with the Vietnam War, with a lack of self-determination—but magnified because we were in the public eye, and it started to piss the band off. Me, I'd been pissed off since the '50s!"

Sinclair's stated cultural agenda of "rock and roll, dope, and fucking in the streets" also gained attention, and police harassment became so unrelenting that the band and Sinclair were effectively driven out of Detroit, taking refuge thirty miles west in the slightly more tolerant college town of Ann Arbor.

Though still just a lowly "local" band, a journey in August 1968 to appear at the demonstrations coinciding with the Democratic National Convention would change all of that. It was there that the MC5 made national headlines after an impromptu concert turned into a full-scale police riot, and the group suddenly became the darlings of the growing hippie underground as "the only band with [the] balls to play Chicago!"

After blowing them away in the Windy City, the Five signed with Elektra Records and recorded their debut album live over two nights at the Grande Ballroom. It was an audacious move for a new rock band to make their first album a concert recording, but perhaps not as audacious as what came next. Born out of a desire to "create the illusion of something bigger and badder; that if you fucked with us, you were fucking with a whole organization." Sinclair, the band, and an alliance of leftist insurrectionists formed the White Panther Party, an anti-racist political collective created to support the Black Panthers, the revolutionary Black socialist movement.

And that was just the beginning of their adventure. What happened next is one of the wildest and most culturally relevant rock-'n'-roll stories ever told.

Intrigued? We certainly were.

The creation of *MC5: An Oral Biography of Rock's Most Revolutionary Band* is almost as intriguing as the content itself. Beginning in 1990, Ben Edmonds, the respected *CREEM* editor and *Rolling Stone* contributor, spent more than a decade interviewing the MC5 and their inner circle, many of whom are no longer with us. Unfortunately, Edmonds also died in 2016, succumbing to pancreatic cancer. However, as his health was failing, he asked us to organize his extensive notes and turn them into a definitive book on the band.

Little did we know, Ben was never a fan of the computer and had written out his interviews in longhand on literally hundreds of sheets of lined paper, which had been organized haphazardly into massive file cabinets. Over the next year, we went about the seemingly impossible task of organizing the intimidating jumble into a semi-linear story line. And then the genuine work began. We spent another year writing narrative bridges and filling noticeable gaps with new interviews.

What slowly emerged was this genuinely exciting, funny, and thought-provoking portrait of rock's most uncompromising band.

The MC5 dissolved in 1972, but the timing of this book could hardly feel more relevant. Their antiauthoritarian politics and raw punk rock are remarkably pertinent and speak to how far ahead of the sociological curve they were.

But this isn't the first time the MC5's urgent music has felt important or timely. Every decade since the band split, a new generation of musicians and music aficionados have discovered their albums and found reasons to call them their own.

Starting in the late 1970s, while their memory was still fresh, the first wave of punk rockers from New York were inspired by the band's wild insurgency. The Ramones, the Dictators, Blondie, and Patti Smith (who eventually married MC5 guitarist Fred Smith) would all claim affinity with the Five.

"The MC5 really believed they could change the world," poet/singer/composer Smith told *Rolling Stone*. "They didn't just say it. They were intoxicated with the feeling that they could stop the war in Vietnam, that they could stop prejudice. And their music reflected that."

Across the pond in London, they elicited an equally passionate response. "We wanted to be more like [the MC5], using our music as a loud voice of protest . . . punk rock, at the heart of it, should be protest music," Joe Strummer of the Clash told journalist Antonio D'Ambrosio.

Brian James, of the pioneering British punk-rock group the Damned, was also an acolyte. "They wiped me out," said James, who saw the band firsthand at one of their rare U.K. gigs. "Live, it seemed like Kramer and Smith were mowing down the audience with their guitars—these white guys beating the shit out of their guitars and ripping off Chuck Berry riffs at ten times the speed. I was impressed big-time."

Throughout the '80s, hard-rock icons Motörhead would also spread the word in the metal community. "I wanted our band to be sort of like the MC5, since that was the big hero band of most of the underground, and throw in elements of Little Richard and Hawkwind," said singer/bassist Lemmy Kilmister.

The band's influence continued to loom large over the next couple decades, serving as a template for some of the biggest groups of the grunge era. Rage Against the Machine, who saw themselves as the spiritual sons of the MC5, recorded a memorable cover of "Kick Out the Jams" in 2000, while Soundgarden's Kim Thayil called them his favorite band, and demonstrated it by joining Wayne Kramer on a fiftieth anniversary MC5 tour in 2018.

"The MC5 has influenced a number of genres," said Thayil. "There are obvious ones like acid rock and heavy metal and, later, punk rock, but I could draw a line from their song 'Shakin' Street' directly to Bruce Springsteen's work. There's a lot there."

Of course, Detroit's own White Stripes, who spearheaded a serious garage-rock revival in the 2000s, wore the band's influence on their sleeve by regularly performing covers of MC5 songs like "Looking at You," and playing them with the same intensity. To complete the circle, White Stripes drummer Meg White would eventually marry Patti and Fred Smith's son, Jackson.

Being ahead of your time, however, is not always the best thing for a rock-'n'-roll band, and the MC5's cultural impact was considerably larger than the dent they made on the *Billboard* charts. This might explain why they were consistently overlooked by the Rock & Roll Hall of Fame, considered the pinnacle of legitimacy in the industry.

Historically, the Rock Hall has been slow to embrace music that was influential but not commercially successful. The Stooges, another Detroit band, endured eight ballots and fifteen years before finally being inducted in 2010. Similarly, cult favorites Velvet Underground faced five ballots before gaining entry. Despite being eligible since 1992, the MC5 had to endure six rounds of voting before finally receiving their invitation to the Rock Hall's 39th induction ceremony in 2024.

Still, their long wait was somewhat puzzling given Jon Landau, one of the group's staunchest supporters, chaired the Hall of Fame's nominating committee for years. Landau—best known for his work with artists like Bruce Springsteen, Jackson Browne, and Shania Twain, and producing the MC5's second album, *Back in the USA*—expressed frustration at the group's prolonged wait for recognition.

"It all comes down to voting," he explained. "The MC5's importance was more apparent to some of us than to others; in some ways it's as simple as that. However, there was never a doubt in my mind that they belonged."

The 2024 induction announcement was bittersweet, as none of the band members lived to attend the actual ceremony. The news came shortly after guitarist Kramer's passing, followed closely by manager Sinclair's death. Drummer Thompson, recovering from a heart attack, learned of the honor, declaring "It's about fucking time," but passed away three weeks later. Tyner, Davis, and Smith had already died years prior.

But perhaps bittersweet is fitting. The MC5 were always at their best when they were underdogs—spitting in the face of authority and fighting to be heard in the face of tremendous odds. Battling the "establishment" was often the source of their energy and power, and perhaps a perfunctory pat on the back would only dull their legacy of righteous civil disobedience.

"We were never a 'hit' band, and we never made any money," said guitarist Kramer in recent years. "But our work stood the test of time and people still appreciate what we've done."

As the song goes: "Let me be who I am . . . and let me kick out the jams!" One thing is certain, the MC5 done kicked 'em out.

—Brad Tolinski & Jaan Uhelszki

PREFACE

When somebody comes to my house and wants to know about the MC5, it's my responsibility to provide some answers. I've always been aware that one day I was going to sit down and tell the story, but I'm not delusional. I know we weren't the Beatles. Our whole appeal was so far off-center, and our whole approach was so oblique, that the best we could ask for was to go down in history as colorful figures that defied traditional rock-'n'-roll conventions.

The people that influenced me most ended up in insane asylums. I loved Van Gogh and Artaud, but how's Van Gogh doing lately? We wanted to act as an inspiration to a whole new generation of rebels and fight against repression, even though it's a tough and disgusting road. You're given this time and this life, and if people try and restrict you, you gotta fight; otherwise, how are you gonna go down in history? As somebody who just went along with the mob? That wasn't going to happen to the MC5.

—Rob Tyner, MC5 vocalist

CAST OF CHARACTERS
(IN ORDER OF APPEARANCE)

ROB TYNER— MC5 vocalist
WAYNE KRAMER— MC5 guitarist
RUSS GIBB— Detroit mover and shaker and owner of the Grande Ballroom
GARY GRIMSHAW— psychedelic poster artist and early band supporter
CHRIS HOVNANIAN— Wayne Kramer girlfriend
MICHAEL DAVIS— MC5 bassist
BECKY TYNER— Rob Tyner wife
DENNIS THOMPSON— MC5 drummer
JOHN SINCLAIR— MC5 manager and leader of Trans-Love Energies and the White Panther Party
RON ASHETON— Stooges guitarist
BOB RUDNICK— DJ and writer
DANNY FIELDS— Elektra Records A&R executive
LENI SINCLAIR— John Sinclair wife and MC5 photographer
GREIL MARCUS— music journalist
JON LANDAU— MC5 producer

CHAPTER I

COME TOGETHER

> Wayne called me one day and asked if I had any ideas for a band name. I had two. One was the Men; I liked that because it was very macho. The other one was the MC5.
>
> —Rob Tyner

As sure as the clear blue waters of Southern California shaped the sun-kissed harmonies of the Beach Boys, the belching smoke and gasoline smell of Detroit fueled the high-octane squall of the MC5.

Technically, the band members grew up just outside Detroit in the small town of Lincoln Park, but the boundaries between the two cities were practically meaningless. Like a small satellite filled with robotic drones tethered to a larger Death Star, Lincoln Park had the primary purpose of supplying Detroit's network of steel mills and automobile plants with an inexhaustible supply of hardworking men. It was often referred to as a "bedroom community," mostly because after a long day toiling on a Motor City assembly line, all you wanted to do was go home and sleep so you could wake up and grind through the next day.

"If you grew up in Lincoln Park, you had three options," said MC5 singer Rob Tyner. "You could go into the army, go to college, or, like most people, work at one of the many auto factories. But there *was* one other option, which only a few dared to do—play in a rock-'n'-roll band."

It was in Lincoln Park that Tyner met a handful of teens who dared to be different, viewing the draft, higher education, and factory work in much the same way—as a death sentence. And they were all looking for a reprieve.

The genesis of the MC5 can be traced to the early friendship between guitarists Wayne Kramer and Fred "Sonic" Smith, two musicians whose difference in temperament bordered on the comical.

Kramer (born Wayne Kambes on April 30, 1948) was a wiry motor-mouth, bursting with energy, ideas, and grand ambition. A natural entertainer, he devoured the spotlight, shaking and shimmying with his Fender Stratocaster while peeling off one hyperactive lick, riff, and lead after another.

Smith (born Fredrick Dewey Smith on September 14, 1948) was Kramer's stoic opposite. Even though he was born in his family's kitchen during an electrical storm, Smith's personality was almost excruciatingly low-wattage. When engaged in conversation, he often made people uncomfortable by offering only grunts for answers or perhaps an occasional shrug. While some thought he was brain-damaged, in reality Smith was a keen observer and overachiever, especially when it came to playing baseball (he was once scouted by the Detroit Tigers) or playing rhythm guitar, which were the only two things that really mattered to him.

"As soon as I could play guitar, I wanted to start a band," recalled Kramer. "I loved Booker T. & the MG's and wanted to model it on that instrumentation—guitar, bass, Hammond organ, and drums. I started asking around if there was anyone that played music. Someone told me there's this guy, Fred Smith, who played the bongos. We were both thirteen and lived in the same neighborhood, and we went to the same school, so I thought to myself, Sure, why not have a bongo player in the band? Luckily, Fred's dad, who played and sang country music, had a guitar in his house.

"I don't think Fred played very much at that point, because once we got to be friends, I remember going over to his house every afternoon and showing him guitar parts. I would show him how to play the chords while I played the melody. From then on, Fred and I played together in various bands. One of them had Fred's sister as our lead singer. She wore a prom gown and sang stuff like the 1960 ballad 'Angel Baby' by Rosie and the Originals.

"During that period, Fred would join other bands, or I'd join another for a minute, but we stayed partners throughout. We just naturally played well together. It was symbiotic, and we never competed. We felt competitive, but it was always *us* against *them*. The only time there was tension was when Fred thought I was playing too much. 'Be cool,' he'd say. 'Lighten up, man, quit showing off.'"

In 1963 the pair eventually settled into a semi-stable garage-rock unit called the Bounty Hunters, named after a famous dragster owned by the legendary Detroit driver Conrad "Connie" Kalitta. After enlisting two additional local musicians, Bob Gasper (drums) and Pat Burrows (bass), they started playing a teen club circuit that was just beginning to flourish, thanks to early promoters like local DJ and schoolteacher Russ Gibb and future Bob Seger manager Punch Andrews.

Their set list consisted of tough, rock-influenced R&B songs by artists like Bo Diddley, Chuck Berry, and the early Rolling Stones, which distinguished them from many of their peers who played whatever happened to be in the Top 40. They were as solid as a rock, but Kramer knew his band was still missing something—an "X factor" that would make them stand out from the dozens of other bands emerging from the garages of the Detroit metro area. And that something was sixteen-year-old Robin Tyner (born Robert Derminer on December 12, 1944), an aspiring illustrator with a startlingly original mind.

"After Fred Smith, I met Rob," said Kramer. "He had a younger brother named Ricky that I used to hang out with. Ricky said to me, 'My older brother's a beatnik. He listens to jazz. Stays up all night.' That sounded interesting to me, so I went over to his house and started telling Rob how cool being in a band was, and he shut me right down. 'Nah, rock music is jive. Now, let me tell you about *jazz* . . .' But the next time I saw him, man, he was drunk in a White Castle playing harmonica, and he was rock-'n'-rolled out. He was ready to be in a band."

Tyner's "weirdo" vibes greatly appealed to Kramer, and he started lobbying the older boy to join the Bounty Hunters. Tyner was intrigued but skeptical. He had never even remotely contemplated being in a band and suggested becoming the band's manager instead. But after it was clear that he had neither the drive nor the organizational abilities to manage a musical group, Tyner attempted to play bass instead, until he finally shifted to the role of lead singer.

He was an odd choice for a front man, and it was a decision the rest of the group would often wrestle with in future years. As a singer Tyner had excellent pitch and a great bluesy shout, but with his glasses, frizzy hair, and doughy physique, he was no teen idol. And his almost perverse delight in going against the grain annoyed just about everyone who came into the band's orbit.

"I felt that our responsibility was to stretch the boundaries of music, and that meant that our climb to success was gonna be weird," said Tyner. "I would always encourage the band's most outrageous ideas, and there were many times when they would push back, saying, 'We gotta stop this crazy shit and get our act together.' But that was not *my* main motivation. I loved crazy shit.

"There were many great examples of me going off the deep end. We'd get a well-paying gig at a fraternity party, and I'd wind up clearing the room by using the PA to create feedback. The band resented it, and they embarked on a seemingly lifelong effort to straighten my ass out.

"The band also had problems having me as their spokesman, because they really felt that I could lose control at any minute, which was precisely what I was very, very good at. My behavior wasn't always received with open arms; in fact, rarely was it taken in the spirit that it was given. They wanted to get rid of me many times, but they saw the value of my creative side and hedged their bets."

Ironically, as the psychedelic '60s began to unfurl, it was precisely Tyner's eccentricities and contrarian spirit that allowed the group to evolve from being the Bounty Hunters—a small-time cover band—into the MC5, a world-class unit that would compete artistically with the likes of Janis Joplin, Jimi Hendrix, and the Doors.

If Tyner gave the group an air of dangerous unpredictability, it was Kramer and Smith's unrelenting proto-punk guitar attack that provided the music with its brawny backbone.

British bands like the Rolling Stones, the Yardbirds, and the Who showed the duo how to construct compelling music out of a couple of amplified guitars and a rhythm section. But it was ultimately the influence of the driving funk and uncompromising performances of James Brown, combined with the exploratory spirit of avant-garde jazz musicians like John Coltrane and Sun Ra, that provided the inspiration that made the MC5 truly unique.

The synthesis of all these elements was no accident. Much of it had to do with the proximity of Detroit's Black population to Lincoln Park and the extraordinary diversity and quality of Michigan radio in the early 1960s.

It would be tempting to call the Motor City "a melting pot," but in the 1960s it would be more accurate to describe it as a hot mess of segregation and racist "redlining" laws—the discriminatory practice that systematically denied mortgages to residents based on their color or ethnicity.

The *real* reason the borders between Lincoln Park and Detroit were created was to keep Black people out of the largely white suburban town via dubious legal technicalities. But no matter how hard racist policies conspired to separate Blacks from whites, they couldn't prevent the airwaves from reaching the ears of teens of all colors. With the flick of a radio dial, you could hear all the latest R&B sounds coming out of Motown, Stax, and Chess; the wild jazz improvisations from labels like Impulse! and Atlantic; or the hottest pop songs, which at that time were dominated by British guitar bands. Parents called all of it "jungle music," but the kids called it heaven.

Gigantic Detroit Top 40 AM stations like CKLW out of Canada and WKNR played the music of the Beatles and Stevie Wonder with equal frequency, but just as important was WCHB, the nation's first Black-owned and -operated radio station, which played an exciting combination of R&B hits, jazz and gospel music, and also talk shows where you could hear bracingly honest perspectives on racism by Black hosts and guests.

The musicians in the MC5 were exposed to all of this, and it shaped their music and attitudes in profound ways that would later be expressed onstage and in their inclusionary politics.

"I realized there was a difference between white music and what the Black musicians were playing," said Kramer. "The Black music had more drive. That's how we wanted to play."

It would take a few years for the MC5 to achieve that goal, but it was after bassist Michael Davis and drummer Dennis "Machine Gun" Thompson joined the band, in 1964 and in 1965, respectively, that they came much closer.

"Once we found this great rhythm section, we started working on this concept of drive—the music had to have this forward power," said Kramer. "I think it came from that kind of adrenaline you have when you're sixteen or seventeen, when your hormones are pumping so fast that you're almost insane. There was this sound that gave us what we needed. We weren't getting it from what parents and teachers were telling us but from what we called 'high-energy music.' Our show was based on the general dynamics of a James Brown concert—we were going to start at ten and a half and go up from there. On a bad night we were going to be great, and on a good night we were going to be unbelievable."

Below, members of the MC5 and their associates recall these formative years.

ROB TYNER [MC5 vocalist] When Black families started moving into Detroit, my family was part of the Great White Flight to the suburbs. We moved to Lincoln Park, a town just south of the city, in 1954, when I was ten years old. But before we moved, I picked up a lot of Black influences I still carry with me today.

When I was in Detroit, I learned to play harmonica and to "hambone," which was a Black style of music that involves stomping as well as slapping and patting the arms, legs, chest, and cheeks to create a groove. It was sort of an early version of beatboxing. If you could do that, you were cool with the Black dudes who used to hang out on the corner. Every now and then, they'd stop and pick a white kid at random to hambone for a laugh. Little did they know I had spent hours practicing, practicing, and practicing, for just that moment to happen, and when it did, I blew their minds. Even at that early age I knew you had to rehearse.

The funny thing was, even though my family moved out of Detroit from a misguided fear of Black people, Lincoln Park was just as dangerous as Detroit. Maybe more so. There was a possibility of serious physical violence every day. Just by wearing your hair a little different, or just by looking at somebody the wrong way, you could receive a serious beatdown from white kids in the neighborhood.

Lincoln Park had the worst juvenile delinquency rate per capita in the entire United States, worse than the worst of New York, Newark, L.A., or Chicago, and there were kids working twenty-four hours a day to hang on to that title. They looked upon delinquency as being a badge of honor. My school was extremely turbulent and very violent, and we were at war with all the surrounding suburbs, like Allen Park and Wyandotte.

My dad installed windows, and my mother worked in small shops and factories. I guess we were typical, but I always felt very alienated. I'd do terrible in school because there was no challenge. I'd just sit and draw. I really liked girls a lot, but I was very clumsy around them. Then I got glasses, which was good in one way because I could finally see, but then that made you dorky because you wore glasses.

My aunt Joan was a rock-'n'-roller who looked like the Hollywood sex bomb Jayne Mansfield. She was talking to my dad one night, and I said something about liking [Big Band jazz musician] Woody Herman. She said, "Man, you are so square." So she started dragging me around to early rock-'n'-roll shows featuring people like Little Richard and Bill Haley. For a young boy, she was *very* exciting to be around!

Despite my aunt's best efforts, being cool was still an uphill battle for me. I had frizzy hair and glasses, and my dad had a pink-and-beige Rambler station wagon. You try and be cool with all that going against you—it's just not possible! For a long while I devoted myself 100 percent to drawing hot rods, reading sci-fi, mooning over girls, and being frustrated about being stuck on a bland death planet.

WAYNE KRAMER [MC5 guitarist] Before our family moved to Lincoln Park, I lived on Elmer Street on the west side of Detroit. A kid up the street had a snare drum, and that was my first real introduction to music. I thought, Man, that's great, you can beat that thing and everybody *has* to listen to you. I played drums for a while and joined the school band. At the same time, Elvis was hitting and he played guitar. I liked drums, but it became immediately apparent to me that guitar players got to stand in the front, wiggle around, and get all the attention.

Simultaneously, my mother was dating this guy from Clarksville, Tennessee, and he would come over with his guitar and play country songs and sing for my mother, who would visibly swoon. I could see that playing guitar worked!

Soon after, I got a six-string of my own and discovered Chuck Berry. He was a major influence for a while. Then the Ventures. In the beginning, that's all that was happening with the electric guitar. It was still undeveloped territory.

My mom ended up marrying the guy from Clarksville and we moved to Lincoln Park when I was twelve or thirteen, and it was *very* white. There were no people of color, and most of the whites were from the South and racist. But the suburbs were surprisingly violent. People got into fights all the time.

ROB TYNER In 1964 I had just begun listening to the Rolling Stones, and I thought, They're playing the harmonica. Jeez, I have one of those from when I was in Detroit. I had a kind of a flair for it. Even the Black kids in the old neighborhood would go, "Y'know, for a white kid you're pretty good." They were being a little condescending, but hey, any faint praise from those guys was solid gold as far as I was concerned. I was probably the only nine-year old white kid in Detroit who knew who John Lee Hooker was.

Overnight, the harmonica had become tremendously hot because of the Rolling Stones, and that was a major breakthrough for me. I'd just gotten their first album and had been listening to it a lot, and the idea of being in a band started kicking around in my head.

RUSS GIBB [DJ and concert promoter] In the early '60s I was a schoolteacher in Howell, Michigan, but on weekends I was a disc jockey doing a Top 40 show on a local radio station.

The school system didn't allow kids to have dances at school because they thought dancing was immoral, so the kids were all bummed out. They had to go out of town just to boogie or have their own parties.

Around that time, record companies started sending groups on the road to promote their albums by talking to disc jockeys or playing a couple of their songs at local record shops. For example, I remember going around with Bob Maxwell, who was one of the biggest radio personalities in Howell, Michigan, and Stevie Wonder, who played "Fingertips" at a couple places, including a Ukrainian church in Detroit.

People were just thrilled because they could hear the record and actually see the star. Television was still in its infancy, so it was rare to see rock music on any of the channels.

One day I said to Bob, "What if we just rented a space, created our own event, and charged money?" So, we rented a VFW hall up there, put on a dance, and made good money. I made more money in those four hours than I did in two weeks of teaching.

In those days, teachers' salaries were something like $4,200 a year, and you had to drive the school bus when the driver was ill. If you wanted a drink, it was in our contract that you had to go thirty-six miles out of town, and you had to show up in town for at least two church services a month. It was a very, very strict society. All of those restrictions made me nervous that I'd lose my job because I put on dances. But I wanted the money, so we started to do them in a bunch of different places out of the county.

ROB TYNER Teen clubs just started sprouting up all over the place. It gave kids a place to dance and listen to music. Kids were really dancing back then—it was a big social thing. There was this little franchise in suburbs like Allen Park and Warren called the Chatterbox, which booked bands and DJs and served sodas that looked like phony mixed drinks. Now that I look at it, it was probably a way of getting kids into the habit.

RUSS GIBB There was a very popular DJ, Gary Stevens, who knew what I was doing, and he approached me with an idea. "Instead of dragging everything all over hell, why don't we see if we can rent a hall and keep it in one place?" So we found a big VFW hall out in the sticks and started a club called the Pink Pussycat Club. Stevens stole the name from a movie house in L.A., which I later found out was a porno joint! Who knew any better? We were from Detroit. Every week he would have the record guys bring in an act. You name 'em, they were all out there. We particularly took advantage of the Motown groups. You could always get a Motown group to come out.

Gary and I put on shows every week and, frankly, we were making good bread. However, it wasn't all smooth sailing. Some parents had real issues with what we were doing. Kids were beginning to listen to this music that their moms and dads thought was African—animal music—and the fear was that their teenagers were going to go to hell, literally. Parents would take records away. It was like if they found pot or cocaine in the kid's room these days. Back then, if they found an R&B record, they'd go crazy. Parents would go to the school counselors and say, "Oh my God, I found this record. What should I do?"

Fashion was changing too. Kids started wearing cleats on their shoes, so they would click, and wear Levi's and leather jackets. Every girl had tight, pegged skirts that would hobble them when they walked.

ROB TYNER At the same time, hot-rod culture was going strong. The younger people who worked in the car factories would get hooked in their job, because they'd want money to buy auto parts so they could build serious hot rods. That'd be their whole life—racing around in their car. Committing to a car meant payments, which meant they'd stay in the factory.

GARY GRIMSHAW [poster artist] The first graphic images that left an imprint were probably paint jobs on custom cars by guys like Big Daddy Roth and, later, Stanley Mouse. Mouse was a Detroit guy who later became famous for designing posters for San Francisco bands like the Grateful Dead and Journey. I never saw him work except one time at the Detroit Dragway when I was kid. I watched him draw for a few hours, which I thought was more fun than watching the races.

Art ran in my family. My father was a draftsman and engineer, so his tools were always around at home: drawing boards, French curves, and rulers. My uncle was the printer who produced all the Grande Ballroom posters at Crown Press in Dearborn, and his wife was an illustrator. My grandfather was a window dresser for stores all through the Great Depression in the 1930s, and later he worked at General Motors as a stylist.

I'd hang around with Rob Tyner, and we'd build model cars and draw pictures in the basement of his house. We were both big fans of Millar, a cartoonist for *Hot Rod* magazine who contributed illustrations to the technical column. Rob was more diverse than I was. He was the cartoonist for our high school paper, the *Rail Splitter*, and I was just single-mindedly into drawing cars. I was intrigued by pin-striping techniques and multicolored paint jobs.

I did learn something about figure drawing—which is probably the most difficult kind of drawing there is—from Rob, because he was good at it. I think he wanted to be an artist when he was in high school, but about halfway through he started shifting to music.

ROB TYNER One night in 1965—after drawing my millionth hot rod—I decided I couldn't stand being alone anymore. I threw my coat on, jumped in my old Chevy, and went down to the White Castle, where all the rockers used to hang out. There was nobody there, so I pulled out my harmonica and started playing the blues. As fate would have it, Wayne Kramer pulled up on this motorcycle and I just blew him away.

GARY GRIMSHAW In the early 1960s, Rob and I listened to a lot of jazz and blues. The British rock-'n'-roll explosion hadn't happened yet, and all the artists that started rock 'n' roll in the '50s had died or stopped having hits. Other than the Brill Building, rock was hijacked by what I called the Philadelphia Mafia—it was all mainstream pop garbage like Frankie Avalon and Fabian.

The Atlantic Records sound was still strong during that period. We listened to a lot of Black radio like WCHB, an urban gospel station, or Frantic Ernie on WBBC. By our senior year, we both had cars and we'd pick each other up to drive to school in the morning and turn on WCHB and blast it all the way. We needed to get a dose of R&B before we had to go to school.

We were also listening to jazz. WCHB would go off the air at sundown, and for the last hour or so, a DJ named Larry Dixon would play music by John Coltrane, Yusef Lateef, and all that stuff, and that's where we learned about it.

I have one great memory of our high school days that says a lot about who we were and where our heads were at. It was a Saturday afternoon in 1962, and Rob and I were walking past Hudson's Department Store at the Lincoln Park Plaza on Fourth Street and there was an entrance that was all boarded up and closed. It was raining and I had my cream-colored Japanese transistor radio with me. We were big fans of the Ugly Duckling on WCHD, an R&B show that would also play jazz—wild jazz—really adventurous stuff. Suddenly, the station started playing "My Favorite Things" by John Coltrane. It's now considered a milestone in jazz history, but it was the first time we'd ever heard it. We just ducked into that boarded-up entrance at Hudson's, with half of the radio on my shoulder, and half on Rob's shoulder so we could each get our ears right into the speaker.

It was like fourteen minutes long, and we just stood there in the rain, completely transfixed. We didn't say a word through the whole thing, and when it was over, there was nothing we could say. We just walked around in the rain getting wet.

During this time, Rob and I also used to go to this club called the Minor Key, which was the biggest jazz venue in Detroit. But to get in we had to bring our parents. I remember the first time we went there and we saw [saxophonist] Cannonball Adderley. We were thrilled and made our moms get there early so we could get a table right up front. We listened to all of Adderley's records over and over again, so we knew all the tunes.

I think our moms were afraid to be in a Black Detroit club, but by the end of the night they enjoyed it. In some ways, it probably wasn't too weird for my mother. She had grown up in that neighborhood, but I don't think she'd been down there since she graduated from high school. I don't know what the club and clientele thought of us—these crazy white sixteen-year-olds with their parents, jumping up and down. They probably thought we were nuts.

One time we went to see Coltrane, and [drummer] Elvin Jones came out onstage eating a *big* turkey leg. He was the first one to come out, and he just sat behind his drums chewing away and scowling at everybody. When he finally finished—when he got all down to the bone—the rest of the band came out. That was great.

His drumming was overpowering. Real loud, real fast, and real full. But we sat right in front of Coltrane, so the bell of his horn was, like, right in our ears. But what was even more impressive was bassist Jimmy Garrison, because he was just ripping at the strings with his fingers. Halfway through the first song he was drenched in sweat. He had this stand-up bass, and it was soaking wet. That's the way he played. He played with the same intensity that Elvin played drums. I'd never seen a bass player do that. I guess if he didn't play that hard, he'd be totally drowned out. The feeling you got from the band was that all of them were pushing each other so hard that they were creating a wall of sound.

ROB TYNER After I ran into Wayne Kramer at the White Castle, I gave some serious thought about playing in his band but decided I didn't really have any experience. But I had read about Andrew Loog Oldham, the manager of the Rolling Stones, and I found him to be an interesting character. I thought, I don't have a lot of musical talent, so maybe being a manager would be a cool thing to do. It seemed like something you could just bullshit your way through.

WAYNE KRAMER Instead of playing in our band, Rob decided he was going to manage us, but then Fred and Rob had a couple dustups. We were sitting in a restaurant, and he was telling us what he was going to do for us, and Fred was being defiant. Rob just kept calling Fred's bluff, but every time Fred would raise the ante, and Rob would say, "So what. Fuck you."

Finally, they decided they were going to fight about it. So when we finished eating, we all went out in the parking lot. Fred and Rob squared off and threw a few blows at each other. I scored it even. You might have put your money on Fred, but Rob was a big guy and he wasn't afraid of Fred. That was the main thing; he wasn't going to let Fred intimidate him. Both of them landed a couple of good, clean shots, but it was in the winter, they slipped on the ice, and Fred luckily ended up on top. He had Rob down and said, "I could smash your face in right now."

Rob said, "Why don't you?" That fucked Fred up, and he got off of Rob and said, "Oh, I don't know what I'm doing." Then we talked for the next six hours about what just happened. "How did we get to this? What caused this?"

I was really impressed. I was thinking, Oh, man, Fred's going to really lambaste this motherfucker. But Rob's defiant attitude just knocked the wind out of Fred's sails. He respected it. After that, we decided Rob was going to be the bass player because we didn't have one.

ROB TYNER Out of curiosity I went to a couple of band rehearsals. Wayne was on guitar, Fred Smith on bass, and they had a drummer named Leo [LeDuc]. I listened to 'em and they sounded really good. But Fred wanted to play guitar, so I stopped thinking about being their manager and tried to play bass. They gave me about three weeks and then fired me.

WAYNE KRAMER After Rob didn't work out on bass, he recommended his friend Pat Burrows, who was great. But Fred wanted to get Rob back in the band because he liked his nuttiness. Fred said, "We gotta have a guy in the band who's nutty! A guy with a lot of crazy ideas and shit." I agreed, and that's how Rob became our lead singer.

ROB TYNER Wayne called me one day and asked me if I had any ideas for a band name. I had two ideas. One was the Men. I liked that because it was very macho. The other one was the MC5. Wayne didn't like the Men at all, so MC5 it was. He asked, "What's it stand for?" and I said, "The Motor City 5, I guess." But it was also my variation on Einstein's $E = mc^2$. I wasn't a physics major, and it's not like I understood what it meant, but it sounded modern and there was something about that equation that just looked great.

I also gave myself a new name. My family name is Derminer, and for some reason no one could pronounce it or spell it right. It didn't seem tough to me, but they'd say Deeder-meyer or Doodie-meaner, and that always bothered me because I was very into identity.

I had a real passion for John Coltrane's pianist, McCoy Tyner, so I became Rob Tyner. Everybody else in the band that had a weird name changed it as well. Wayne Kramer took his name from the country pianist Floyd Cramer. And later, when Dennis Tomich joined, he became Dennis Thompson.

Once I started calling myself Rob Tyner, I started expressing myself better on all levels. I was very into self-invention; I always believed it was my inalienable right. I think that is the process of rock 'n' roll; with every album you're reinventing yourself. I felt like a weight was off me, and that's the connection to the freedom I heard in McCoy Tyner's playing with Coltrane.

Even though I was introverted, I didn't have any problems making the transition to front man. If you think about it, the stage is a very isolated place. You're completely alone out there, and it made me feel strangely at home. I had the feeling that nobody could tell me what I should do, and I liked that.

WAYNE KRAMER The MC5 was really launched with our original rhythm section of Pat Burrows on bass and Bob Gasper on drums. Man, that band rocked! Unlike Michael Davis and Dennis Thompson, they were so solid and so in the pocket. But we were so vain in our pursuit of fame, we forced them both out of the band because they didn't look cool enough. Pretty vicious shit.

GARY GRIMSHAW I was working like a dog at the end of high school. I decided I really wanted to go to college but my grades were terrible, so I started studying. Since I was occupied, Rob started hanging out with a bunch of musicians. I would go to the shows and sometimes I would work as a roadie.

ROB TYNER Wayne was always the practical one. His mom was very supportive of him, and she was very motivated to help get the band going for him. He would talk to his mother and she would offer advice. In turn, he'd give us pep talks and the band would hear all this wonderful stuff that we were supposed to do. They'd cook up these ideas, like playing a benefit for this school for the blind or playing a Halloween party for the mentally ill. In some ways, that's where our social and political involvement all started. We were trying to create this "we are the world" vibe long before [future manager] John Sinclair stepped into the picture. We always had the idea that we wanted to use our music for more than profit and self-gain. That's probably what made us so ripe for conquest by Sinclair.

That said, Fred Smith didn't care about any of that. He had this stoic thing: never show emotion and never show pain. He never liked school or working, but he did have a deep affinity for the guitar, and that was enough. That's enough for a person.

Fred understood the automatic transmission of playing rhythm. One of the highest callings in music is to play rhythm, because as a rhythm player you control the dynamics. Unfortunately, there was this real hierarchy among guitar players at that time. The dumb guy was supposed to be the rhythm player. I always felt it takes a special mentality to be able to play that position. By starting out as a rhythm player, Fred developed an incredible sense of how to build our songs. The combination of Fred and Dennis Thompson was dynamite. They could get things rolling. When Fred started playing lead later on, things got more complicated.

In our early days, Fred toyed with the idea of committing petty crimes. Breaking and entering were glorified in Lincoln Park. Fred and I got into a couple of little things. Let's face it; we were hoodlums, running the streets with nobody telling us what to do.

GARY GRIMSHAW The MC5 attempted to steal some equipment from a local music store. One night, at three in the morning, they backed a truck up but set off an alarm before they could get anything. Fred probably masterminded the heist. They were regular customers, so they were paranoid about getting caught. But they needed the stuff so bad.

ROB TYNER The other guys in the band were rock 'n' rollers, but they were fundamentally conservative. They had a suburban mentality. Wayne was really obsessed with "How do you do this stuff? How do you get a sound?" He was the one with all the practical questions. I was more into asking, "How weird could we get?" I wasn't interested in procedural stuff.

There's a certain security in doing things the right way, but at that time I thought it was way too early to start worrying about the right fucking way. Doing things "right" meant eliminating all the interesting ideas. But that's why it was also good that Wayne tried to keep things organized. We were a good balance. If it would have depended on me, I doubt we would have been successful.

The band wanted to get rid of me many times, and I don't blame 'em. Looking back on it, maybe it would've been better for everyone if we had just become like [pop singer] Bobby Goldsboro or something more mainstream. They knew that they needed me, but they would've liked it if I was more measured, which was exactly what I was fighting against. Their attitude mobilized my defenses, and it got to the point where things were very complicated. Very complicated.

There were many times they sat my ass down—in front of people—and tried to straighten me out. They'd come over to my house and bitch me out in a most cruel manner. They were on me every second, and when I made an infraction the boot came down. It didn't work. I'd already been fighting all my life to be Rob Tyner. The only thing they could do to hurt me was to shut me up, and later in the band's development, that's exactly what happened.

I wasn't easy to deal with. I knew that, and acknowledged it. But if they'd let me go, I'd have gotten in another band, and then I would've been the competition. There were other people in town that would've gladly done any freaky-ass thing that I would've wanted. I wanted to be like my British idols. I liked more obscure bands like the Troggs, but the guys in the band didn't care for 'em because they weren't mainstream enough. I liked 'em precisely because of that!

I really liked the Pretty Things' first album. You had to dig through the rocks to enjoy it, and I liked that. The Yardbirds also meant something to me. I could point to them and say, "Look at these guys. They play weird music and have hit records. Let's be more like that!"

WAYNE KRAMER We all loved the songs on the Rolling Stones' first album. They were among the first things we learned to play together as the MC5. In fact, about all we played were Rolling Stones songs up until the point where we thought we were going to get to open for them. We were sophisticated enough to understand we couldn't go on in front of the Stones and play their material.

ROB TYNER Our early gigs were always kind of strange. We played record hops, teen clubs, but we never did play the upscale places like the Chatterbox much, because we were never popular enough. We played what we liked instead of the hits—lots of deep cuts by the Rolling Stones, Chuck Berry, Animals, and the Kinks. We'd play more obscure things like the Who's "Bald Headed Woman."

WAYNE KRAMER When the Stones first came to Detroit, nobody came to see them. The next time they came, in 1965, they were much more popular and we were supposed to open for them but got knocked out of the box at the last minute. That was a real heartbreaker.

ROB TYNER Playing gigs wasn't about money. It was mostly about picking up chicks. I'm not sure what our aspirations were, but we certainly understood our limitations. I was a white guy singing in the same city as Marvin Gaye and Smokey Robinson. Forget it. It was like, "You're the wrong color, man, hang it up." As a white vocalist in a town dominated by Motown, it was ludicrous. You had to be really gifted as a singer to survive, and we probably wouldn't have been able to make it in Detroit if we were a commercial band. We made it in the suburbs, out in the boonies, where it was just kids.

The whole Black music thing was very popular with white and Black audiences. There was an incredible amount of music being released in the mid-'60s. Ten classic songs would come out in the space of a week, and it would be difficult to keep up. We'd be playing a gig and somebody would invariably come up and ask us to play some impossible Motown tune.

There was this tussle between the indigenous music of Detroit and the British Invasion music of the Beatles and the Stones, which was all lily-white. It was a musically turbulent situation.

Additionally, we had some tremendous competition. A local band called the Satellites were the absolute greatest. I'm not kidding. Had they been anywhere else, or gotten any kind of a break, even just a small one, they would've been unstoppable. They were energetic onstage, could sing four/five-part harmony, and play their instruments with real precision. They had long hair and could sing things like Smokey Robinson's "You've Really Got a Hold on Me" and actually make people weep. And they were our competition!

We couldn't beat them, so we began to use that Beatles-versus-Stones territorial thing. The Satellites were like the Beatles, and we were the scruffy guys. We wore all black, had big Vox amplifiers, and were real macho. Also, nobody else was putting the energy into the tunes like we were. We had found these little pockets of places we could play. There was one place in Flat Rock, which was about fifteen miles south of Lincoln Park, that loved us. We didn't get paid, but every weekend, or every other weekend, we could go down there and slam for those guys. There was an actual stage, so we could begin working our act. As we played around the city, we began to formulate this idea of putting a lot of intensity into the music. We grew up playing Chuck Berry songs, and with Fred Smith around there was a lot of drive on that rhythm guitar.

WAYNE KRAMER It was a real competitive scene in Detroit. The standards were really high. The best bands made a lot of money, which was a wild concept. Billy Lee & the Rivieras was one of the bands to beat. They eventually became famous as Mitch Ryder & the Detroit Wheels, and they were monsters. They could play all sorts of wild shit that nobody knew yet. I mean, here's this white kid, Billy Levise [Mitch Ryder's real name], up there singing James Brown shit. Damn, how could he do that?

ROB TYNER A crucial person in our story was a guy named Bruce Burnish. He worked at Ford, had some money, and he cosigned a loan for us to get some top-of-the-line equipment. The Beatles, the Stones, and all the top British Invasion bands used Vox amplifiers, and with his help we bought two Super Beatle Vox amps, a Westminster bass amp, and a PA. If it had not been for Bruce, the MC5 would never have existed, because after that, we weren't just another band.

When we walked in with that gear, the crowds would stop whatever they were doing and gawk. At that time, a Super Beatle was the biggest amp anybody had ever seen. So when we came in all dressed in black with all this gear, people knew something was cookin'. Something was going down. And then when we hit those first couple of chords and it was so fucking loud, it really grabbed people's attention.

WAYNE KRAMER We kind of considered ourselves junior confidence men—junior hustlers and manipulators. We talked this guy Bruce Burnish into buying all this Vox equipment—thousands of dollars' worth of stuff, which none of us or our parents could afford. We made him the manager.

ROB TYNER We were booked to open for [British Invasion superstars] the Dave Clark Five at Cobo Arena in Detroit in December of 1965, and it was the moment that the band had been living for. I think we sleazed in there through one of our record-hop connections. We knew that if we got to the right place and played in front of a big audience, we'd do well. The Dave Clark Five were as hot as a pistol, and they jammed the place. It was such a shock to me that we were gonna do it.

I was backstage and the place was filled with screaming girls. It was like heaven. At one point I peeked through the curtains at center stage and the whole crowd erupted, and I said, "Goddamn! This is great!" It was the first time I saw how you could play with hysteria, which was heady stuff. I said, "Man, I'm home."

During our set, my pants got stuck in the top of my boots, and I was stumbling all over the place, scared and nervous but also exhilarated. The whole thing was so expansive. I literally was never the same after that. You moved this way and the crowd would break the same way. We had these green corduroy coats and black pants and vests, and white shirts, and Beatle boots. That was our outfit. I liked that because it gave us a certain unity, even though there was very little unity in the band, personality-wise. It was depressing afterwards to go back to the same old stuff, but that gig did increase our standing in the community. Somewhere there's a picture of them and us—the DC5 meets the MC5.

WAYNE KRAMER Opening for the Dave Clark Five was our consolation prize for not getting the Stones slot. That was our first taste of the "big time," and we rehearsed hard for it. I think there were a couple of other acts before us, but I can't remember who they were. Four acts total. Everybody got twenty minutes, then the Dave Clark Five. I was so high on just being there, it was like taking acid or something.

GARY GRIMSHAW In 1964, after I graduated from high school, I started going to Wayne State University in Detroit, and immediately moved downtown into a building filled with beatniks. Rob would hang out with me, and that's when he met his future wife, Becky. Becky was also living downtown and going to Wayne State.

This guy Ron lived a couple doors down, and he showed me the first Beatles album. He saw my record collection of jazz, blues, and rock 'n' roll, and said, "You'll like this too."

But I really didn't. The Beatles were the kind of band your parents would like. They were cute. My mother used to go out and buy Beatles albums. The Stones, however, were a whole different story. But the interesting thing was that before they had even heard the Stones, the MC5 were doing basically the same thing—covering blues tunes. They glommed onto the Stones right away. Once we knew about the Stones, we just forgot about the Beatles. The hell with them. We'd buy those records for our parents. That said, we did like Beatle boots. They were like greaser shoes but with higher heels.

ROB TYNER I was always looking for a party, and I was English at the time. It's an embarrassing story to tell, but true. I pretended I was from England to get into all the cool parties. I'm good with accents and I had the jacket and the little black dickey with the white shirt, right? The little Peter Gunn hairdo and the English accent, and I would flash my way into any party.

On weekends there would be these mad, wild, existential, insane, debauched parties on the Wayne State University campus in Detroit. All the houses would just be rocking! The Student Non-Violent Coordinating Committee threw some parties over on Fourth Street that would blow you away! There would be drinking, carousing, and a little bit of pot here and there. You'd meet these people who were like . . . militant anthropologists! Stuff like that. I loved these people. I didn't go to college, but I always was hungry for the intellectual stimulation they offered. A lot of guys in the band thought that was all horseshit, and maybe on some levels it was, but I loved it for the sense of intellectual possibilities. No thought was taboo.

I met Becky at one of those parties. I was out prowling in the city—"lurking," as we called it. Boy, I was trying my damnedest to get into this one party. There were rumors that there would be pot, so I had to get in, but even the English accent was failing me. I was walking down the street, feeling dejected, and I saw this girl walking up the other side of the street. And I said, "'Allo, love, where's the party?" with my English accent. And she said, "It's right in there." And I said, "I know, I can't get in!" "Well, I'm invited, let's go to the beer store first." She could buy! I couldn't believe it! She was my age, but she could buy.

BECKY TYNER I was on my way home and I met this guy with an English accent in front of my building who asked me about a party. I didn't think twice about it. I just told him it was at my friends', Neil and Sandy. I wasn't going myself. I was going out with my boyfriend who had a red Corvette. When I came home later that night, my roommate Donna, who had been at the party, told me that the guy I had met wasn't really English, but he seemed nice enough, so she invited him to *our* party the following weekend. After that, Rob started hanging out at our apartment, even though he had a girlfriend and I had a boyfriend.

ROB TYNER Towards the end of 1965, things were changing rapidly in the band. We were not commercial enough for the Top 40 bars, and we were getting too old for the teen clubs. We started realizing that soon there would be no place for us. I started pushing for the band to go in a more artsy, experimental, psychedelic direction. Our bassist, Pat, however, could not deal with it. He was a great player, but he was not interested in getting freaky at all.

WAYNE KRAMER Pat wanted to play Motown-style funk, but we started taking acid and wanted to get weird.

ROB TYNER I had moved out of my parents' house and into an apartment on the campus of Wayne State University, and Mike Davis was a guitarist and singer who lived across the hall from me. He was this real handsome guy and had a real pop-star look. The band decided that even if he hadn't played bass before, he would be better for us than Burrows. So he was in and Pat was out.

Around that time, Becky's best friend married this architect who owned this huge house in Southfield, Michigan, with glass walls—it was really far-out. They had this big artsy-fartsy party and invited the MC5 to play. All the local artists and heavies were there. It was very heady for me. Even though it was Mike's first gig with us, we just really went for it.

At some point in the evening, I discovered that if you took the microphone and stuck it into the speakers, it would feed back like crazy. I also started making all these weird metallic, xylophone-type sounds by running the mic up and down the speaker columns. Suddenly, what we would eventually call "avant-rock" was born, and the hip people at the party loved it.

We found out quickly that not everyone was receptive to that kind of weirdness. We tried it at fraternity parties and forget it, they just wanted to hear "Gloria" and that was it. But I didn't care, because it pointed the way for what became one of our biggest anthems, "Black to Comm," and the band's later sound. I saw it as pure research and pure experimentation.

WAYNE KRAMER Michael was recruited as much for the lifestyle as he was for his looks. Lifestyle-wise he fit into our program: he was a beatnik, he liked downtown, he was an artist, a hipster, he smoked reefer. Pat, our current bassist, was the other end of the spectrum: a white suburban working-class kid who wanted to get a nice day job and do the right thing. Michael had a lifestyle we were aspiring to.

Since he played some guitar, in my youthful enthusiasm I thought I could just teach him how to play bass, like I taught Fred. I told him, "Don't worry. I'll take care of the music. We'll show you how to do that. You're in the band." He would play the exact notes I would show him to play, but we lost that feeling we had been getting with Burrows, because Burrows was in the pocket. We didn't really appreciate what we had because we were coasting on the enthusiasm.

But when Michael joined the band, everything really started roaring. We'd get these jobs around Wayne State playing for the beatniks, so we were just—AGGGHHH!!!!—blasting through this new counterculture thing.

CHRIS HOVNANIAN [Wayne Kramer's girlfriend] Before Wayne and I became a couple, I was friends with Michael. He was an incredibly talented painter, and in a way it's too bad that Wayne talked him into becoming a bass player. And after they did, they were critical of his musicianship and made him feel like garbage.

Michael used to flip me out because he looked exactly like Paul McCartney. He'd sit there and play Beatles songs and you had to keep telling yourself that this was not Paul McCartney sitting there on the couch.

Everybody thought he'd be great up there with the band because he looked great. Wayne looked goofy, Rob was overweight, and Fred was sort of ugly like a Rolling Stone. Michael *was* handsome. Incredibly handsome and nice. It was too bad that's the only reason they hired him.

MICHAEL DAVIS [MC5 bassist] Yes, I was the ladies' man. That was my area. Fred was the quiet tough guy. He was the Charles Bronson of the band. Wayne was the show-off—the guy that was always in your face. Wayne had to always have the spotlight on him. He was the one that was dancing the boogaloo out there. Rob was our beacon of enlightenment, and Dennis was like a little caveman. He was Bamm-Bamm.

CHRIS HOVNANIAN Wayne pushed everybody around except Fred. They were all afraid of Fred. Fred, though, didn't push anybody around. He just didn't say anything, which made everybody afraid of him. He'd just grunt and did whatever he wanted. They didn't even really try to force him to do anything. Plus, they had a lot of respect for his guitar playing.

WAYNE KRAMER Michael had limited technical experience and facility, but he thought like an artist and he played like an artist, which meant that he ignored half the rules of how you're supposed to play and would go off on these weird musical tangents. If you just listened to him, he sounded fine, but I would've preferred someone who had a more traditional approach.

MICHAEL DAVIS I was interested in classical music; rock 'n' roll was like the farthest thing from me. Then the Beatles and the Stones came along, and it was like, Whoa. What is that? When I joined the MC5, my vision wasn't that I was joining a rock-'n'-roll band. I saw it as kind of a living, breathing sculpture. To me, it was the whole thing: five individuals contributing to a whole kind of art piece. It wasn't just the music—it was the look, it was the attitude, it was the words, it was the clothes, it was the performance, it was kind of everything. So, I looked at the thing like a huge painting, like working on a living sculpture. The MC5 was never just a rock-'n'-roll band.

When I joined them, they were pretty much a Lincoln Park cover band, and the most that was going on was an occasional bar gig and playing at the teenager clubs and sock hops. And it was all about covers. When I joined, my vision was to create something that no one had ever done before. When Dennis Thompson started playing, that completed the wheel.

ROB TYNER During the whole period of the band's formation, there was always this question of whether they were going to get rid of me because I was not consistent as a person. My standards of cleanliness were not like everybody else's and I was always late. I also had a penchant for oblique literature and art, and that just didn't do it for them. There was this real pressure to be just one of the guys, and I would never be that. Never will be that. I'm not cut out for it, and I'm not motivated towards it. I'm my own person; I like the things I like. In those days, I was very nihilistic about everything because I didn't think I would live for very long. I felt that most things didn't really matter, so why not stretch out while I can?

I took a lot of criticism. There was constant criticism about my weight and even about my age. When I turned twenty, the band was like, "You're over the hill, you're too old." I was old at twenty! They kept that up constantly. They even worried about whether I was going to lose my hair! My dad lost his hair at an early age and I was expected to do the same.

I also took a lot of flak for my relationship with Becky, who would become my wife. She was one of those intellectual girls—not your regular band chick. We got married at a very early age, and that was very taboo and uncool. The idea that you would get married was so nuts, but as weird as I was, I also wanted some stability in my life. My parents had a difficult marriage and stayed together for the kids, which was miserable for everyone when I was growing up. I really wanted to feel a sense of home and I found that with Becky.

MICHAEL DAVIS The first thing that comes to my mind when I think about Rob Tyner is that he was a loving person, and he always had his head above water. He wasn't somebody that could be duped into believing in fantasies or was frivolous. He was pretty serious, although he had this humorous side to him too. In fact, when we first started hanging out, Rob and his brother Rick were like a comedy team. We'd go up to the burger joint and just sit and eat fries and watch Rob and Rick tell jokes and clown around. I mean, we'd just be in stitches.

The second thing I think about with Rob was he was so not cut out to be a rock star. He wasn't skinny. He wasn't pretty. He just had all this shit going against him. But what he did have was drive. And he was determined to be a lead singer. He was determined to be in a rock band, and that was how he was going to make his mark.

The third thing I think of is that he was frustrated. He wasn't a trained singer. I mean, he had to kind of, like, pull it out of his ass, as the saying goes. He was like a student of performing artists, so he was always trying to reach that level. Which is a great thing because he wasn't satisfied with just mimicking a song. He needed to master a song. He aimed high. I mean he named himself after McCoy Tyner. That tells you something.

ROB TYNER After Mike Davis joined the band, we played at a wedding reception for a friend of ours who knew all the "right" people in Detroit. We were crackling, droning, and making all this feedback noise, and they were dancing to it! I couldn't believe it. It was a breakthrough for us. That paved the way on some levels for our involvement with John Sinclair.

We were playing a lot of Yardbirds and starting to connect with the college crowd and the freaks. We got to "avant-out" for the people, and they dug it. And then the band started to dig it a little. It was a period of expansion, and we were making the transition from being a sock-hop band to something more interesting.

WAYNE KRAMER After we discovered feedback, we ended a lot of record hops by clearing the room. We knew if we could make people react that strong, we were on to something. We knew we were on the right track. Maybe it wasn't the exact right application, but it was *something*, because, man, we could drive people out of clubs in droves.

Our drummer at that time, Bob Gaspar, didn't like when we got too experimental either. He wanted us to be a lounge act, and we wanted to be a rock-'n'-roll band. He used to yell at us about playing too loud all the time. One evening he stopped playing, got up on the mic, and yelled to the audience: "How many people in here think this band is too goddamn loud?" Nobody said anything. "You think it sounds okay?" And the crowed went, "RAAAGGGHA!!" He went back to his drums with his tail between his legs. That's probably when he knew his days in the MC5 were numbered.

ROB TYNER Bob hated "Black to Comm." That was the song where we would really get weird. I mean, he *hated* it because it was loud and real demanding to play. There was only one way you could do it—flat-out.

Bam! Bam! Bam! He'd be tired at the end of the gig and want to go home. One night he protested by just sitting there and refusing to play along.

ROB TYNER That pissed Fred off, so he turned his amp up all the way; in his hands, a Gretsch Tennessean guitar and a Super Beatle amp were lethal weapons. Bob wasn't playing and we kept going. Finally, Gaspar did this big single slow roll and came on it, the whole band hit all at the same time, and the whole place just took off. Ironically, it became the signature of the song.

WAYNE KRAMER Wow! It took people's heads off. Thermonuclear war. I don't think it was quite so cathartic for Gaspar, though. He was still pissed off.

ROB TYNER Not long after that, we got a residency at this itty-bitty place called the Crystal Bar in Detroit. It was a place where friends and some of the freakos would come over and bounce off the walls as we'd play. Mostly, it gave us a chance to develop our sound.

WAYNE KRAMER We weren't a good bar band because we didn't want to play the jukebox songs, which is what most people wanted. We did covers that we wanted to do. Bar owners would pressure the band: "You gotta play the Top 10." But at the Crystal Bar things were different.

It was around then we knew we *had* to write our own songs. At one point we just said, "Rob, go make up some other words." He could go in the other room and come back in a couple of minutes and say, "Here, I wrote a song." "Great, let's do it!" He got enthused with that and he started writing more. Later, Fred and I started writing too. Like they say, "When the going gets weird, the weird get going."

ROB TYNER We wrote "Looking at You" at the Crystal Bar. Some nights could be pretty dismal, and one evening the place was completely empty. Out of sheer boredom I said, "Hey, check this out, try this." I just started singing, "Do, doo, do, doo," and the band just took off on it and created a groove, and I started improvising. That song was exactly what I was always hoping to do. I love the idea of spontaneous composition, and the structure of "Looking at You" flowed in a way that allowed me to create and sing lyrics on the spot like a jazz player.

BECKY TYNER Rob wrote all the lyrics in the beginning. To him it was poetry. He was very well-read and creative. I can remember when he wrote "Kick Out the Jams" in my bedroom, then brought it out to the guys.

WAYNE KRAMER When we settled into the Crystal Bar, Gaspar wanted out. He wanted a girlfriend and to buy a new hot-rod car, and that meant expenses and getting a day job. He wanted that American success thing. It was no surprise that Gaspar didn't like the Crystal. We weren't contributing to his bottom line. One night he said, "You guys are fucked up," and left.

When Gaspar couldn't make a gig in the past, we used this kid who used to play in the Bounty Hunters named Dennis Thompson, so we asked him to come down.

DENNIS THOMPSON [MC5 drummer] When I was in the ninth grade, I was in a band with Wayne called the Bounty Hunters. We played instrumentals like "Tequila," "Walk Don't Run" and "Wipe Out." After the Bounty Hunters broke up, I just started playing weddings. One night, Wayne popped over to my house on his motorcycle. I hadn't seen him in over a year, and he asked, "Hey, Dennis, what're you doing? Our drummer has girl problems. You want to sit in on this gig?"

I said, "Sure." I was only in tenth grade, but I went into the vortex. I was a little square at school. Tyner, Smith, and Kramer had become bohemians, and I was still straitlaced and conservative and was planning on attending college. I was playing little bars with my brother and weddings and whatnot. I agreed to fill in for their drummer. They were playing all the hippest tunes that I was hearing on the radio, and it sort of caught me off guard.

Initially, I *didn't* like the guys because they were rough around the edges. They were all really rebellious. If I had rebellious feelings they hadn't surfaced yet, but I guess they were there. My interest in math was an indication of a very orderly mind, which was everything they were not. Fred Smith's hair was so long you couldn't see his eyes, and he used to stink. He wouldn't take a bath for weeks at a time. He had already been kicked out of school. Fred said he dropped out, but he was kicked out. But their music drew me in. I didn't like them, but I liked the music they were playing.

WAYNE KRAMER Even though Dennis was straight, we convinced him to join. We hornswoggled him in with a typical Machiavellian move: We just promised him everything. If you join, you can have everything you've ever wanted. He held out for a very long time. Dennis was afraid to smoke reefer in the beginning, and he was the last one to become a stone-cold junkie. But he eventually started smoking that reefer, and the boy lost his mind!

DENNIS THOMPSON The first time I took acid, I got it from someone I considered to be my mentor. He got me through doing it without a bad trip. Then I did it every day for like two weeks. Just stayed in an LSD frame of mind, until it became who I was. And I was just a very smart, very perceptive, and happy guy. LSD was a happy drug. At that time it wasn't laced with belladonna or speed.

The guys smoked pot and had dodged the draft before me. I was always one step behind them, until I finally caught up. When I quit school, I just fell right in step with them.

ROB TYNER Wayne and Fred had known Dennis long before I did. I liked him because I thought we would be able to make a show drummer out of him—a drummer that was capable of real wildness. Pat Burrows and Bob Gaspar had been a rock-solid rhythm section, but we were looking for something more adventurous.

The strange thing is, as soon as Dennis joined the band, I started antagonizing him. It's stupid, but that's the way kids start showing their affection on some levels. I kept tormenting him just to see if he'd get pissed off, or what he would do behind the drums. I was taking a real chance by doing that because Dennis was a very volatile person. But in a way I felt it was good, because I liked it when the band was a little unpredictable.

On one early gig we were playing a party, and at one point we turned it loose. And Dennis stayed right in there. I remember looking behind me and saw that his seat had fallen over. He just stood up and kept going, sweating and raging with the rest of us, and I thought, Well, he's a blood brother, a comrade in arms.

I really liked Dennis, but he was weird. On the other hand, he was probably the straightest out of all of us. He had a college mentality. He was very mathematical, and I was interested in that side of him because I believed that mathematical concepts had potential in our "avant-rock."

I was thinking that it would be cool if you could write out drum parts on a blackboard and do calculus theorems on drums. Drums fascinate me. I like drummers; they're the most primal of people. They're hard-headed and impossible to deal with, and this makes me love them dearly. Put a crazy drummer along with an aggressive guitar player and you can do something with that.

Dennis was a very cerebral person but a very physical player, and I wanted to have access to somebody that had real brute strength. In rock 'n' roll it's such an asset to have a drummer that's physically imposing. I figured that whatever personality differences we had, they were secondary to what the band really needed.

I think he also saw our potential and commitment—that we weren't gonna stop. We had a plan for world domination; I don't think he completely understood it, but neither did we! We just knew there was something there. We'd already proved ourselves in combat against an incredible list of entertainers. I think he could relate to our aggressive attitude.

After several nights at the Crystal, we asked him to join. We had a little ceremony onstage. We presented him with a plunger from the toilet in the dressing room, and there we were, the MC5!

DENNIS THOMPSON By playing with the MC5, I felt like I was part of a movement. They were legitimate—legitimately rebellious. Fred Smith was living the part, playing the part; he quit school and *became* the part. It was scary at first to be a part of something that big. I was a little frightened of it. It took a big commitment to pull it off. It meant you had to change your life, change your lifestyle. You're going down this nice, narrow straight path, smooth road, and suddenly, you've got to go through the rough rocks and the bramble woods and the briars. The rest of the band were already living that life. They had the image, the look, and the feel. They were living the part. They'd committed to it. Me? I was just a little shaky about what that meant. "Do I *really* want to do this?" But then I would hear the music, and the music made me want to do it.

We were all big, combustible personalities that emitted a palpable sense of danger. I don't think any of us could've created the kind of attention and attraction that the whole group did together. We were like five spokes in a wheel who appreciated that we all had this kind of equal membership.

CHAPTER II

BALLROOM BLITZ

Oh yeah, that's them! Rock 'n' roll, sex, and drugs? That's them.

—Rob Tyner

By 1966, all the pieces of the MC5 had neatly fallen into place, but they were essentially a stick of dynamite with no place to explode. They were too loud and wild to function as noisy background music at frat parties, and they were too weird, dangerous, and high to keep playing underage teen clubs. The band knew it was time to either "go big" or throw in the towel and get an assembly-line job like everyone else.

But that was precisely the problem—they had no real clue how to "go big." Fortunately, Rob Tyner, who had moved to the hip Cass Corridor area of downtown Detroit with his girlfriend, Becky, had a small inkling.

"It would've been depressing for us to continue on as just another band—maybe even impossible—but we were being indecisive about our direction and going nowhere at the Crystal Bar," said Tyner. "I had a gut feeling that the best way for us to go was to embrace this whole hippie thing that was just emerging in Detroit around the Wayne State University campus. In a lot of ways, we were perfectly suited for it. At least, I thought we were. We had already gone beyond the pale, even for some of the hippies! You had to be beyond hard-core to deal with us."

And what better way to woo "the hippies" than grab the attention of John Sinclair, a man who had achieved near-mythical status among Detroit's growing army of beatniks, weirdos, and political activists. None of the band members knew him, but they were determined to get his ear.

"We figured Sinclair was going to be the King of the Hippies," said Kramer, "so if the King of the Hippies was our manager, all the hippies would like us. We recognized that there was a wave developing in Detroit, and that if we played our cards right, we would be at the forefront of it. The idea of courting him was pretty calculated."

Born on October 3, 1941, the son of a career employee at Flint, Michigan's Buick Assembly Plant, John Alexander Sinclair was involved in just about every aspect of the downtown Detroit hipster scene. One could even argue that he created it.

Towering well over six feet tall and crowned with an unruly tangle of pitch-black hair, he was a husky, imposing bear of a man with a formidable intellect and seemingly endless reserves of enthusiasm and creative energy. He detested traditional American values and the standard nine-to-five workweek—something he referred to as "the death system"—but he was no lazy bohemian stereotype. He had the soul of an artist, but the indefatigable work ethic of a Fortune 500 CEO. He labored tirelessly to champion the arts and his right to live the way he saw fit, which primarily revolved around churning out reams of prose and poetry, producing avant-garde events, listening to the free jazz of John Coltrane and Ornette Coleman, and doing anything and everything to subvert societal norms.

Sinclair's radical life began in earnest in April 1964 after he entered graduate school at Wayne State University, where it didn't take long for him to make a big impression. At a time when marijuana was still highly illegal and only whispered about in back alleys, he had "the only steady reefer supply" in the campus area, due to a connection he had through the jazz scene.* "My apartment got to be the meeting place for all different kinds of heads, musicians, poets, and other incipient freaks," he said.

In October 1964, his notoriety grew exponentially when he was arrested for the first time and charged with "sale and possession" of marijuana after being set up by a "friend" as part of a sting operation by the Detroit police. He received two years' probation and was given a $250 fine and an elevated place on the authorities' shit list. Not that Sinclair cared. For him, police harassment came with the territory of being a beatnik and a freethinker.

During this period he began an intense relationship with fellow student and photographer Magdalene "Leni" Arndt, who had emigrated from East Germany in 1959 and was putting herself through school at Wayne State.† The two became almost inseparable, and on November 1, 1964, they, along with fourteen friends, founded the Detroit Artists' Workshop (DAW), a "neo-beatnik self-determination center for musicians, poets, photographers, painters, filmmakers, dope fiends and lovers of all kinds."‡

The embryonic DAW took advantage of the cheap housing available in the inner-city neighborhoods close to the Wayne State campus, and within a year they were occupying seven houses and two storefronts, which provided them space for a printshop, a performance center, and places for other outsiders to crash and live communally.

While all of this was happening, Sinclair completed his coursework for a master of arts degree in American literature with a thesis on

---

* John Sinclair, *Guitar Army* (Port Townsend, WA: Process Books, 2006), 164.
† David A. Carson, *Grit, Noise, and Revolution: The Birth of Detroit Rock 'N' Roll* (Ann Arbor: University of Michigan Press, 2006), 108.
‡ Sinclair, *Guitar Army*, 46.

William Burroughs's subversive novel *Naked Lunch* before dropping out in the fall of 1965 to better pursue his activities in the Detroit jazz and poetry community.*

To those in tune with the Detroit underground in the mid-'60s, it seemed like Sinclair was everywhere. Just a small sample of his output included the publication of two magazines printed by the Artists' Workshop Press—one devoted to poetry entitled *Work*, and another devoted to avant-garde jazz entitled *Change*. At the workshop itself, Sinclair booked numerous jazz concerts and poetry readings, as well as photography and painting exhibitions by local artists. Additionally, he served as the Detroit correspondent for *Downbeat* magazine and wrote jazz reviews for *Jazz*, *Coda*, and *Sounds & Fury* and published three books of poems.

In October 1965, after returning from the Berkeley Poetry Conference in California, where he rubbed shoulders with fellow counterculture luminaries like underground publisher/musician/activist Ed Saunders and beat poet Allen Ginsberg, Sinclair was busted again for selling weed.

He pled guilty to charges of possession in order to avoid a more serious conviction for sales and was sentenced on February 24, 1966, to six months in the Detroit House of Corrections. The authorities hoped that spending half a year in the pen would curb some of his radical zeal, but it was not to be. Upon his release, Leni and the DAW didn't hesitate to throw a wild shindig in his honor they called the "Festival of People" where Sinclair held court as jazz groups improvised, dancers danced, and poets spouted antiestablishment free verse.

It was at this gathering the MC5 saw their opportunity to seize Sinclair's attention. Kramer and Tyner in particular had become fascinated by the firebrand, as had many who closely observed the steady rise of the Detroit underground. They had learned about the Festival of People gathering through their network of friends and had the band bring their

---

* Bentley Historical Library, University of Michigan, John and Leni Sinclair Papers: 1957–2003, Biographical/Historical: findingaids.lib.umich.edu/catalog/umich-bhl-850.

instruments, hoping to snag an opportunity to perform for the Hippie King. They finally got their shot at three in the morning, but their signature ear-shattering volume caused a redneck neighbor incensed by their racket to knock on the door with a shotgun in hand. Fearing more problems with police, Leni immediately pulled the plug on the Five before Sinclair had any real chance to hear them play.

Disappointed but undeterred, Tyner decided to take a different approach. After Sinclair wrote a column in the Detroit-based antiauthoritarian publication *Fifth Estate* attacking rock 'n' roll and the people who played it as puerile, Tyner wrote a sharp response. The singer rightly surmised that Sinclair would enjoy a good argument, and the two met soon after and immediately became friendly.

"As much as I loved jazz," said Tyner, "I didn't feel that it was ever destined to break into the mainstream consciousness, and that rock 'n' roll was the vehicle. The letter was printed, and John dug it, because he enjoyed confrontation."

Intrigued by Tyner's street-punk intellectualism, Sinclair started attending some of the MC5's shows and was surprised to discover how much he enjoyed them. "I saw they were doing the same sort of things as Coltrane and the other free jazz artists," he said. "Yeah, they were playing rock and roll, but with more creativity and improvisation."*

Soon, he began allowing the band to rehearse at one of the DAW's performance spaces and started advising them in an informal way. It was the beginning of an intense relationship that would eventually alter Detroit's music landscape, generate national controversy several times over, and land at least a few of them behind bars for lengthy periods of time.

But before any of that could transpire, the MC5 still needed a place to "go big." A playground that would allow them to develop their strangest ideas and indulge in their most extravagant conceits in front of an audience and turn them into the force of nature they would become.

---

* Carson, *Grit, Noise, and Revolution*, 111.

Through sheer luck and timing, such a place would fall seemingly out of the sky and into their laps. It was called the Grande Ballroom, a venue whose name was as majestic as their dreams.

ROB TYNER I was lurking around the Wayne State University campus in downtown Detroit, and I'd been hearing about this John Sinclair guy, who ran this counterculture performance space called the Detroit Artists' Workshop, so I went there to check it out and hear some music.

After the show, Sinclair got up in front of the audience and ranted, "You can't expect to come in here for free and listen to this beautiful music without giving up some money. You *gotta* pay to support the arts. These people work really hard and they deserve some money for their labors!" He really impressed me. He was almost brutal about it.

I figured the best possible way to align yourself with the counterculture was to go to the man himself. After seeing Sinclair in action, I knew that he was really motivated and organized. He had the Artists' Workshop, and I was beatnik enough to know that took a lot of work, and a lot of balls to do it.

JOHN SINCLAIR I grew up during the first wave of rock 'n' roll in the '50s. I loved it, but when I went to college I got into jazz. By 1960, rock music was a dead issue to me. I wasn't even interested in Motown, because it sounded like bubblegum music to my ears. I was just out there! All I wanted to listen to was progressive jazz musicians like Archie Shepp and Cecil Taylor.

But by the mid-'60s, everything was changing. Bob Dylan was the first one to really bridge it. He was a beatnik that also aspired to being wealthy. Before that, being a beatnik was really an underground thing inhabited by starving artists. The only people that knew anything about the Detroit Artists' Workshop were in our neighborhood, around Wayne State University. We used to promote the DAW events very selectively, because we didn't want a lot of squares around because we knew they'd blow the whistle on our activities. It was kind of a hothouse atmosphere, and that's what was so beautiful about it. A lot of people weren't even poets or musicians or performers; they just came every week and supported it.

It was especially beautiful because we were so fucking naïve. We'd read about things happening in New York or San Francisco, and thought, Maybe we can do that here.

ROB TYNER I thought John could be helpful, so I started looking for a way to introduce myself. He had a column in the *Fifth Estate*, a Detroit underground newspaper, and he wrote something to the effect of "These rock 'n' rollers, they ought to just open up their souls and listen to some jazz." As a gambit to get his attention, I wrote a critical response that said, "Listen, Sinclair, you jazz guys ought to drop all this bullshit and really listen to some rock 'n' roll, then you'd know what's going on for real."

JOHN SINCLAIR I didn't know Rob Tyner, but he was in my orbit. He was friends with Gary Grimshaw and Frank Bach, who both worked with me at the *Fifth Estate* offices on Plum Street, which was sort of Detroit's counterculture center. Grimshaw had returned from Vietnam and did the layouts, and Bach was a regular columnist.

Tyner and Grimshaw were best pals, but I met Rob through Bach, who brought him by the office one day. We talked, and I played them some flipped-out Cecil Taylor records, and we became friends. The MC5 were playing what they called "avant-rock." Wayne Kramer was the leader of the band, but Rob was the brains of the outfit. Tyner was emblematic of the kind of thing that was happening then: a high school intellectual and weirdo who embraced the energy of rock 'n' roll.

We just rapped, and discovered we had a common ground. That motivated me to want to see the MC5. Rock 'n' roll was so foreign to the beatniks. Beatniks appreciated folk and jazz but felt rock 'n' roll was hoi polloi music for chumps. But we were becoming aware that, in 1966, weirdos were starting to play electric guitars.

I first saw them at a battle of the bands or something in Northville, Michigan. They were like a gem in the rough. They were different enough from your typical rock-'n'-roll band to be interesting. I was coming from a jazz place, so most rock-'n'-roll bands just weren't that interesting musically. But the MC5 had an idea of something beyond that form.

When they did "Black to Comm," man, that fucking *killed* me. That was right up my alley. When I met them, they didn't really have a show. They were raggedy and nothing was together. They had some guy doing their equipment who just fumbled around. They'd be late, their gig would be a mess, then they'd play a handful of tunes and go into a half-hour version of "Black to Comm," and this would be in a teen club! Everybody hated it, but not me.

ROB TYNER "Black to Comm" was one of our first songs and one of the weirdest. There's some debate as to where that song came from, but I accept its existence. Originally, it had an extremely tight arrangement; just a regular three-minute song. It was the set closer. But it wasn't until we were able to stretch out at the Grande and places like that it evolved into the long, noisy free-form thing that it became.

People wonder about the name. It was always a chore to set up the PA in those days. You had to connect all the little wires, and connecting the black wire to the ground, which was "Comm," was essential. So "Black to Comm" was the connection that allowed our whole sound to happen.

Later we nicknamed that song "The Hydrogen Bomb." It was like a Tet Offensive against the music of the time. That song was our attempt to bypass all restrictions. It was a good excuse to let loose and totally let go and express all the vitality and energy overload that we felt in the city at the time. It became the song that I waited for at the end of the night, when I could unleash all the frustrations I was feeling inside.

I believe that the amount of screaming I did in the MC5 was a consequence of being born in Detroit. You're always screaming in this fucking town. We grew up in this city that was being built up and torn down at the same time. There were steam engines and big pile drivers, building freeways and tearing down buildings. There was all this turbulence and turmoil everywhere you went, and the cars were loud and real fast. We tried to express all of that in our music, especially in songs like "Black to Comm."

JOHN SINCLAIR I picked up a lot of my ideas from the West Coast. A lot of Detroiters that shaped what happened in the '60s like Russ Gibb, Gary Grimshaw, and Jerry Younkins [often referred to as Detroit's first hippie] traveled to Northern California frequently and met via the San Francisco poetry scene. I was there in July of '65 for a month, for the Berkeley Poetry Conference, and then hung out in the Bay Area and I met all these people from Michigan, and we reconnected when we got back into the city.

GARY GRIMSHAW I bounced back and forth between Detroit and San Francisco for quite a while. I came back to Detroit in fall of '66. Then I went back to California in early '67 and came back a couple months later. Just back and forth.

I was living in a rooming house maybe three or four blocks north of the Panhandle, by Haight-Ashbury. I started noticing these interesting psychedelic posters on the city buses advertising concerts at the Fillmore, the legendary San Francisco venue.

The early color Wes Wilson posters caught my eye first. He was the pioneer of using colors that were really electric. They'd be all over town. Every clothing store, record shop would have his posters in the window. If you lived in San Francisco, you saw them daily. The Fillmore really used the posters as their primary source of advertising.

I never really considered being a graphic artist until I saw Wilson's work. I realized it was something I could do, so I started working at that.

RUSS GIBB I was invited to San Francisco by a fellow DJ named Jim Dunbar. We'd been roommates in Detroit until he got a job at a

Chicago station doing a late-night shift. Even though he wasn't hosting a prime-time show, it was a giant station and went all over the country, so he was building a great reputation.

In the summer of 1966, he left Chicago for San Francisco, where he was doing radio and had a television talk show. I went out to visit, and one night he said, "Look, I've got these passes. I had this concert promoter named Bill Graham on my show today, and he's running some crazy club called the Fillmore where the kids go and dance."

He knew I'd had the Pink Pussycat, so he thought it might be interesting for me to check it out. We went over, and the Fillmore turned out to be this big auditorium with lights on the wall, things flashing, and long-haired people, which neither one of us had really seen before. It just blew me away.

Jim said, "I knew you'd like this; this is right up your alley." We stayed that evening and had fun. We were voyaging—going into a culture that wasn't ours. I was only twenty-five, but most of the people at the Fillmore were younger. I started thinking, This would go down well in Detroit. Jim said, "C'mon, let's talk to Graham."

Bill Graham turned out to be a character and a half. We went back to his office, and the noise level was incredible. There were all these strange people roaring around smoking pot—which I knew nothing about—and it was complete chaos. I finally got a moment with him and he said, "So, Jim says you have a club." I said, "Yes, I'd like to do something like the Fillmore." He said, "Detroit? How far is that from San Francisco?" I said, "Oh, 1,500 miles." He looked a little relieved and said, "Oh, okay. I'll tell you what you want to know."

When I got back to Michigan, my first task was finding a place where I could re-create the Fillmore experience. I was a bit older than most of my peers, so consequently, I had a little greater depth of knowledge of where things were in old Detroit. I remembered the Grande Ballroom from when I was a kid, and I set up an appointment with Gabe Glantz, who owned the building. I was totally out of my depth. Here I was, a twenty-five-year-old naïve schoolteacher, dealing with Gabe Glantz, who was much older, very smart, and swift with the dollar. I said, "I wanna rent this place," and his eyes just glistened.

The building was empty and completely dormant. He had tried to make it into a roller-skating rink, but that hadn't worked. He took me upstairs, and I saw the place was dirty and falling apart. I told him I wanted to rent it, and I think he said, "Well, that'll be $400 a week," which was an outrageous sum for this beat-up old place at the time. I told him I'd call him back, but I didn't . . . so he started calling me, over and over.

I finally called him back and told him that I couldn't afford it. He said, "I'll tell you what I'll do. I'll throw in the building, just give me half of what you make from the events." I'm sure in his mind, something was better than nothing.

Around that time, I went out to do a record-hop gig at the Wayne Memorial Civic Center in Wayne, Michigan, and there's a live band called the Motor City Five. I was introduced to John Sinclair, who was sort of managing the band, but with his long, shaggy hair, I thought he looked like a total madman. I told him I was thinking about opening a club and asked whether the band would be interested in playing.

He said, "Sure, and I can help you get other bands too." I was sort of fascinated with John and the whole scene around him. To make a long story short, we put on the first show at the Grande, although Sinclair really put it all together. He knew more bands than I did, but I knew the record side of things and I could plug the show on the radio.

GARY GRIMSHAW All the famous big bands played the Grande during the 1940s. It was the high-class, fun place to go. We think of the '60s as the Grande Ballroom's heyday, but the '40s were its *real* heyday.

Its stage was surprisingly shallow, but when you looked at it from the floor, it was very impressive. It also had a lousy backstage area—there was barely any room for the bands to hang out. When I first walked into the place, it was totally empty, and I thought it was big and scary. It hadn't been used for quite a while, and it was dirty and messy, and the carpet stunk. But when you filled it up with young people, and you had bands and a light show going, and you had all these little boutique concession tables filled with clothing and incense, it was fun. The ambience came with the people. It wasn't built into the place, that's for sure.

I came back to Detroit from San Francisco in the early fall of '66, and I stayed with Tyner, who was living in the city with Becky. I was right next to him when Russ Gibb called to book them to open the Grande Ballroom. Russ asked Rob if he knew anybody who could do a poster, and he just handed the phone to me. That was my first gig as a graphic artist.

San Francisco was a beautiful place, but I always felt like a visitor. I mean, I never really felt at home there, plus things were starting to happen in Detroit. Rob was in a band, I met John Sinclair, the Grande was opening, and I could work at the *Fifth Estate*. I was set!

It was weird. San Francisco was really like an outpost for people from Detroit and Texas. The moving forces in San Francisco weren't San Franciscans—except for the poets, which was a whole different thing. Chet Helms, for example, who ran the legendary Bay Area concert-production company Family Dog, was from Texas, and half of the people in the Family Dog production team were from Detroit. Larry Miller, who started underground radio in San Francisco, was also from Detroit. Tom Donahue liked to take credit for it, but Larry Miller was the first.

JOHN SINCLAIR The opening night of the Grande was a beautiful thing. I would say there was about 100 to 150 people there. Almost everybody knew each other. The crowd consisted of Workshop people, plus these suburban déclassés, and Russ's little crowd of post–high school West Side weirdos. Frank Bach was the announcer and stage manager.

It was great because we finally *had a place*. It was definitely the next level up from the Workshop, but it wasn't a big scene until they started bringing in the famous bands a bit later. For a year, it was like a family.

There wasn't any advertising except for the posters and maybe something in the *Fifth Estate*, so it grew by word of mouth.

RUSS GIBB For the opening, we put posters up all over town. I remember these hip kids from Cass Technical High School were very helpful, because they tended to live in very happening suburban areas like Oak Park, Southfield, and Birmingham. I think the first night we opened, we had, like, sixty-nine kids. It wasn't that big. But we had a black light; we had bought a couple toys at some cheap toy shop and spray-painted 'em, and we bought a strobe for $300, which was a lot of money. But the kids loved it and freaked out, and the next night—if my recollection is correct—we had maybe forty more people.

We met everybody, we talked to everybody. It was a great, open place, and the hippie kids were starting to really run free. It was like a lunatic asylum in the best possible way. The Detroit hippie culture finally had their own playground. I remember putting up aluminum foil over the archway because we wanted a little more color and sparkle, and we didn't have much money.

People think the Grande had a bar, but we never got a liquor license. We didn't really need drinks in those days. There were plenty of other ways to get high.

JOHN SINCLAIR Right from the beginning, the Grande had a great light show. I think it was developed by Grimshaw, Emil Bacilla, and Robin Sommers—that group of people. I can't remember who started it, but it was spectacular. They had a "disco ball," which nobody had never seen that before, a strobe light, and *everybody* was on acid.

GARY GRIMSHAW We put together the light show on a scaffolding before the opening. It was wobbly, but after a month or two, John Sinclair's friend Pun Plamondon and I designed a new setup and went out and got the lumber, and built a real solid light stand.

The main difference between the kind of light show we were creating and what they were doing in San Francisco was speed. The San Francisco light shows moved rather slowly. They were very subtle in the way that one image would change into another, whereas the light shows we did were frantic. Fast-spinning, flashing—we gave it more of a strobe-light quality. The light show was affected by the fact that we were all dropping acid. Taking acid was like a prerequisite for doing the show. Not every night, but it was certainly something we looked forward to.

And acid in Detroit during that period was not particularly clean—it was usually speed with a little bit of acid in it—so the light shows were real high-energy. San Francisco would work on their light shows at rehearsals, and it was very synchronized, and very personal with the band. Ours was more slam-bang.

A lot of the bands that would come in from out of town would complain, because we would do the light show *right on* the band as well as the walls around them. And they'd be there playing and there would be this barrage of colored lights coming at them. And after two or three tunes they were, like, blind and dizzy. We were kinda crude and rude; we'd just blast it everywhere. If we'd been paid a little more and could concentrate on it, we'd have worked out something a lot better. But... it was like 6:00 p.m. Friday night, drop everything, grab all the equipment, run down to the Grande, and bang it out. And then do it again the next night, and then do it again the next night, and then collapse on Monday.

There was no such thing as a rehearsal. We did all our rehearsing during the show. But it worked out well: we got a rhythm together and we learned to communicate with each other.

RON ASHETON [guitarist for the Stooges] Pete Andrews had a club in Ann Arbor called Mother's. I often played there with a band called the Chosen Few, and when we weren't playing, I would go down to see what was happening.

One night I went there, and a Detroit band called the MC5 were playing, and at that time there was still kind of a hostile element about long hair. I remember seeing Fred Smith, who had hair down to his shoulders, and some drunk kid tried to take a swing at him. My brother Scott stepped up and literally beat the shit out of the guy.

I had long hair, but my brother was still kind of an Elvis type. He had greased-back hair and sideburns, but he was used to protecting me, because I'd been through so much shit. I'm sure that Fred probably could've handled the kid himself, but my brother was so incensed that he jumped in. That's how I met the guys in the band.

My next real experience with the MC5 was when the Chosen Few played with them at the opening night of the Grande Ballroom. I actually struck the very first note at the Grande! I was playing bass, and we started our set with "Everybody Needs Somebody," the Stones song which began with a bass riff.

That night is one of my fondest memories. We were so anxious. We had our little van, and we arrived way ahead of time. Scott Richardson, our singer, drove, and he went up, knocked on the door, and no one was there yet. We were thinking, Whoa, this is a kind of scary part of town, man. I ain't getting out of the truck till that door is open.

Finally, somebody showed up. I remember walking in the place and being impressed when they switched on the lights.

It was a very different situation from playing the teen clubs. Even though they had security guards, you didn't feel like you were being chaperoned, and that's what I super loved about the place.

ROB TYNER The word "grande" was just a fancy way of spelling "grand." It was meant to add a little class to the ballroom when it was built back in the 1940s. But people are so literal in the Midwest, so everyone pronounced the Grande Ballroom the "Gran-DEE," and it just stuck.

The MC5 had a home-court advantage when we played there, because we understood the acoustics of the place and knew how to get a good sound there. It was originally designed to complement the unamplified sounds of the big-band era. The room was a circular-shaped thing, with this funny walkway all around it. The ceiling was domed slightly, which would add warmth and richness and beauty to the sound of a clarinet. And that would've been great if we played fucking clarinets, but it was a whole different ball game if you were plugging a Stratocaster into a Marshall, because the sound would rumble and roar. The trick was to control all the overtones. If you weren't careful, the music would bounce back off the walls and you'd get this slap-back echo that would garble your sound.

One night, after everyone was gone, I walked across the dance floor, a lone figure, the mirror ball still going around. And I stopped and stomped my foot, and the sound went *DAT-DAT-Dat-Dat-dat-dat-da-d*. It just ricocheted around the room. The place had the most bizarre acoustical properties. I didn't know anything about acoustics, and I don't profess to be any more of an expert now, but I know that if you didn't take them in consideration at the Grande Ballroom, your band would sound terrible.

We decided we would just overpower the echo, and this is where the sound came from because we had the technology to overpower it. We had Vox Super Beatle amps, and then after that big Sunn amplifiers, and after that Marshalls. We discovered that if you hit the "slap" with something harder, the problem disappeared. And on more experimental songs like "Starship" and "Black to Comm," we discovered we could also use the echo to add to noise and feedback. You can hear that extremely liquid echo on our live *Kick Out the Jams* album. It's just like throwing a rock into a pool.

RUSS GIBB I knew we needed bouncers to help us keep some semblance of order, but I had no idea where the hell to get bouncers. Upon a friend's recommendation, I drove out to an early McDonald's way the hell out in the sticks and met these two hillbilly guys. They worked at the Cadillac plant during the day and were looking to make extra money at night. They were the only people I could find that were dumb enough to entertain the idea of being bouncers at some hippie club in Detroit. But I guess they weren't that dumb. They thought the job was the funniest thing, because the kids turned out to be no trouble at all.

Back then, you hired a bouncer to clobber kids when they got out of hand. But the kids convinced me that all they had to do is talk to them, not clobber them. That "alternative" peace-and-love hippie attitude was already becoming prevalent. And they were right. The early kids were so nice and supportive. They felt they were creating a new world, and that's what made it interesting. They all helped.

RON ASHETON I was only sixteen or seventeen when the Grande opened, but I drove almost every weekend to go and just hang out.

ROB TYNER We wanted to give people more show for their money and be the hardest-working band in show business and all of that jazz.

We tried to put a bunch of different elements in our show, so even if you saw us more than once, each show would feel different and unique. We didn't have flash pods or anything like that. It was more about our physicality.

Most times the stage moves just happened. But you gotta remember, there was barely any room to move at the Grande at all. No room whatsoever. It was like a snake pit. Just look at the cover of the first album; there's millions of wires all over the place. There was this little railing you could stand on, and I used it a lot. The drum riser was right there. But what it made you do was jam-pack as much movement into whatever space you had. Occupy every inch of the space that you were allowed. When we began playing the bigger stages, that's when things began to open a little bit.

Putting on a great show was important. We didn't have the money, fame, or power; some of the bands we played with did, but could match or exceed them in aggression. When you were playing on the same bill as Janis Joplin or Jimi Hendrix, it became pure survival instinct on our part.

WAYNE KRAMER That's the thing about success: most of the time it doesn't have anything to do with talent or even luck. It's sheer force of will. You *make* something happen. But taking acid helped: it gave us some ideas about intensity and energy.

DENNIS THOMPSON Our music either scared the shit out of you or you were immediately attracted to it. It was one or the other. There was, like, no standing in the middle because it was an assault on your senses, and you were either with it or you were appalled by it.

Intuitively, we realized that energy could play tricks on people, and it would make them hear things that weren't there. The excitement we'd get back from the people was tremendous. The more we'd crank it up, the more we'd apply this intensity, the more intense the responses we'd get back from the crowd.

ROB TYNER To motivate the crowd, you gotta be motivated yourself. And I want to make sure I say this: being pitted against other bands was not our attitude—it was the attitude of the audience. The locals wanted to see how the MC5 would hold up against these famous bands. We didn't create that idea, but we didn't shy away from it either. If that's what the crowd wanted, of course we had to give it to them.

I mean, you'd come in and people would be patting you on the back, saying, "Go get 'em, man, go get 'em," and by the time you got ready to go onstage, you're just like a mad dog. Every time we were on the bill with somebody more successful than us, we stood up and fought. Detroit audiences will always give you an A for effort, and that is the greatness of the Detroit audience! If you get out there and bust your ass, then no matter who you are or where you're from, they'll give you your due.

People would always marvel at how we would kick the asses of much bigger bands, and it became like a blood sport after a while.

Audiences are extremely powerful—the crazier they'd get, the crazier we'd get. I was playing at a club in Paris one time, and I was doing this bit where I'd stand on the edge of the stage and fall off into the crowd and they'd grab you and throw you back on. It was a fun little game that

I used to play. But at one point, they just picked me up and passed me around the room. Now, I'm a large person—a big, broad-shouldered guy—the place was jam-packed and they just picked me up and passed me around over their heads. And I'm going "*L'étage! L'étage!* Put me back on the stage!"

RON ASHETON I became a great fan of the MC5. They had Detroit by the balls. High energy—that's what I liked about them. That's what was so daring and different, and that's why I fell so much for them, because I was interested in doing something similar.

They certainly paved the way for the Stooges. When the Stooges were just forming, we'd hang out with the MC5, and we shared the same sort of—for lack of a better word—contempt for bands that were more famous.

They'd show the respect due to somebody like [singer] Bob Seger for what he was doing, but when you were just sitting around, shooting the shit, they'd say, "Fuck that shit, man, we can kick on that." They were very street-level, scrappy guys. There was a lot of "Hey, fuck Ted Nugent, he can't play guitar."

Their idea was to do their own fucking show and kick some ass. I'd seen the Who at the Cavern Club in 1965, and for me, the MC5 were the first musicians that carried that kind of attitude locally. They were cultivating a whole new situation. I don't think they cared what people thought about them, and isn't that the whole idea of that period? Not caring what people thought? They had a mission, and they were going to carry it out.

RUSS GIBB The Grande was a spooky place when you were by yourself. You'd go in, and if nobody'd be in there, that old building made all kinds of noises. The story I heard was that there was a trumpeter who had been in a band, and he had gotten word that his girlfriend was killed in an automobile accident and committed suicide. He didn't kill himself at the Grande, but it was said his spirit came back there and that you could hear his trumpet.

We'd hear about the sound of the trumpet from the kids that would clean up. I always thought, Well, do they hear it because we tell 'em it's there, or does it actually happen? From an engineering point of view, I'm sure it had something to do with the ducts. We didn't have air-conditioning in those days. Instead, we had these large fans that would blow in, and they were in these metal vents that could pick up distant sounds like a big giant shell. I think maybe certain sounds, or certain winds, would create this noise, but it's more fun to think of it as the ghost of the Grande. There were a lot of people that did see ghosts there, but it was probably due to the circumstances—a lot of drugs were being consumed.

One legend I loved was that we kept the windows closed during summer heat waves to make people drink more soda. But the real reason we kept them shut was that we were afraid that the cops would shut us down because of the noise level of some of the bands.

ROB TYNER You're talking to a believer. One night I was stuck at the Grande when people that were supposed to take me home split without me. At first, I felt something, and then I started to hear something. Let's face it, it was a spooky place.

RUSS GIBB After the Grande opened, it didn't take long for newspaper reporters to start checking it out. Rumors were circulating that dope was available, and of course I knew it wasn't just a rumor—there were drugs *everywhere*. But I also knew I had to try to keep it on the down-low. From a business point of view, I had to side with the police. At one point I even offered to allow the Detroit police to send in undercover drug men if they wanted, but they didn't do it for some reason.

Anyway, this very conservative newspaper reporter came in one evening, and he started to ask kids questions like, "Is marijuana available here? Is it true that the potato chips have LSD on them?" The young people at the Grande thought it was hilarious. They knew he was digging for dirt, and they were quite willing to oblige. One kid said, "Yeah, man, we buy packages of potato chips down here, and take 'em home and sell 'em."

Now, the only potato chips we were selling were prepackaged and sealed, but the guy published what the kid said in the paper anyway. We thought it was funny. People to this day will ask me, "Did the potato chips really have LSD?" and I say, "No, it was the bananas." The misinformation was incredible.

To say that drugs weren't around would be less than candid. But I will tell you this, after the Grande had been going for a good eight or nine months, I was invited to a very prestigious party with some famous businessmen in the city, and on a table in this magnificent office was a tray of rolled joints intended for the guests. That started me questioning what the rules were. If you're rich enough, it seemed like you could do just about anything, and get away with anything. Some of the very people who were speaking out against drugs back then were the ones that were using them.

ROB TYNER My idea when we first started playing the Grande Ballroom in 1966 was to produce a live record of our arrangements of all this seminal garage-band material like "We Gotta Get Out of This Place," "Gloria," "Satisfaction," and so on. Instead, we decided we were going to have a smash hit with "Gloria," which was originally the B-side of "Baby, Please Don't Go" by Van Morrison's band, Them. We had it all worked out. Every time we played it, the people from the record hops would go nuts. Everybody loved it. Then the Shadows of Knight—those little rats—beat us to the punch and had a Top 10 hit with it. They pulled the rug out from under us, so I said, "Look, there's this other tune that Van Morrison did, called 'I Can Only Give You Everything,'" which, ironically, was Van's attempt at covering somebody else's song to try and get a hit record.

Truthfully, our first recording session ["I Can Only Give You Everything" b/w "One of the Guys" (1967/AMG)] scared me. I was nervous, because I knew the band was wondering whether I could pull it off.

The band nailed the basic track in just a couple takes, but I couldn't sing at all. My throat just stopped working. We had just rehearsed the day before with no PA system and I had strained my voice, but I also think it was a bit psychosomatic. The band tried to talk to me, but nothing worked because I was just not ready.

I gave it some thought and talked myself down, and went back in with a much healthier attitude, and nailed everything quickly. It sounded great and everyone was pleased with the outcome. We gave it to Jerry Goodwin, a DJ friend of ours, to get it played on the radio. That's how we thought it worked. You go in the studio and make a record and they start playing it on the radio! They played it a couple of times, but it never got into rotation. The station said something about a problem with the bass and the drums.

There was no shock when the song didn't take off, because it wasn't what we wanted to do in the first place. We knew that if we had done "Gloria," we would have been able to ride that sucker around the world.

However, we put one of our earliest original songs on the flip side, "One of the Guys," which was inspired by our early days. Before we moved to Detroit, we hung out at a White Castle in Lincoln Park, which was like the center of our universe. The crowd liked the Beatles and the Stones, but they were still suspicious of people with long hair. I was growing my hair out and changing, so, in some ways, the lyrics were my attempt to say goodbye to that world: "I don't see how you survive being one of the guys."

I'm not sure the band really understood what I was trying to say with the lyrics, because they still shared those Lincoln Park values. Fred still believed that if he didn't become a professional guitar player, he could still just pick up a bat and glove, become a pro ball player, and go all the way to the World Series. He still had those fantasies. You can't mess with people's sacred beliefs, and the other guys in the band believed in that world, but I was trying to move beyond it. When you're a kid, you have to work to free yourself from that perspective.

I grew up in an environment where my best friends were saying, "You're gonna be in a rock-'n'-roll band? With these kids? It's crazy. They're hiring at Chrysler, and you're going to chase around and throw your time away, and fuck it up, and, man, you're not getting any younger." And I was all of eighteen at the time! My hope was that the release of the first single would cool things out for me. Finally, the people who were always telling me that I couldn't do this for a living, would say, "Well, he did it. He's a real recording artist."

CHAPTER II (PART 2)

MOTOR CITY IS BURNING

> When I got to the door, there was a shotgun pointed right in my face. I said, "What the fuck? Is there a warrant or something? What's your problem?"
>
> —John Sinclair

In early 1967, as the activity around the Grande Ballroom started to heat up, the police were plotting with equal enthusiasm to bring the hammer down on Sinclair once again. However, this time they were also going to go after anyone in his widening circle.

The Special Investigative Bureau of the Detroit Police Department had opened a file on Sinclair after his first arrest for possession in 1964, and ever since they had been keeping a watchful eye on his activities. Sinclair had been smart enough to stop selling weed, but his enthusiasm for cannabis only grew and he continued to poke the establishment in the eye by doing things like starting a Detroit chapter of LEMAR, an organization whose name was short for "legalize marijuana."

In his book *Guitar Army*, Sinclair recalled, "We didn't think about the police at all. We were too busy trying to get all this shit together *and* we were dropping acid one or two times a week on top of that . . .

"They thought they were going to put a stop to us when they sent me to the Detroit House of Corrections a year earlier, but the whole fucking thing just started growing and intensifying and we were right in the middle of it. So, [the police] laid out this whole strategy for breaking up the expanding community before it could consolidate itself."

His rant might've sounded a little paranoid, but if there was any question whether there was a target on Sinclair's back, the answer came decisively at the dawn of 1967. In mid-January one of Gary Grimshaw's strikingly designed psychedelic posters began dotting the streets of Detroit promoting the "Guerrilla Lovefare," a January 29 event organized by Sinclair featuring the MC5 and what promised to be one of "the most explosive gathering of freeks [sic] in Detroit's history."

The Detroit authorities were clearly not amused by this citywide promotion of what promised to be a drug-fueled gathering and had other ideas. On January 24, a few days before the event, thirty-four cops staged a massive six-hour drug raid around the Wayne State area, arresting John and Leni Sinclair and fifty-four of their associates. While the raid succeeded in scaring the flared pants off the local hippie community, it proved to be somewhat of an embarrassment for the police, yielding only negligible amounts of marijuana. Less than a dozen "long-haired types with beards" were immediately released on bond, and forty-three suspects were not even charged.

Desperate to save face, the authorities held one person—John Sinclair. Sinclair was clean but was detained for allegedly giving two free joints to two undercover cops posing as a hippie couple at the DAW the month before. As this was his third arrest on drug charges, Michigan law at the time called for an automatic ten-year sentence. Sinclair's lawyers kept him out of prison by arguing against the constitutionality of the state's marijuana statutes, but the arrest would haunt him two years later when the case would go to trial and he would be found guilty.

But, for the meantime, he was free and determined to double down on his various pursuits. "The duty of the revolutionary," he would say, "is to make the revolution."

Unfortunately, there would be more chaos to contend with. John and Leni and poster artist Grimshaw decided it was time to give the Detroit Artists' Workshop a rock-'n'-roll facelift, renaming it Trans-Love Energies Unlimited (TLE). The name of the new organization was inspired by the song title "Fly Translove Airlines," by British folk-rock musician Donovan, and the goal of the "hippie cooperative" was to generate money by producing rock concerts and publishing books, posters, and magazines to feed and house its members, with Sinclair declaring that "the commune is the life-form of the future."

While the TLE sounded an awful lot like the DAW, there was one crucial difference in Sinclair's mind, and that was LSD. "Before acid, we didn't want to turn anyone on," he said. "The Detroit Artists' Workshop was created to be an underground club for jazz heads and beatniks. We were very wary of outsiders." The Trans-Love Energies Unlimited, on the other hand, was going to be a very public endeavor that would strive to effect political and social change.

The organization's first event, however, was nothing less than a total nightmare. On Sunday, April 30, 1967, Sinclair meticulously planned an afternoon of peace, love, and music to be held on Belle Isle, a six-hundred-acre island park located in the Detroit River, featuring local bands including the MC5, the Up, Seventh Seal, and Billy C. and the Sunshine.

The day went according to plan, but the positive vibes quickly soured when the sun began to set and a local motorcycle club called the Outlaws began to menace people in the crowd. The police, waiting for an excuse to bash a few hippie skulls, responded with a small army of

150 reinforcements, many on horseback, and turned the event into a total melee. As MC5 guitarist Kramer told journalist David A. Carson, "Mounted police galloped toward the running people and clubbed them like they were playing polo."

The Belle Isle Love-In was anything but, putting Sinclair's name once again in the middle of lurid newspaper headlines. Its memory, however, was quickly erased by the truly horrific events that followed two months later. On July 24, a raid of a Black after-hours club unleashed eight straight days of rioting in downtown Detroit that would result in 43 dead, 467 injured, and nearly 1,400 buildings burned to the ground, resulting in some 7,200 arrests.

The so-called 12th Street Riot is to this day considered one of the worst uprisings in U.S. history, occurring during a period of racial strife and similar race riots across America. The Detroit Police Department, which had only about fifty Black officers at the time, was viewed by the African American community as a white occupying army. Racial profiling and police brutality were regular occurrences, and when a vice squad raided an air-conditioned illegal after-hours club in a Black neighborhood one hot and sticky evening, the locals decided they had had enough. Some two hundred onlookers lining the street began to pelt the officers with bottles, and within an hour, thousands of residents from nearby housing filled the streets and began looting shops and setting Twelfth Street buildings on fire. As the rioting continued, snipers reportedly took aim at firemen and fire hoses were cut, causing Governor George Romney to request President Lyndon B. Johnson to send nearly two thousand U.S. troops, who began patrolling the streets of Detroit in tanks and armored cars.

The city's Black population was targeted, but sympathetic long-haired white radicals like Sinclair and the MC5 were second on the list. And when the shit hit the fan during the sweltering and tumultuous week, it was no surprise that they, once again, found themselves in the eye of the hurricane.

JOHN SINCLAIR Most of the time, my attitude was essentially, "Fuck this!" Because that's obvious that the police were always trying to intimidate us.

For example, we organized a benefit at the Grande we were calling the Guerrilla Love Fair, and it was going to feature music, poets, and there was going to be a lot of weed and acid. Then, a few days before, fifty-six people were arrested and put in jail during a campus dope raid. It was like a Vietnam-level body count, and it included most of the weirdos in the area. They arrested everybody that was standing around. If they had a warrant for you, and your friends were there, they all got crocked too. The intimidation was a real factor. My strategy was to not be intimidated: "Fuck this!"

Russ Gibb and the Grande Ballroom ended up backing out of the event, which was going to benefit Trans-Love's various activities. He was scared. I remember how let down and enraged we were. But there was too much heat, and we were so far gone on LSD at the time, so we had no perspective.

For many people, the raid was a mammoth discouragement. It was meant to bully the people from being part of what we were creating, and to some extent, it succeeded. People were afraid of going to jail. But from my outlook, it was important to oppose that sort of police intimidation. We really had to work hard to keep everything from shriveling up.

The Grande had only been open for three months, so the thing was just beginning to burgeon, and the raid was supposed to be the clamp. Everything had been so cool, and then the raid happened. I was angry when Gibb didn't support us.

GARY GRIMSHAW After the cancellation of the Guerrilla Love Fair, we worked like dogs preparing for the Belle Isle Love-In. The whole afternoon was really nice. It was just what it said it was gonna be—a love-in. Then, later in the afternoon, the bikers showed up, and they were all our friends, so they joined in the party. Then the police showed up, and the bikers started confronting the police, and that's when it turned into a riot.

By that time, we were all so buzzed that we just split. The whole riot thing happened after we were gone. It was basically just rock and bottle throwing. Philosophically, we were on the side of the bikers, but we didn't want to have a riot. In some ways, the event reflected the society it happened in.

JOHN SINCLAIR "Love-In Turns to Hate" was the headline in the *Detroit Free Press*. It started out as a beautiful April 30th Sunday in 1967. It was Wayne Kramer's birthday and Trans-Love Energies took a pavilion on Belle Isle, an island park in the middle of the Detroit River. We got a power generator and had a few bands play for free. Unfortunately, there was a community of bikers hanging out and they were engaging in their typically offensive behavior.

The police rode down on it on horseback and chased everybody off the island. It was like the Cossacks descending. It was disgusting. The media took kind of a triumphant tone: "See, this shit is crazy. It won't work. You can't have a love-in and have it come off right. Let's just keep celebrating war."

WAYNE KRAMER The Summer of Love never came to Detroit. It didn't fit. The Summer of Fear and Paranoia was more like it. The draft board would come around and fuck with you, patrol guys would fuck with you ... it was endless. The Belle Isle mess was immediately followed by the Detroit riots in July.

JOHN SINCLAIR The day before the Twelfth Street Detroit riots ignited, a bunch of us jumped into a van and went out to the northern suburbs somewhere to visit with these people that belonged to Mensa, the organization for people with high IQs. We were their guests of the month. They wanted to see if hippies were a new form of intelligence or something.

From there, we went to Grosse Isle, where this hip doctor was playing host to either Ralph Metzner or Richard Alpert, I can't remember which. Both were psychologists that participated in psychedelic research at Harvard. The part I remember is that the host's wife greeted us and then went off and reappeared naked to the waist. That was very outré, exciting, and hip to me. It was something you'd always dreamed of—women walking around without tops on. Very chaste, but . . .

The crowd was relentlessly hip, rich and hip, in a New York way. We spent a very pleasant evening and we got totally smashed. We finally left early in the morning on a Sunday, six or seven o'clock, higher than goats. That was the morning the riots started.

We went home, and when we woke up that afternoon, it was going full blast. You could see the fires. We were right there at John Lodge and Warren. Grimshaw created a banner that said, "Burn, baby, burn," with a picture of a black panther on it, and hung it out the window. We were so excited: We had our own riot! We thought we were going to win. Detroit was a hard place to have a Summer of Love. They didn't want that for some reason. The riot, though, that was big fun! We saw troops, tanks, convoys, and police of every description converge. We watched one convoy come down the street, and it came up to *our* door! Suddenly the police came charging through our little hallway and started banging on the door.

When I opened it up, there was a shotgun pointed right in my face. I said, "What the fuck? Is there a warrant or something? What's your problem?"

"We hear there are snipers up on the roof, and we're investigating."

"Bullshit, there's no snipers up here; are you crazy?"

I was kinda belligerent. This one police officer called me by name and said, "Aw shaddup, Sinclair, or we'll blow your head off."

That made me snap. I started hollering at them, "Go ahead, blow my head off, I don't give a fuck if it's going to be like this, if you can just walk in here and stick guns in our faces. I don't even care to be here. I'll go to another planet, start over again. This is unacceptable. Now, either blow us away or get the fuck out of here. Ain't no snipers here and you know it. I'm not going for this shit."

I just ranted and raved. These guys kinda looked at each other and backed off, because they could tell I just literally didn't care. That was a turning point in our development. It just blew our minds. I was just so pissed. Afterwards, we left town and went to Pun Plamondon's hometown, Traverse City. It was obvious that the riot was over, and the police had won.

For a minute, during the riot, it wasn't so clear who would win. There was one point when the 10th Precinct was pinned down by sniper fire. We thought the revolution had arrived, and I remember designing a flyer calling for a Bastille Day—let's go down and free all the prisoners from Wayne County Jail! I had the stencil on the mimeograph machine, when suddenly I had a moment of sobriety. I thought, Wait a minute, this is sedition. This is big trouble if we don't win. Ultimately, we knew it was over when we saw tanks rolling down the fucking street. Tanks!

BECKY TYNER John tells this story, during the Detroit riots, about being at John C. Lodge and Warren and being threatened by a policeman who held a shotgun to his head. The riots gave the police free rein to oppress the community. And the local cops knew what was going on within their area, and they took advantage of that situation to violate people's rights.

ROB TYNER Yeah, carte blanche and a shotgun.

BECKY TYNER After, John said, "I gotta get the fuck out of here," so he went to Traverse City for the duration just to escape. You couldn't blame him.

ROB TYNER We lived through that. We saw the city in flames, and it was scary. Becky and I were off camping someplace, Canada I think, and we came home and we were really tired, so we crashed out until about four in the afternoon. I woke up a few hours later smelling this smell, like somebody's fireplace backing up or something. Then I started to hear sirens. I got up and looked out the window and the whole neighborhood was full of smoke! I thought, Jeez, the building is on fire! So, we went outside and it wasn't our building burning, but there was something on fire. Then the phone rang and it was my parents out in Lincoln Park. They said, "What're you doing?! Get in the car and come out here; the whole city is rioting!" What? Rioting? We just got back from camping.

The authorities were so arrogant, they called our own National Guard on our people, right here in this country! There were so many bad things that happened during the riots. The police and National Guard were just out of control. The Michigan National Guard was issued live ammunition, real guns, and there were snipers all over the place. It was bad. We were really worried about being able to get out. So, we got in the car and we were driving down the freeway, and you could see on either side of the freeway whole neighborhoods going up in flames.

Other people in the band didn't get out of the city, and some of 'em wound up going to jail. Cops just came and picked 'em up and threw their ass in jail. Wayne was walking around in just a pair of pants, no shirt or shoes. They were just picking people up, even if you weren't doing anything.

We were looking out the window just before we got out, and these cars were pulling up in front of the house; guys would jump out, open up the trunk, take out all this stuff they'd looted from the stores, put it in the trunk of another car, slam the trunk, and drive off in search of another load. Afterwards, we got all kinds of stuff from people. It was bizarre. We got clothes and an assortment of other things that had been looted from stores. They knew that our ladies used to make our clothes for us, so they gave up all kinds of material. Because of the Detroit riots, we ended up with some good stage gear!

WAYNE KRAMER Frank Bach, me, and a couple of girls, and another guy went out to the beach on the Sunday that the riots started. It was really hot. I remember thinking earlier that week that the nation was going up in flames left and right. We were driving back from our picnic when I saw these big flames bursting out. I said, "Oh, goody, a fire. Oh boy." We were getting closer. "A big one too."

Then we noticed the shop windows all broken out, with TVs and shit laying in the street. Then I saw the whitewashed words "Soul Brother" written on some of the buildings. When we got to the corner of Beverly, where the Grande Ballroom was, I saw the National Guard on the corner, flanked by police convoys. It was anarchy. I said, "Whoa, what's going on here? The shit has hit the fan; let's get home." We kept driving and we got onto the expressway. There were more flames everywhere. It was like Dante's *Inferno*. On the expressway cars are racing every which way, lights out, sirens, smoke everywhere.

When we made it back to our apartment house, we went up on the roof and started watching as this police car pulled up and two Guardsmen got out. Two cops got out on the other corner, and we watched them run into a house. Then we heard shooting. The next day we found out that they had shot and killed an old drunk guy with a broom on a fire escape. They thought he was a sniper.

It went on for a week, and it was like a war zone. Sinclair, Tyner, and Fred split town, but I stayed. My mother called and said, "Wayne, are you all right? Do you have any guns or anything?" I said, "Ma, I don't need any guns." "Well, what are you going to do about the Blacks?" I said, "I'm not worried about the Blacks, I'm worried about the police. I'm afraid of the police. I don't care about the people in the neighborhood. They're just people."

We had a telescope in the window that we were using to watch shit. The police thought we were using it as a sniper scope, and they busted in the house Sunday morning. Everybody was asleep. They stormed in yelling, "Everybody get up! You're going to be shot! Everybody lay down on the floor! You're going to be shot!" So, everybody's laying on the floor with shotguns in their faces.

All they found was a knife and a bag of seeds. The fucking white troopers didn't know what the seeds were, so they yelled, "Go get that Black officer! He'll know what this is!" And he did. He yelled, "Yow, this here is marijuana, you're all going to jail!"

We went downtown and the detectives wanted to know what happened, so we told them how they'd broken into our house and clubbed a couple guys, and we didn't know anything about any seeds. They took me up to the jail, and as we walked past cellblock after cellblock we saw Black guys just beat to fuck. And they were all screaming, "Yeah, put the white boy in here with me! I'll fix his ass! Put him in here!"

I thought, This could get *really* unpleasant. But they put me in my own cell, and then they let us go. At the end of the day they just said they had their hands full and what did they need with us? It was an experience!

It wasn't too much longer after that we moved to Ann Arbor because Sinclair had been through the whole thing with the neighborhood: the robbery, the harassment. When he decided to move to Ann Arbor, we stayed for a little while longer, but then Michael's girlfriend got raped. Finally, we said, "Fuck this, this ain't living," and went out to Ann Arbor.

RUSS GIBB People in Detroit really liked the folk-rock singer Tim Buckley. He built quite a following at the Grande. He always struck me as the quintessential minstrel—the poet with an acoustic guitar.

On many occasions, Buckley and his conga player, Carter Collins, stayed at my house when he came to town. One evening, they were scheduled to play the Grande, and both came in early, so we decided to go out for a picnic. It was warm, hot, and muggy, and we hired the Grande cops to go out and stake out an area in Kensington Park, and invited the kids that worked at the Grande and a few close friends to join us.

The reason we had the cops was, in those days, if you got caught smoking pot you'd go off to jail, so we hired the cops to protect us from the cops! They thought that was funny, and we did too.

At the end of the picnic, we rode back into the city. Little did we know the riots were just starting to break out and pick up steam. We heard sirens, but you heard sirens all the time on hot summer nights, so it was no big deal. I do remember someone saying there was some kinda rhubarb down on Twelfth Street by the Grande, but that wasn't such a big deal either.

It was about 5:30 p.m., and I think Tim was gonna play that Sunday night. We got closer to the venue and ran into a police barricade. We saw a lot of black smoke, and I said, "Oh my God, there's a big fire." Then somebody came to their senses and turned the radio on, and then, of course, we heard about the riots. I took everyone back to my house, and we turned on the television and they were talking about "the great riot, citizens, please stay away, the police are blah blah blah." And then it hit me: "Oh my God! The equipment, the equipment!"

I thought about my $7,000 PA system at the Grande and panicked. The TV kept warning, "Please stay home. Do not go into such and such a zone." Which of course was where the Grande was. What were we gonna do? So, I decided we would try and run the blockade. I called my lawyers and asked what we should we do. They said, "Well, dumbass, you better go down there and get your equipment, if you can."

We were in Dearborn, which was totally segregated. It was the mayor of Dearborn who said the police should just shoot anyone causing a disturbance. That was his solution to the problem.

Tim, Carter, and I jump into my Thunderbird. Because Carter was Black we were worried he might get hassled, so we had him duck in the back. Then, as soon as we crossed Joy Road where it started getting Black, we had Carter take the wheel and we got into the back!

When we finally got to the Grande, there were people just running around. There was a Good Housekeeping store right where the Grande marquee was, and people were just looting the place—but it was sort of a joyous thing. There was a lot of smoke, but mostly it looked like a party. It was like a sale, but this time the customers were just bashing windows and pulling refrigerators out.

Carter had sort of a sense of humor about it. I remember him saying, "Hey, this Detroit shopping is the way to go!"

But we were afraid that if we opened the doors to the ballroom, everybody would swarm in, so we just hung around for a few minutes. It's interesting to note, there were white people doing their share of "shopping" too. There weren't as many, but they were helping themselves as well.

We were just about to go into the Grande when we looked across the street and saw someone throw a gasoline bomb in our direction. When that kind of bomb hits, it spreads. I thought, Oh my God, they're gonna burn the place.

We quickly opened the door to the Grande, and this one little Black kid ran in with us. I said, "What's going on?" and he said, "Oh man, it's crazy out there, man. It's crazy. Those fucking cops."

Then he peeked out the door and saw his buddies running by, so he drew them in. Carter took command and asked how they were doing. They told him that they were having fun, but added, "Hey, man, a hand grenade went off, and some dude was shooting from the rooftop."

We asked whether they were burning buildings, they said yeah, and identified a building that was on fire just three blocks away. We asked them to give us some help getting the stuff out, and they said sure. I asked one of the kids how come the Grande hadn't been torched, and he said, "Hey, you got music here, man." And that was it! The Grande did not experience a single problem. Nothing was burned, nothing broken, not even a window.

It was a music place, and to Black people, you didn't destroy that. Especially because by that time, we were booking people like Bobby Bland and Buddy Guy. While our audience was primarily white, Black kids from Cass Technical High or Wayne State would come to see shows. There was no difference. They were just bright kids doing their thing. Every so often, you'd get some Black kids that would laugh at the white kids freaking out, but it wasn't a problem. Certainly when we put on some of the more famous Black acts, we'd get Black people in, but it was more what we used to call "black and tan." The hippies didn't care.

CHAPTER II (PART 3)

RAMA LAMA FA FA FA!

> That night the MC5 played one of the greatest shows
> I have ever seen in my life. They were just incredible.
> It was hard to believe it took place on a stage.
>
> —John Sinclair

Even with his many distractions—taking drugs, being busted for drugs, organizing a massive commune, and God knows what else—Sinclair never lost sight of his commitment to the promising rock band he had taken under his wing. The truth was, he couldn't afford to.

Of his endeavors, the MC5 were his most lucrative, and it was the money from their countless string of one-nighters across Michigan that was keeping his Trans-Love dreams afloat. It's been endlessly debated whether Sinclair took advantage of the group, but it was easy to see that it was far from a one-way street.

With Trans-Love in their corner, the MC5 had an extraordinary advantage over most other struggling rock bands. The organization provided the quintet with management, roadies, a light show, a publicist, poster artists, clothes designers, photographers, food, shelter, and a small army of enthusiastic hippie influencers who cheered them on at all their shows. Not to mention, it was Sinclair's connection to the Grande Ballroom that gave them an extraordinary place to showcase their music and perform with national acts like Cream, the Who, Janis Joplin, and scores of other 1960s superstars.

Sinclair's involvement also brought the band massive amounts of publicity and enormous credibility within the hippie movement that was spreading rapidly across the United States like the sweet scent of patchouli oil in a tiny head shop.

To the MC5's credit, they didn't take his mentorship lightly, and they worked diligently to take full advantage of every opportunity he brought their way. The band approached every show, no matter how small, with rigorous determination, inspired by the standards set by their musical heroes like James Brown, the Who, and John Coltrane. While they lacked some of the God-given genius of those artists, they made up for it in explosive, unrelenting energy that struck fear into the hearts of many national headlining acts whom they were often hired to "support."

"We started developing a vision of what the band should be when the Grande appeared," said Sinclair. "We set out to destroy every time."

The band could be notoriously uneven musically, but they were almost always exciting, and on their best nights they could be the best rock band on the planet.

WAYNE KRAMER Our relationship with Sinclair developed on a philosophical level. His initial attitude was "I'll help if I can. I'll do what I can do." I couldn't ask him to do any more. John always maintained he was never in it for the money—he was in it because of the music and that's why we never had a contract. He had a cultural point of view, and he never wavered from it.

ROB TYNER You gotta remember that in those days, money was looked upon as being not so cool. We wanted to get rid of money and share things with one another. If you tried to sell that idea to kids nowadays, they'd just look at you like you're from a different galaxy. Back then there was this heavy anti-materialist thing. Travel light, live fast, die young, all that stuff, and don't bother about this money jazz.

JOHN SINCLAIR Not long after the Detroit riots, the Grateful Dead played the Grande. I was helping the MC5, but the idea of managing hadn't occurred to me yet. That changed when the Dead came to town and I met their manager, Rock Scully.

The Dead had an album on Warner Bros., and they were on a national tour, and here was a guy who was just like me: long hair, dope fiend, crazy motherfucker. But he was their manager! Until then, I'd always thought the manager of a rock-'n'-roll band was a guy with sunglasses and a cigar.

Although my function in the Workshop and Trans-Love was to organize its activities, it was more of an experiment in artists doing business for themselves—publishing our own books, doing our own concerts and performances, and maintaining our own quarters. Self-determination was the concept. So, I just thought that to go from that into rock 'n' roll, which was big business, required much more expertise and background than I had. It had never occurred to me that it was something I was capable of.

It was after speaking with Scully that I became the MC5's manager. It was just an organic outgrowth, and then a leap of consciousness that I finally said, "I can take responsibility for this!"

It was sorta ironic that the Dead would play such a pivotal role in our story, because the MC5 *hated* San Francisco music. They thought I was daffy for liking it. They kinda liked Moby Grape a little bit. But the

Dead ... they thought they were all just charlatans. They just looked at them like they were some lower musical form, because they were fans of more high-energy music.

MICHAEL DAVIS It's true. We didn't respect a lot of bands. The Who, they were dynamic. We wanted to at least match those guys because they were heroes to us. But I can't think of any American band we admired. There wasn't anyone that was doing what we did.

Other bands would always have a standard show, so how could they excel? How could they break out beyond their own barriers? We made it a point to break out beyond our own barriers every time. Nobody could ever predict what we were going to do because we would constantly change and evolve. We would always take chances. It didn't always work. Sometimes we had shitty shows for one reason or another, but I'll tell you, when we felt confident, we always had a good show.

RUSS GIBB When we first started to book the acts it was easy, because they were quite anxious to play. However, I was in a constant tug-of-war with Sinclair. He was always an advocate for using local bands. I guess I sided with that idea to a degree, because I felt my audience on the radio was also local, so it was politically smart for me to think that way. But we were also hearing these other bands like the Who, Cream, and Janis Joplin, and a lot of the kids wanted to hear them too. When we first started to book national acts, we'd get 'em at good prices. We'd guarantee them $500, and they were fine with that.

The first time Cream played for me in October of 1967, they were young and innocent. They were in awe of being in Detroit, and I remember Eric Clapton asking me about John Lee Hooker, who lived in Detroit. They were also really into the music of Motown, so I drove them by Hitsville, where all the Motown groups recorded their music.

They were overwhelmed by the reception at the Grande, and I think it was probably one of the best they got. People knew their tunes. Jeep Holland got me the record, and I started playing their stuff like "I'm So

Glad" and "I Feel Free" on air. Clapton was very easy to deal with. I'm thinking, They're rock stars from England; they must be special. But as I got to know 'em, they just came from ordinary backgrounds, so they could associate. And I think they always thought it was amusing that a schoolteacher was dealing with something like this. Jack Bruce was more aloof. He was slightly cold, and his eyes would shift more.

Clapton said he wanted to get some cowboy pants. Chaps. And I thought, Where the hell do we get chaps? Maybe they thought we were in the West. Then Dave Miller, the MC, said there was a costume shop down in Royal Oak. So, we proceeded to go up there, and he finds a pair, and wants to buy 'em. The guy says it's gonna be $150. Probably cost him $20. But Eric bought them and you can see them on one of the albums, where they have all the little pictures cut up. There he is with these furry pants on, which he wore onstage.

We also took him down to Montgomery Ward's department store down on Schaefer and Michigan in Dearborn. We passed it, and he saw this shirt in the window that he liked. So we took him in. Remember, he had long hair and was wearing bell-bottoms, and there's a bit of an entourage. Some kids hollered out, "Are you a boy or a girl?" That was the insult if you had long hair at the time, and he just ignored it. And the clerk couldn't understand why Clapton wanted this sun-faded shirt that was in the window. They had others, but the faded color appealed to him. Eric was particular about his fashion from the beginning. They finally took it off the dummy for him.

JOHN SINCLAIR The first time we played with Cream in 1967 was not a good experience. The MC5 liked Cream and the guys were looking forward to playing with them, but then they came in with their asshole English roadies and set up Ginger Baker's drums to take up the whole stage. We were forced to set up around them, which was humiliating. Dennis had to shove his drums into this little cranny, so everything was off-balance and we couldn't do our show the way we wanted to.

From then on, we were determined to kick their asses—as well as anybody like that who tried to pull shit like that. We protested, but Russ, of course, just sputtered, "But . . . Eric Clapton!"

You could tell Gibb considered them to be "legitimate" guys from England! Not just some scumbags you could get for $125 . . . like us! So, we didn't get any sympathy on that count. But it was a powerful stimulus to kill. Eventually we would get our chance to destroy them when they returned in the summer of 1968.

WAYNE KRAMER We had a little confrontation with Cream. They came in and played these endless solos. They just improvised for *hours*. At the time, I was listening to John Coltrane improvise. John Coltrane can improvise for twenty minutes and keep you interested. Eric Clapton can't improvise for twenty minutes and keep it interesting, I'm sorry. We started getting bored with it. It was pissing me off, because I could see the audience was going for it, and they just thought it was really something. I thought, This is bullshit.

During one of Eric's big solos, Jack Bruce walked into our dressing room, because he was on our side of the stage. We were back there grousing and trying to fuck girls—our usual backstage activities. Fred walks over to him and says, "Hey, you guys, you overdub on your records. I can hear two or three guitar parts on your records. How come you don't have two or three guitar players in the band. Isn't that being a little dishonest?" Jack Bruce said, "No, we find that Eric's capabilities are quite good enough for us. He can handle it all." Fred said, "Ah, bullshit. This is all bullshit." Jack Bruce went back to Russ Gibb and told him that Fred had been "insolent" to him.

JOHN SINCLAIR The MC5 built their reputation by blowing other bands off the stage. For example, there was a band on Verve named Beacon Street Union. They came here, and they plastered big posters all over. The hype was mammoth for the time, and, oh man, we just fucking *killed* them. They could hardly go onstage. We almost had to take them out in an ambulance.

ROB TYNER Jimi Hendrix's second album had just come out, and we were booked in February 1968 to play with him at Masonic Auditorium, a medium-sized venue in Detroit. We went on before him and tore it up. Then he came out and had all kinds of problems. He was very frustrated because his amplifiers were blowing up. Everything was as bad for him as it went good for us. I guess by default the audience gave us the night, another feather in our cap.

But let me tell you, Jimi Hendrix saved my ass. At one point, it was real bad within the band because of my hair. It was starting to get long, and nobody was digging it. I was walking around with my hood up in the middle of summertime. I had this whole complex about it. I felt like an alien. I didn't know what to do. I couldn't go Dylan's way, because it wasn't that cool, and I didn't even like Bob Dylan. I was totally brain-damaged about it for a long time. I'd try to straighten my hair out, but it just was not happening.

One night, some crazy son of a bitch walked in with Jimi's *Are You Experienced* album and I looked at the cover, and wow, I ran in the restroom and pigged my hair out and I was cool instantly!

Jimi Hendrix saved my whole fucking life. I went from being the most fucked up that I'd ever been to being absolutely on the cutting edge of cool. Overnight. Everybody's going, "Oooh, righteous hair, man." It was great. Till then I was still using hot combs and brushes and all kinds of crazy shit on my hair. The fashion thing at the time was very important, and you had to have just the right attitude about it. If you didn't have the right kind of hair, you were out. But after Hendrix, I'd walk around and people were out there perming their hair to try to get it to look like mine. A very strange concept! But that's one of the things I love about rock 'n' roll; when things get quirky, it can quirk your way.

When I allowed my hair to run wild, it became like a symbol for what was going on inside my head. Because I'd look at myself in the mirror, and that's exactly what I always saw inside: everything going haywire. Now my interior physiology was being exteriorized. I was bringing the inside to the outside. It was very liberating for me. It also consolidated the opposition. Walking into a place with hair like mine was a real statement of fact, and it's a little too real for a lot of people, which was damn good! This entire thing is a story about American freedom, and the freedom to exercise freedom.

The MC5's music was symbolic of my freedom, my struggle against people who said, "You can't." Ultimately, I guess they might've been right, but we gave 'em a damn good tussle. We came out of it kind of beat up, but that happens. It's what happens in the fight that counts. Right?

BECKY TYNER I used to set Rob's hair on big, huge rollers to make it straight. You can see a couple of early pictures where he has like this little bowl haircut. It was crazy, but you had to have this image. Then he'd start playing and sweating, and those bangs would begin to creep up and it really became tiresome. But one day he said, "Screw this. God gave me beautiful hair. I'm just going to let it be." And he did it on his own. He just let it go curly. That was great and fun too. That became a thing with the fans: "Yeah, I saw the band before Rob got his permanent."

JOHN SINCLAIR There was a huge anticipation for the Big Brother & the Holding Company show featuring Janis Joplin. They'd been at Monterey Pop, and they were the new thing that was going to happen. We were waiting for them. The band had no respect for them, or their guitarist, James Gurley. They were very arrogant. Even Eric Clapton wasn't really up to snuff. That's why they were always eager to get on bills with these people, because they knew they could blow them away. The MC5's idea of great guitar playing was Keith Richards and Brian Jones.

We *killed* Big Brother & the Holding Company. They were just cruising in, and they had reached a point where they were getting some respect and adulation, and they were enjoying it. We knew it'd be easy and we were laying for them, and the MC5 fucking *killed*.

ROB TYNER The first thing I thought was that Big Brother had no rhythm section. There was no drive. See, that's the difference between Detroit music and the music of almost *any* other place in the country, is that Detroit music has a drive underneath it. It's built into the attitude of the players. I mean, c'mon, Chicken Hirsh from Country Joe and the Fish? I'm going to get nervous about this guy? Jesus Christ, I could kick his ass on drums. No offense, Chicken, but hey...

DENNIS THOMPSON We had to blow those bands off to make a name for ourselves. It was easy to stomp the smaller bands like Beacon Street Union and the Vanilla Fudge, but soon we were up against the Who, Hendrix, and Janis Joplin. Although Janis and her band Big Brother was no competition. Janis was a bitch. She was an asshole. We saw her at sound check, and she would just browbeat everybody in that band. She used to yell at them like a screeching bitch, stopping them in the middle of a song: "Can't you get that part right? Can't you get that part right? I'm not going to do this anymore unless you concentrate. Will you fucking concentrate?!"

JOHN SINCLAIR What will it take to destroy the audience? We used "Black to Comm" like an atomic bomb at the end of the set, leaving them with an experience they'd never had before in pop music. So, the question was: How do we build up to that for maximum effect?

On the way to the gigs in the van, we'd smoke joints and listen to *James Brown Live at the Apollo* or Coltrane *Live at Birdland* cranked all the way up and we'd rap about what we were going to do that night. The energy and the power of James Brown! He was the model.

MICHAEL DAVIS I used to say, when everything else fails, we just kick shit over. It was kind of a joke. If the music isn't there that night, if the crowd isn't responding, just like knock all the shit down and everybody will go crazy. And it worked every time.

ROB TYNER The Detroit frame of mind is a car frame of mind. I think the band would agree with me that that's where we found the pulse, that's where we found the energy, and that's where we found the excitement. Here, in Detroit. The cars coming off the assembly line at that time... I'll never forget coming out of the Grande one night, and this guy almost hit me with a Mustang, and on the side of the car, of this Detroit machine, it said "Mustang Grande." It was a major Detroit experience. We had been playing and playing trying to get notoriety, and to see this Mustang, this new Detroit machine that said Mustang Grande? For a car boy, this was an intense omen. A wild moment.

Unequivocally, we were from Detroit, a product of Detroit. Detroit was *to blame* for the MC5. It bore the burden—they *asked* for it. Detroit was to blame for making me as crazy as I was.

DENNIS THOMPSON Russ Gibb kicked us off a bill with the Blood, Sweat & Tears, because he knew we would blow them to pieces. There was a big stink about that because we were scheduled to open for them in March of 1968. Beacon Street Union told them, "Watch out for the MC5, they're gunslingers. Don't let them on your bill." So, Blood, Sweat & Tears wouldn't play with us. We got canceled, and the Stooges were added to the bill in our place.

JOHN SINCLAIR The Stooges... that was not a randomly chosen name. The concept of the stooge was he didn't care. They basically created a wall of sound that Iggy could dance in front of. That was the concept, and it worked. When you'd *see* the fucking Stooges, it was incredible. Jaw-dropping.

It was funny. Blood, Sweat & Tears had heard of the MC5 and how good they were, and wouldn't let us open for them. But we fixed them by putting the fucking Stooges on.

GARY GRIMSHAW When the Stooges first started playing the Grande, they'd do these fifteen-minute sets. Instead of bass drums, they'd have these big oil cans for the drums. They'd come out and just do a wildly insane fifteen minutes and collapse, and then they were gone. It wasn't a set—it was just fifteen minutes of the "Stooges experience." The crowd liked them; it was like, "Did you see the Stooges? They only played for fifteen minutes but . . . wow!" It wasn't until they started getting booked regularly that they started doing real songs.

RON ASHETON The MC5 camp liked Iggy, but they thought the rest of the band was kind of a joke. They didn't think we were anything, musically. I don't want to gloat about it, but it's kind of ironic that we really made more of a mark in the long run than they did, with the limited musical talents that we had at those times. They really burned out fast.

MICHAEL DAVIS Were we jealous of the Stooges? No, I don't think so. The reason that the Stooges—well, Iggy really—stayed in the business the whole time is he stayed visible. He became an icon on his own. The whole time I was in the post-MC5 band Destroy All Monsters with Ron Asheton, he never stopped bitching about how Iggy had dumped the band, and now he was the big shit and poor little Ronnie Asheton was still living in his mother's house. He was always bitching about Iggy, but Iggy was hanging it out on the limb for the world to see. Ron was always upset that Iggy became such a star. Whatever. That wasn't anything I cared about at all.

RON ASHETON The MC5 could be aloof and very arrogant in a lot of ways. Admittedly, they were doing something right, so the arrogance didn't offend me, which was amazing because I don't like "arrogant." Period. But I would let it go with those guys. They didn't go out of their way to intimidate me, but they did always let me know I had my place. Fred and Wayne especially always treated me kinda weird. Not badly, but they acted kinda superior—you know, "You're lucky you're hanging with me" and shit. Still, I had a great respect for them.

They were volatile individuals. When they were younger, they could tolerate each other's bullshit better, but as they matured, they became such different guys. I knew that they were doomed. I saw them engage in fistfights over band business. They really were street guys, and that's why they died the way they did. They were the real essence of Detroit.

Wayne Kramer was always sort of deemed the leader. But each guy had his own subversive way to try to get his point across. Dennis Thompson had the loudest mouth. Fred would weave his quiet kind of "Fred Smith thing." And Rob would just leave. Rob was more an ally of John Sinclair. I would even forget at times that Rob was Rob Tyner and not Rob Sinclair, because he was like John's son. I really enjoyed Rob because he reminded me of me. Instead of yelling, he would go away and formulate some sort of logical way to express himself.

He was so different from the rest of those guys. Kramer and Thompson would argue all the time. They'd scream at each other. Kramer usually had the edge because he'd get Fred to be on his side. Rob would go, "Okay, whatever you decide." And somehow, they would work it out.

Dennis was a very opinionated, very strong person. You get the combination of Fred Smith, Dennis Thompson, and Wayne Kramer together, and it was like fucking mixing nitroglycerin. They were roughhousing guys, lots of punches . . . and arguments all the time.

They used to make fun of Rob, but I related to him because I was sort of an outcast too. But I also enjoyed the freak side of these street fuckers who would overindulge with alcohol or anything. Drugs. And fighting! We never, ever came to blows in the Stooges. But those guys would just wreak havoc.

CHRIS HOVNANIAN I don't know if Wayne was officially the leader, but John Sinclair used to talk to him a lot. It could be that John felt he could manipulate Wayne more than anybody else.

MICHAEL DAVIS The MC5 didn't have a leader. Reporters would always ask you who's the leader of the band, and our response was always "We don't have a leader. Leaders suck." Wayne later said he was the leader. You know, that's baloney. Wayne was probably the most aggressive, and always trying to get his way with things, but it didn't fly because everybody had to wait for Fred to get on board. I mean Wayne wanted me in the band and it didn't happen until Fred said it was okay. There just wasn't any leader in the band. But there was Fred.

We had our checks and balances; each member of the MC5 had their own kind of force field. No matter what kind of personality it came out of, it was an equal sharing. I think the reason the band started unraveling towards the end was because we started following somebody else's direction—namely Jon Landau [the producer of the band's second album *Back in the USA*]. And that's when things fell apart.

WAYNE KRAMER It's absolutely true that we would regularly sit Rob down and try to straighten him out in the most awful way, and I must admit that it was all Fred Smith. It was *all* Fred's doing. I did it with him for a while. We'd have these group therapy sessions where we'd all fishbowl Rob and just tear him apart. It was merciless.

In a lot of ways, Rob was uncomfortable onstage. He wasn't a natural performer. Talking to the audience didn't come easily to him. He was self-conscious about his appearance, so it was a difficult thing for him to get up and do, and I could see why he'd kind of wanted to get out of it. I don't think he had any kids then, but he liked to stay home, smoke reefer, eat, read books, and write. So, almost every year he would go through a period where he would threaten to quit.

The first couple of years I was involved in big brainwashing sessions. We'd be in a motel room somewhere, and we'd all take speed and stay up all night and browbeat poor Rob into submission. It was merciless, man. We just tore him apart. After a while, I just told the rest of the guys, "Look, you want to convince him to stay in the band, *you* do it.

Because I'm not going to be involved in it. Because if I had my way, I'd have him leave the band and get somebody else to sing who wants to be here who's better than he is."

I started thinking, Well, here's this kid Bob Seger. I know he could do the job. Then I thought, Maybe we can get Scott Morgan, somebody that's a good singer that looks good, and we'll do the rest. But after a while, I just didn't want to be involved in this psychological torture with Rob. I was the leader, and the one who found the most fault with Rob, but then Fred would come in and try and confront the situation and deal with it.

MICHAEL DAVIS We were always looking for a scapegoat. If things didn't go off well, we could always pick on Tyner. I mean, the guy had a gap in his teeth you could drive a truck through. He had this kind of foul hair; I mean, he wasn't handsome like Mark Lindsay, the singer of Paul Revere & the Raiders, or anybody like that. We gave him shit. He had to wear glasses, and so we told him, "You can't wear glasses onstage. What's wrong with you? And that dance step you're doing, you look silly. You're making us feel like we're a bunch of, like, candy-asses." We gave him a lot of shit. But part of being in the MC5 was being scrutinized by your fellows, but he got it the worst.

CHIS HOVNANIAN Rob was made to feel horrible. They'd call him fat. Is this how you treat your friends? And he had frizzy hair, which later became the big thing; then it was okay. Then it was like, "Hey, look at Rob, we love your hair. Isn't this great?"

Rob also got criticized because he and Becky wanted some time alone: "He should be spending time with the band. Why is he spending time with his wife?"

ROB TYNER The people you surround yourself with can affect everything about you. You have to be really strong in who you are in order to avoid being hemmed in and having your options cut off. My physical appearance was not that of a star; I was more like a working stiff who got lucky.

I was completely unsuited and genetically inferior to be a rock star. But I brought a lot of humanity to the stage. If you don't have outsiders, then you're gonna have people with skinny legs, long hair, and a guitar to identify with, which is exactly what happened when MTV got big. I felt it was my job to bring some reality to rock 'n' roll, or else it would become fake, just like everything else.

I had different motivations than the other guys in the band. I was already married, so I wasn't into it for the chicks primarily, or the adoration, whatever. I was in it for the art. Wayne and Fred and those guys were unattached, and that was their reward. But when you put on a performance that is intentionally abrasive and confrontational, the chicks split and it gets lonesome. Artistically, some of those performances were really satisfying to me, and I didn't give a damn whether anybody else liked it.

I saw absolutely no future for me at all, in the mid-'60s. I did not believe that I was going to live to see twenty-five. The animosity directed toward me by strangers was so intense that I figured that, if I kept along the way I was going, pretty soon one of 'em was gonna stop and kill me. Or society would stop me somehow. So, I got to the point of, "Well, what the fuck, then?" It was all the more reason to be weird and outrageous. I was under fire from so many different directions that I didn't think it was going to last much longer anyway.

My whole psychological situation had deteriorated, but when I moved in with Becky, all that kind of went away. I got a handle on some stuff. However, the band didn't like the fact that I was spending so much time with her. It took my time and input away from them on some levels. But, hey man, you gotta have a life.

WAYNE KRAMER Our second single, "Looking at You," backed with "Borderline" [A2 Records, 1968] was radically different than our previous attempt. By that time, we were full-blown acidheads. Our goal was to tear down the walls and uplift the spirit! John Sinclair produced that one, and John's idea of record production was "Go for it. Floor it and risk everything." Whereas, before that we recorded with supposed music business "professionals" and whatnot. Unlike [our previous] single, the Ann Arbor single doesn't sound like a band trying to make a hit single. At that point, we thought doing what we were doing *would* be the hit. We knew we were doing something weird, and something different from what any other band was doing. The sound was different. We got deep into it. John was like a cheerleader. He got us all pumped up, and then we went in and rocked the house.

JOHN SINCLAIR When we recorded "Borderline" and "Looking at You," we made the engineer, Danny Dallas, crazy! Poor guy. We had next to no experience in a recording studio, but we had a clear idea of what we wanted that band to sound like. We thought the best way is to just turn everything on and let us play live in the studio.

I wanted to capture the chemistry of the band. The MC5 made something happen while they were playing together that wasn't in the arrangements or in the tunes. If they tracked their parts separately, how could the chemistry happen? How could you get the feeling between Fred and Wayne, and the interplay with the drums? That was what made the MC5 so exciting. You wouldn't get that if they tracked their parts one track at a time, as Jon Landau so thoroughly proved when he produced *Back in the USA*.

We had, like, three hours. "Borderline" was recorded in one take, and the mix was just as quick. We concentrated more on "Looking at You." Wayne and I went in and mixed it while we were on acid.

We paid for a three-hour mixing session, and two and a half of it was spent on "Looking at You," and it came out perfectly from my perspective. I mean, I can listen to it today and I'm still struck with the perfection of what we achieved without having any idea of what we were doing.

Dave Dixon was a DJ on WABX, Detroit's big underground FM radio station, and he hated it. It was the very opposite of his taste. The kids would call up and ask Dave to play "Looking at You," and he wouldn't do it. He would accuse them of just having been put up to it by us, but it was genuine response. They were fans and they wanted to hear it. Of course we urged people to call in and request it, as any band does, but kids wanted to hear it, and Dixon would tell them, "Oh, it's terrible, the production is awful." When we came out with the album on Elektra, he completely changed his position on the band.

ROB TYNER When we started playing the Grande, we used to headline the damn place, and then they started bringing in all these established people from the outside and we had to adjust. We didn't mind, because a lot of the acts were great. For example, I think we were third on a bill behind the Fugs and Sly and the Family Stone.

Ed Sanders, Tuli Kupferberg, and the rest of the Fugs were into the poetry of the thing. Ever hear "Venus Rising"? That's a wonderful piece. I think that's where modern poetry and music is going to be someday. A masterpiece.

And Sly and the Family Stone were fantastic. "Dance to the Music" had it all! But once again, that echo problem at the Grande hurt them. Despite that, everybody liked Sly. How could you not?

But goddamn, you want to talk about the British Invasion? We got invaded, that's for sure. There were Brits crawling all over that place. Initially, I had this mentality of "They're on our turf and we gotta open for them? Jesus Christ." But we were powerless, because, of course, Stevie Winwood and Traffic were going to pull down a larger buck than the MC5.

JOHN SINCLAIR Jeep Holland was the most powerful local booking agent at the time. Despite our growing popularity, I often had to beg him to give us gigs so we could pay the bills. He booked all the frat parties and the teen clubs, and he had the hot teen acts like the Rationals. He was still into the concept of uniforms and all his bands dressed in matching outfits. Each group had their own distinctive uniform, like the Apostles all wore capes, which was pretty corny.

The Rationals and those people only played the Grande because Jeep was booking it; otherwise, they wouldn't have played there. The Apostles, the Thyme were all Jeep's groups, and he'd just bring them in when he had openings. I always hated the way Jeep booked the Grande. I always had beefs with him, and it was such a humiliating experience to beg him for $125 gigs. Plus, the MC5 were drawing! We eventually had to pull out of there for three months in order to create a new term of agreement.

I'd spend hours sitting in his office trying to get a meeting with him. I'd always badger him for "TG gigs," which is what we'd call TGIF fraternity parties on Friday evenings. They were lucrative, and if you played early enough, so you could squeeze in another gig later the same night.

To be fair, the MC5 had a terrible reputation, because they would regularly fuck up gigs. Part of my job was to guarantee that everything would go smoothly. The shows might be loud, and it might be weird, but at least they would be on time and they would play the allotted length of time. I wanted to establish regularity. Not of the music, but of the conditions of the performance.

Before I started helping the Five, they'd show up forty-five minutes late; they'd set up, that'd take another hour, and then they'd play "Black to Comm." They'd be drunk by then and totally pissed off. The people would be pissed off, and the players would be pissed off. So, there'd be an orgy of hatred and negativity.

That problem with Jeep wasn't a real problem, though. We were just trying to convince him to give us some action. It wasn't like he was actively trying to shut us down or anything. We were a big headache! If I were an agent, I would've flipped too. If I'd had to send a band to a frat party, it wouldn't have been the MC5.

RUSS GIBB When the Grande started exploding, suddenly, bigger agents and people like Premiere Talent started to intercede, and the prices started to go up, and the demands were ever increasing. I felt like I was being raped. First it was the money, then they started into dressing rooms. They were demanding this and demanding that. It started to get crazy. Then they wanted percentages. My Scottish stubbornness started getting the best of me and then I started thinking, The hell with 'em.

But Gabe would say, "Do the math!" And he'd figure out what we could expect to get, and he'd say, "Pay the price." He was willing, and he would never renege on payment to a big band. But to little ones he'd weasel, and that used to bother me, because I'd have to deal with the local bands and guys like Sinclair daily. He'd say, "Nah, nah, they'll play for nothing." We had a constant battle on that.

JOHN SINCLAIR In May of 1968, Detroit had gotten too intense. When Martin Luther King was assassinated in April of 1968, the police created a curfew and just shut everything down on weekends. It decimated us financially, because the only way we could keep Trans-Love Energies afloat was by working Friday and Saturday nights at the Grande. I remember borrowing money from my parents to be able to feed everybody for the week. We thought they were going to shut Detroit down for the whole summer, and that's when we decided to get the fuck outta the city.

We moved to this big turn-of-the-century house on 1510 Hill Street in Ann Arbor. Our reputation had preceded us, and immediately, Lt. Eugene Staudenmaier, from the Ann Arbor police, came knocking on our door to see what we were all about.

We invited him in for a heart-to-heart conversation. We were very reasonable, but the first thing we said was that we planned to stay. We explained we weren't a criminal enterprise or anything. We were just a rock-'n'-roll band and a light show, and that we looked forward to the peaceful, calm environment of Ann Arbor after Detroit. We didn't anticipate any trouble, and we weren't looking to cause any trouble. However, if there were any trouble that we didn't cause, that we would resist to the utmost, and if there were any unprovoked type of raids or any kind of police action, we would defend ourselves to the death against this.

If they had a problem, or if they had a warrant for somebody, or somebody did something wrong, call *me*. Don't bring a bunch of police here to ride down on the house and to pull a big show of strength, because it won't work. We didn't care about dying.

And we developed a relationship. We had ups and downs over the next year or two, but it worked well, and we didn't have any trouble.

WAYNE KRAMER I can't say a bad word about Lieutenant Staudenmaier. I remember him coming over to the house, stopping in. He was very low-key. Great police officer; he was cool even when I wasn't.

For example, we were performing at a park in Ann Arbor and getting heat from the John Birch Society for being "subversive." Sinclair was sitting up on the hill talking with him, trying to make sure everything was fine with the authorities. I had no idea, and of course, that's when I made the crowd say "Kick out the jams, motherfuckers" three times! It was another one of those times when John was so fucking mad that his face turned beet red.

He came running up to me, and his voice was up six octaves, "Man, I was talking with the police and you had to do it three times! Are you out of your mind?"

John was the master negotiator. There he was, sitting with Lieutenant Staudenmaier, telling him how "Everything's fine ... yeah, nothing too weird here ..." Then: "Motherfucker! Motherfucker! MOTHERFUCKER!"

ROB TYNER Out of all the possibilities of law enforcement officers in that situation, Lieutenant Staudenmaier was probably a miracle, because he was a serious individual and a fair man. His image was that of a total pit bull cop, but he was always very fair with us. There was outrageous shit going down on some levels, but he was the voice of calm, the voice of reason. And as a result, we always tried to be straight with him.

BECKY TYNER I think Staudenmaier had an identity crisis because of us. His frame of reference was "These horrible people have invaded *my* territory, and they're against everything I stand for. But I sort of like them. What can this mean?" He went beyond our stereotype and treated us as people.

ROB TYNER It was extraordinary, because he had all these rabid dogs around him that were just ready to go in.

BECKY TYNER One time he came over to just talk, and Audrey Simon was standing in the front room smoking a joint. Lieutenant Staudenmaier walked right in, because the front door was wide open. Instead of just putting it out, she screamed, "Aiiieeee!" and ran the fuck out of the room.

He just sorta stood there. Remember, this was an incredibly conservative Ann Arbor policeman, who was coming from this real redneck place, encountering this household of hippies who were smoking dope and breaking the law. How do you deal with this? Immediately, Leni Sinclair and Audrey got in his face, yelling, "Fuck you! You don't have any right coming in here; you don't have a search warrant. Get the fuck out of my house."

Rob and I heard the commotion and came in and defused the situation by just being civil. We said, "Hey, man, how ya doing? How's it going," which allowed him to bow out gracefully.

He was ultimately a decent guy. One time, when the band was on the road, Staudenmaier came around the house to check on us. A bunch of women had been murdered in Ann Arbor by a serial killer and he was concerned. He urged us to be cautious of who came and went. He had been around enough times to bond with Chris, [Fred's girlfriend Sigrid], and I, so he had concern and compassion. It was real and very touching.

RON ASHETON I can remember being at the Ann Arbor house when the lieutenant detective of narcotics would come in. He wouldn't bust the house. He just wanted to see "Oh, who's here?" It was more like "At least I'm glad to know where all of the assholes in town are, so I can keep an eye on them."

The Hill Street house was open enough that if somebody came in and just wanted to be a person, they were accepted. That was John—just trying to bring people together. A lot of it was just the power of John Sinclair. He really was a powerful person. John was so unafraid, he took everything so casually and welcomed any kind of weirdness. I don't mean bad weirdness. That was part of his thing. I just think the aura and atmosphere he tried to create was "Don't feel paranoid. Hey, this is it. Feel free. We're doing our thing here, and the goodness and the righteousness of what we're trying to do will save us from any real harm."

JOHN SINCLAIR The only real trouble we had in Ann Arbor was when we decided to play a few free concerts, and it was about our right to be able to play for nothing for people. We just said, "Well, we're going to do this." To say that we couldn't do it was an unreasonable position, and we wouldn't accept it. We told them they would have to bring in tanks and arrest us.

We told them that we wanted to do it in the West Park, because it's perfect and we'd have a lot of fun there while respecting the right of the people around there not to be assaulted with this music.

Other than that, we didn't have any harassment problems. People weren't getting busted for a joint or shaken down on the street as had been happening in Detroit. That's why we left Detroit. We couldn't *move* without being surrounded by police. Guys would simply walk down the street, and they'd have the police stop them three times.

RON ASHETON The Stooges were also based in Ann Arbor, and I liked knowing that John Sinclair and all these Detroit people were in the area. That they were sitting down and actually talking about trying to change things so we could live comfortably as people, because we felt isolated and alienated. I know it sounds weird now, but just having long hair or looking a little bit different put you in great jeopardy. I had been hit on the street. Michigan college kids in cars regularly tried to run me down. I had full beer cans thrown at me for just walking down the street. It was nice to know that in my town, there was a group of people creating a "freak community." Before they moved to Ann Arbor, it was *very* underground. There was no meeting ground. I thought of it as a command post, and that's what it was.

The Jefferson Airplane had played at Ford Auditorium, and they thought, Well, hey, let's check out the Detroit messiah, John Sinclair, our cultural counterpoint in Detroit. They came to the Hill Street house and I remember everyone was a little apprehensive. They wanted to make them feel at ease. Grace Slick was drunk after consuming a bottle of whiskey. People were asking her for a hit of it and she wouldn't do it.

My impression was that the Airplane thought the place was kind of creepy. I didn't feel that they really liked it. I left, because I felt uncomfortable. It was like the inspector general in the military coming to check out the barracks of the Michigan hippie scene. That was my first encounter with the subculture snobbery.

JOHN SINCLAIR In June of 1968, we killed Cream. The Grande was packed, because they were at the height of their popularity. The Cream were like the new Beatles in Detroit. Granted, "huge" in Detroit then was two thousand people. The Grande was packed from wall to wall. There was not an inch of space. It was about 105 degrees; it was so hot you hardly see, but because it was the Cream we were ready and wanted to wreak havoc and exact our revenge.

The previous time we played with them, we had to set up around Ginger Baker's drums, and we weren't going to let it happen again. Did anybody tell you about the special material we had for that show? It really didn't come off, but everything was so cosmic by then, it didn't make any difference. We were going to have Tyner mock-assassinated. I mean, *that's* the way we were preparing for them. We were *prepared*.

ROB TYNER I had a plan to burn the American flag onstage in protest of the Vietnam War, and then have someone in the audience pretend to shoot me with a pistol loaded with blanks. At the end of one song, the flag would be burning, then this straight-looking guy, one of our friends from the Up, would come up with a starter pistol and shoot me. I was going to fall on the stage, bang a blood capsule on my head, then rise up over the footlights covered in blood and fall down dead. Then the band was going to jump him and beat the fuck out of him. A couple of guys would pick me up and take me in the dressing room and we were just going to lock ourselves in until everybody went home.

Unfortunately, people got wind of the fact we were going to do it, and the Grande promoters, Russ Gibb and Gabe Glantz, said, "You burn the flag, you're never going to work in this town again . . . da-da-da-da, the police, they'll take our license away . . . don't you *dare* burn the flag." I said, "I promise I am not going to burn the flag. I promise."

Since I promised them I wouldn't burn it, me and our equipment manager, Steve "the Hawk" Harnadek, tore it to shreds instead, in protest of the war in Vietnam. The guy who was going to "shoot" me jumped up, pulled the gun—I'm standing there waiting to get shot—and the gun wouldn't fire! Click, click, click. So, he turned around and walked away, leaving me standing there with the flag in tatters.

I'm like, Goddamn, the theater's gone! Now, this is real. I have just ripped up the American flag like a goddamn idiot, and I got stuck with that. It was meant to be part of a whole piece to say something about American violence, and how the plastic people were so into the thing that they'd rather kill a person than see the thing being messed with. But the punch line never happened, and I had some explaining to do.

I've taken the American flag onstage probably as much as George Bush ever has. And I've always treated it with respect. We used to cover the amps with American flags. It's a cool symbol, if it stands for something good.

JOHN SINCLAIR After the show, we got called on the carpet by Gabe and Russ. Scores of parents called the club the next day and screamed. But despite all the drama, that night the MC5 played one of the greatest shows I have ever seen in my life. They were just *incredible*, and so fucking good it was hard to believe it took place on a stage. After that Cream show we were really feeling our oats. That was when the legend of the MC5 really began to peak—they were becoming as badass as their idols.

RON ASHETON One time the Stooges came to see the MC5 at the Grande, and we were late. They were already onstage and they were playing "Black to Comm." We slid right in the very front row. I was sitting next to this girl that was a regular. John Sinclair and Steve the Hawk came out and were playing saxophone and freaking out. Someone broke one of the mic stands, and Hawk threw down the base of the stand and it bounced, right onto the fingers of this girl that was next to me. It ripped her up, man, I'm talking *to the bone*. Blood everywhere. But she was so into the MC5 show that she would not listen to my pleas of getting medical attention. She could not stop watching the show!

On another occasion, the Hawk rolled out a cherry bomb onstage and it went right between Wayne Kramer's legs. He saw it, did a backflip. The firecracker went off as he jumped, he flipped backwards and landed on his feet and kept playing. I'm going, "Too fucking cool, man!" That stands out forever.

I liked it when they did their stage moves and it came from a real place. But eventually, they discovered things that the crowd responded to and their show became too staged and pretentious. It was better in their earlier days, when they were just feeling themselves out and doing that stuff organically. That's when it was *hot*, man.

RUSS GIBB I got tired of the Grande after it started to really make a lot of money—and it made a hell of a lot of money. I profited $25,000 off the Cream show alone.

I remember coming home with a brown paper bag filled with cash. My father was sitting at the kitchen table when I got in, and I said, "You wanna see something?" I take this brown paper bag and I pour it out, $25,000 in cash. He said, "What did you guys do? Rob a bank?" In his mind, the way we made money probably was a little illegal. By this time there were stories about dope and so forth, and he was a little suspicious. But he sat down and helped us count it!

ROB TYNER The consensus on the band Blue Cheer was that they sucked. I never thought anything like that. They were good people to me. You won't hear me say anything bad about them.

JOHN SINCLAIR Our show with the Blue Cheer, in June 1968, was another turning point for the band, and our relationship with Glantz, Gibb, and the Grande. Before the gig, somebody called Russ up from the papers, asking, "What about this 'kick out the jams, motherfucker' thing?" Russ trembled and his lawyer, Roger Craig, came down. They were trying to censor us from saying something that had been our rallying cry for six months. We said, "Wait a minute, let's not be silly; this is *us*. We built this place. What are you talking about?"

We were really pissed off. He was literally *not* going to let us play. He had been our friend and benefactor, but that was because we had made him a lot of money. We weren't going to back down on the use of "motherfucker," because we'd said it every time we played the Grande, and, to some degree, it was a big contributor to our success.

It was more than a gimmick. That phrase could express exuberance or rage or whatever . . . a whole complex range of emotions about the way things were. It was all in a phrase that was also sure to offend the squares that offended you. It was a way to get in their face and make them as disgusted with you as you were with them.

RUSS GIBB People sometimes painted John and I as enemies, but I never found him to be difficult to deal with. Some people thought he was always ranting and raving, but I never found him that way. I always found him very straight. In fact, he had a term: "Let's take care of business."

It was funny, because people would say, "Boy, Sinclair really hates your ass." Or: "Boy, did you read what he said about you in the *Fifth*

Estate?" But it was a friendly feud. I never felt a personal vendetta or vindictiveness. He was totally a different guy in your day-to-day dealings with him.

John seldom came on harshly. I saw him mad only once or twice. John would just shrug his huge shoulders and he'd just smile at you. "You can't do it like that Russ. You can't do it like that, man, it just don't work." And he'd shake his mane of hair, and God bless him, he could convince me a lot of times. I figured, What the hell, this guy knows more about this stuff than I do.

John was the only one who really understood in the very beginning what I was talking about, and really drew me in. When I think about it, I was probably sorta like Richie Rich to him—this little teacher with some bucks in his pocket.

ROB TYNER There was all this talk about sex and drugs in the media. And with the way we lived, everybody kind of said, "Oh yeah, that's them! Rock 'n' roll, sex, and drugs? That's them." That's why a lot of people came to see us, and that's why parents really hated us. A friend of mine told me this terrible story about how she was a big MC5 fan, and how much her dad really, really hated us. She sent away to get a Trans-Love poster. And when they sent the poster to the house, her old man got the mail and opened it up. He was so angry, he got her down on the ground and tried to make her eat it!

When we were building our following, there was this tremendous turbulence in the country. Culturally speaking, there were a lot of people experimenting. Drugs, sex, and politics—everybody's mom was flipped out. There were all these individual family wars going on. All over the country: fathers against kids, mothers against kids, kids against their parents. It was a very turbulent time, and the MC5 was a product of that. We got to the point where the "love it or hate it" aspect began to get more and more intense, to match the escalating civil unrest. It's hard to get people to understand what an intense time it was.

JOHN SINCLAIR I remember two things vividly about the July 4, 1968, Saugatuck Pop Festival. Even though we were on the west coast of Michigan and a long way from home, the audience was calling for the MC5 all afternoon. God, my mind was blown! Wow! This whole crowd, man . . . It was like, "Wow, listen to that shit! Goddamn!"

There were intense backstage negotiations about who were the stars, between the Detroit bands like the Rationals, the Amboy Dukes, and the Frost. I tried to tell these guys that it would be better for them if they let us close, but it didn't matter to me when we went on. We would go on whenever they insisted, but if they had to follow us, they were going to be in trouble because we were going to kill those motherfuckers! I don't remember but we went on probably two bands from the end, and just leveled the fucking place. There was something like five thousand people there and it was the biggest audience we had played for.

Bob Seger, the Rationals, Ted Nugent . . . these were all the band's peers. I didn't have any background in the rock world, and it was through the MC5 that I grew to enjoy and appreciate these people. They all became my friends, even though their goals were different than mine—they were all just nice kids trying to be the Beatles and buy their mom a new house.

For beatniks, the possibility of influencing the public was just not even in the deck. We were just hoping to get recognized by Allen Ginsberg. We wanted to go to New York and see Cecil Taylor. That was the epitome of success for a beatnik. Our goals were to have someone like LeRoi Jones welcome you into his home. So, I had to relate to those people through the prism of the MC5.

MC5 was the radical left wing of that world, but they were in it. They were part of that community led by people like Bob Seger and the Rationals, who already had records on the radio. Great records, in my estimation.

Bob Seger's manager, Punch Andrews, always had a different outlook than most people in the Detroit music scene. Punch was an unremitting square, as he is today. He owned the Hideout clubs and came from the greaser teen scene. He always had this idea about the "proper audience." You never saw Seger play benefits or free concerts. He was so concerned about overexposure that it took Bob ten years to achieve national success, even after he had a big hit single.

MICHAEL DAVIS I believe the MC5 put Detroit on the musical map. I mean, there had been music in Detroit, for sure. Motown was there, and there was a blues scene, but Detroit wasn't particularly noted for being somewhere where all this great music came from. Later, Mitch Ryder, Bob Seger, Ted Nugent, and Alice Cooper became bigger stars, but we put the town on the map.

What made us stand apart from all the other Detroit bands? Well, for one thing, we were totally arrogant. We had Fred Smith! So, there wasn't any way that anybody could be better than us.

ROB TYNER Sure, there was jealousy, of course. There were numbers in a damn legion that thought we were an overrated bunch of boobs who couldn't play for shit and didn't know how to tune our guitars. There was a whole bunch of people that really used to look at it like, "Well, yeah, if it wasn't all that bullshit. Yeah, okay, so you got this big fucking stage show." There wasn't universal acceptance to the MC5's music, and I never pretended that there was. Or should be.

WAYNE KRAMER We were definitely on the rise, but that didn't stop us from constantly getting hassled. We played at this club in northern Michigan called the Loft, and the club owner stiffed us on part of the money.

But because he made *so* much money from our show, he apologized and begged us to come back. He said he'd pay us the money he owed us from that show and to give us more money the next time, so we went back and played again. Afterwards, the band was tired, we'd done our show and everything was fine, but this rent-a-cop started woofing at us to "get our fucking equipment out of here." We woofed back at him and told him to go fuck himself.

They were in a hurry to get home, so this name-calling thing went back and forth a little bit. I think the club owner might've burned us again on the money. But then he called and begged us to come back and play again and said he would give us *all* our money. We went out there again, and when we pull up there's all these Oakland County Sheriff's cars all over the place. They told us we couldn't sing "Kick Out the Jams" because it was obscene.

John Sinclair told them, "My contract doesn't say anything about that. It says my band shows up here and we play at this time and we make this much money. That's what we're going to do." But the cops were all whipped up about it. We started to play the show, and we got into "Kick Out the Jams," and they turned the power off on us. They told us they were going to have a folk singer come up and sing about peace and freedom. So, we started packing up our shit, and the kids started leaving.

I walked through the crowd, and the fans were angry and tried to set fire to the place. Outside in the back there was a bale of hay in the back and the kids lit it up. The cops all ran over there and put the fire out. Then this rent-a-cop that John had had the words with earlier went up to the top of the stairs and points over at Sinclair and says, "That's him, that's the bastard who started all this."

He got two or three Oakland County sheriffs, and the rent-a-cop went over and tried to lay hands on John, and John clobbered him. Knocked him down, busted his glasses. John's a big guy. Then, all the sheriffs jumped in. Fred was just close by, and I guess he went over to help John, and they whaled on him too. There was all this screaming and hysteria. They took us all to jail. That was pretty wild.

WAYNE KRAMER The trial over the skirmish was a big deal. John was charged with resisting arrest, assault and battery on a police officer, and Fred was charged with the same thing. When they got to the booking desk, the rent-a-cop wanted to sign the complaint, and the real cop told him, "You can't sign; you're not a police officer." So one of the other real cops said, "Well, I'll sign the thing. I'll say he struck me." They just *lied*, which was typical. "Pigs" was not an inaccurate expression for the police in those days.

They threw Fred's case out, and they convicted John. Everybody's testimony was pretty factual. Nobody buttered it up too much except for Tyner. I think Tyner's the one that lost the case for John. They made a big issue because I swore and I used a clenched-fist salute. The prosecutor made a big deal out of that, demanding to know "What does it mean?" I gave him all my standard cosmic "We are the people" and all that shit.

But Rob made a big deal about how his music was "music of love" and he was pretty persuasive—I thought, Man, he's doing really good, he's swerving the jury in our direction—until the prosecutor did his closing summation and said, "Yeah, that's right, you heard Rob Tyner get up here and testify that the MC5's music is the 'music of love,' well, 'kick out the jams *motherfucker*!' Is that love?"

It was like UHHHHH! That's why we lost it. When the prosecutor said "motherfucker," it was *really* dirty. It wasn't just dirty, it was *unspeakably* dirty. And all the good citizens of Oakland County agreed that John had assaulted a police officer. They cut John's hair off. They took him to jail. He appealed it, but they cut all his hair off. Boy, he wasn't thrilled with that. I was in New York when he had to go back for the sentencing. I talked to him on the phone: "What happened, man?" Inaudible. "What? What'd you say, John?" Still inaudible. "What? Huh? Say what?" "THEY CUT MY FUCKING HAIR OFF!"

That kind of shit happened a lot. Club owners got incensed at what we were talking about. Or what we did onstage. Tyner had this routine when we did "I Want You Right Now" where he'd pull one of our official groupies out of the audience, or some other girl, and feign intercourse onstage. People would get nervous: "Holy cow, look what he's doing." But none of these "outraged" club owners ever objected to the amounts of money they were able to make off the band. And they all did make money too. We didn't really know it at the time; we didn't realize how things worked. At the time when the first album came out, we were probably still playing for $125 if we could get it. We'd still drive out to Livonia or somewhere to play a teen center for $150 or $200.

JOHN SINCLAIR When we all started working together, the attitude was singular. It was shared by about eight primary people, and then by another support group of probably twelve more people. That's a big attitude, man! You had the band and me, [roadies] the Hawk and Ron Levine, and we were all single-minded of purpose. The stuff that I wrote about the indivisibility of the MC5 at that time was sincere and heartfelt. That was the way that it was.

The beauty of it was our sense of community. During that time, there wasn't ever any quibbling over allocations of money or resources. That's another reason why I was so hurt by the stuff they said afterwards, and the negativity that was fanned by Jon Landau and [the accountant] David Newman.

The early supporters of the band just put everything into them, because of the love of their music and the possibilities it represented. Man, that was the thing. If we got any money, it went for equipment and transportation. People did their flyers and posters, promotion, light shows, anything that was needed, without any thought of compensation. It was a whole different type of construct. That had an influence on the development of the band, sure, because they weren't just a band trying to get over. They were part of a *thing* we hoped would take over the world!

The group never resisted any of it. I mean, we had to literally go over and wake them up, make sure they got dressed and make sure they had their instruments. The Hawk and Ron, for example, were like members—they were firmly committed. Then would just take care of everything so the band didn't even have to think about any practical matters. Then I would be there to make sure that the band would leave at the appropriate times. It wasn't like they resisted this. They knew they needed that component.

The MC5: (from left) Wayne Kramer, Dennis Thompson, Michael Davis, Fred "Sonic" Smith, and Rob Tyner. *Michael Ochs Archives/Getty Images*

Robert W. Derminer's dramatic transformation into Rob Tyner—a 1963 graduation photo next to a portrait taken a mere three years later. "Being cool was an uphill battle for me," he said. *Courtesy of True Testimonial*

An early band shot, circa 1965. From left: Rob Tyner, twenty; Wayne Kramer, seventeen; Dennis Thompson, seventeen; Michael Davis, twenty-one; and Fred "Sonic" Smith, seventeen. *Emil Bacilla*

John Sinclair, twenty-eight, manager of the group MC5 and founder of the White Panther Party, poses for a 1969 portrait in Detroit, Michigan. *Leni Sinclair/Michael Ochs Archive/ Getty Images*

Michigan National Guardsmen push rioting Blacks back from a burning building with fixed bayonets on Detroit's riot-torn West Side. Tank crews blasted away at entrenched snipers with .50-caliber machine guns early July 26, 1967, after sniper fire routed policemen from a square-mile area of the Motor City. *Bettmann/Contributor*

The MC5 give a typically spirited performance at West Park in Ann Arbor in July 1968. *Leni Sinclair/Michael Ochs Archive/Getty Images*

The entrance of the Grande Ballroom on opening night, Friday, October 7, 1966. It's promoted as "a dance concert in the San Francisco style." *Emil Bacilla*

Guitarist Wayne Kramer lets his freak flag fly at the Grande Ballroom, Detroit, Michigan. "Clothes became a big part of our show. It was a good thing. Costumes are what entertainers wear," he said. *Charles Auringer*

Gary Grimshaw, childhood friend of Rob Tyner and the graphic artist responsible for many of the unforgettable concert posters that helped put the MC5 and Detroit's Grande Ballroom on the map. *Emil Bacilla*

Gary Grimshaw's Seagull is one of the rarest and most collectible rock posters of all time. It was printed in 1966 to promote the first shows at the Grande Ballroom that featured the MC5 and the Chosen Few. *Courtesy of Laura Grimshaw*

ROB TYNER Becky would make me clothes and I would go through them in one second. She'd work and work and work and make these beautiful outfits and then I would just go right through them. I think that if we hadn't done that, we would have been pretty dumpy-looking. We got into really crazed colors and stuff. We'd rip 'em all up onstage, and Becky and Chris and Sigrid would just go to the store and only buy even more insane material—sequins and sparkly things. We wanted to take advantage of the lights and make it a visual experience that would grab people. I really liked walking in with some totally ballistic jacket and freaking people out.

BECKY TYNER I really didn't know how to sew. None of us did. But what happened was Wayne saw a picture in a magazine of the Beatles wearing that Gandhi kind of jacket, with a Mandarin collar, and said, "I want one like that." That's really what started this whole clothing thing, and so we started to sew clothes, because you couldn't buy anything like that in Detroit.

The jackets we made were really intricate. The first thing I ever made for Rob was a black blazer jacket, and then these shirts with big ruffles at his throat. When the rest of the band saw what Rob had, they all got into wanting these elaborate clothes.

WAYNE KRAMER Rob was a real prick about his paisley shirts; he had two of them and I asked him to loan me one. "Let me wear one; it'll be cool," I said. "You wear the greenish paisley, and I'll wear the brownish paisley. We'll be in the band together . . . fashion statement." But he'd never loan me that motherfucking shirt! Prick. I couldn't understand. But now I realize it was *his* shirt, *his* statement.

BECKY TYNER Making clothes for the band really did evolve. Rob would tell me what he would like, and I figured out how to do it. Chris would sew clothes for Wayne, and then Sigrid came around and she started to sew some clothes for Fred. Michael and Dennis were kind of left out in the cold because they didn't have girlfriends to sew for them. So, if we had time, we'd make something for them. Girls would come around to see Dennis and Michael, and we would say, "You're here to see them; well, first, you sew this. Do it!" We were not always really nice.

WAYNE KRAMER My girlfriend, Chris, could sew. Becky Tyner could sew. We could never find shit that you want in stores, so Chris and Becky said, "Just go pick out the material you want and we can make it." I started to realize these clothes were a big part of the show. This is a good thing. Costumes are what entertainers wear. So, we'd try and come up with more creative, and more outrageous, jazzy, appealing, and exotic [stuff].

CHRIS HOVNANIAN Wayne was wrong. I didn't know how to sew. I'd never sewed before. I'd tried to sew once in high school because we had to for a class, but I got a D in sewing. I found it totally frustrating. I hated it. Wayne told me, "I want this Nehru jacket. Make this." I told him I didn't know how to sew. "You can figure it out," he said.

Of course, they didn't even have a pattern for it yet at the fabric store, because it was a new style. So, I just cut it different. The first one I made, I didn't even know you were supposed to press the seams open. The hem was all different lengths. On the inside it looked horrible. On the outside, it was *sort* of a Nehru jacket. After that, he wanted more stuff, so they ended up getting me a sewing machine. Of course, then Michael wanted clothes, and Dennis wanted clothes; they didn't have anybody to make clothes. Becky would only make clothes for Rob. I ended up making clothes for everybody!

When Sigrid moved in, she took over Fred. I went down to a fabric store in Detroit, and I spotted a tapestry rug lying out, and I thought that would make a nice jacket. It was heavy, but it made a great-looking jacket. After that, I made these orange satin pants, and an orange ruffled shirt to go with it. Wayne put it on, then he took one jump and he ripped the pants. After that he wanted them custom cut.

I saw this photo in *Vogue* where a model was wearing these pleated sleeves. So, I got this idea for a shirt that would have these huge buccaneer sleeves, but they'd be pleated satin. I put glass buttons on it. This shirt took me a long time, and I was really proud of it. He wore it once and it got stolen. What? You let that shirt get stolen?! His attitude was "So what? What do you want me to do? Make another one." I can't believe I did.

When Jesse Crawford started hanging around as their spiritual adviser, I made him a black velvet cape with a red satin lining. At least *he* appreciated it. He loved that cape and prancing around in it.

ROB TYNER Our girlfriends made all the sparkly, futuristic clothes we're wearing on the cover of the first album, like Mike's American-flag outfit. In many ways, our clothes were instrumental in making the MC5's stage show the spectacle that it was. A lot of the material was cheap, because people didn't typically buy it to wear on the streets, which suited us fine, because we had absolutely no money to work with. The girls could take almost anything and make a great stage outfit out of it, and they just went nuts and gave us a completely original look.

Our pants were a universe unto itself, or at least, a system of tailoring. They were made to be worn sans underwear and designed to be as provocative as possible. We all had good legs and we wanted to show them off. The back would have an actual sort of cleavage, then they'd be cut super close to the thighs, and tight at the knees, and end in a slight flare. Then boot-cut—lower in the back than it was in the front to go right over the top of your boots. I used to draw cowboy pants like that when I was a kid.

We each had our own contour, and we did a lot of striped pants, because again that would accentuate the curve of the leg. At the Grande, the audience would be right at pant level, so we tried to make every detail exactly right. But there was an inherent flaw built into them on purpose. A favorite thing was to have mine constructed in such a way that when I'd fall to my knees and get back up, the knees would be gone.

On the first "Kick Out the Jams" video, I fell down in front of the camera and you could see both knees rip, revealing a gash where blood was coming out. You can see all the people—especially the chicks—going *wongo*. Wayne would often have to change his pants at least a couple of times during the set because they would rip at the crotch. They were blatantly made to be as suggestive as possible.

Becky made Iggy's first serious pair of tinfoil pants. He wanted them cut very, very low, and she cut them so that the top was parallel to his pubic hairline. One time he was onstage performing, his thing fell out and he was arrested for obscenity.

WAYNE KRAMER Breakaway pants! They were just made of cheap material. We made them tight. And with all that leaping around, gee, if something were to rip and there was a scandal, it'd be terrible.

We were playing this job up in Dexter, Michigan, and I accidently exposed my "personal self" as the local newspaper claimed. I wrote this great letter back to the editor or to this newspaper saying: "What he was showing was his penis. His personal self is on display all the time."

I didn't actually know I was exposed. I was jamming away. I was on the floor of this teen club. I did a couple of moves, a knee drop or something. I see all these young girls aghast, pointing at my crotch, going "Uhhhhh!" Then I said, "Yeah, baby, there it is. That's right, that's it right there."

Then I looked down and said, "Holy moly!" I was so caught up in the gig that I didn't notice.

On another occasion, we played at this open-air festival, and I ripped my trousers open and walked back into the dressing room with my dick hanging out. And here's Procol Harum, with all their girlfriends and wives, all these low-key polite English people. And I come in with my dick out: "Yeah, baby, here I am, here I am." Suddenly the whole room went quiet.

ROB TYNER There was the whole period where we really did go crazy with the clothes. But later, we adopted a much more casual look: Levi's,

T-shirts, Levi jackets, and rock-'n'-roll boots; that would be the band uniform for a lot of gigs. Once people knew who we were, there was less motivation to dress to impress. Later, when we went to England, I returned to wearing all black.

WAYNE KRAMER Rob wore some wild shit, man! He really got creative. He wore a miniskirt once. He said it was a long shirt, but if it was, then it was a long shirt that *looked* like a miniskirt. He didn't have any trousers on and wore black pantyhose. It was wild. Hell, yes. He's started to deny it later. Clean it up in retrospect. You can do what you want with the information, but he did it. It was *his* idea, but we thought it was great. He just showed up with his new outrageous shit. Everybody was trying to outdo each other. Come up with something wilder, flashier! We went through our taffeta phase, our velvet phase, our lamé phase. Gold lamé was big for a while.

ROB TYNER A lot of times, the stuff was great individually, but when you put it all together it was just fashion chaos. Sometimes it worked. But sometimes it didn't, and I'm still living with it. Like the bullshit about me wearing a miniskirt! Goddamn lie. I wore a green sparkly shirt that was long, had long tails on it. And I had tights on underneath, and high boots, and the press said that I was wearing a fucking miniskirt. But I guess we got a lot of publicity out of that. But that's one thing I really want to have in the book. I did *not* wear a fucking miniskirt. I am not the father of androgyny!

But you know what? When I saw Alice Cooper the first time, down in Florida, he was wearing almost the same damn outfit, except that his *was* a miniskirt. Nobody bitches at him for wearing a goddamn miniskirt. Oh well . . .

CHAPTER III

KICK OUT THE JAMS!

> They filled the Grande Ballroom, they played a great show, their clothes were amazing, and the kids were screaming. They were loud and fast and spun around onstage. What else did you need to see? I mean, if you worked for a record company, you go, Wow!
>
> —**Danny Fields, Elektra Records A&R**

In the summer of 1968 there was no one more surprised than John Sinclair to discover that all the unusual threads of his life had come together to create an astoundingly well-designed psychedelic tapestry. He was a poet, a freak, a leftist agitator, and an ex-con, but somehow, through it all, he had stumbled into becoming the "chief hippie" of a growing revolutionary movement, and the manager of a band that could potentially be as big as the Grateful Dead or the Rolling Stones.

It wasn't all by accident. Sinclair had been as productive as one of the many factories that dotted southern Michigan, and his organizational skills were rare in the radical community, though not unheard-of. In fact, there were several others like him in other parts of the country building small armies of like-minded long-haired extremists who were in the process of doing their best to disrupt society.

First and foremost, there was Tom Hayden, who was the president of the Students for a Democratic Society (SDS), a national protest organization composed mostly of college kids. The SDS held an earnest if somewhat naïve belief that a nonviolent youth movement could transform the United States into a model political system. While Hayden was effective in coordinating some of the earliest anti–Vietnam War demonstrations and recruiting students to head to the South to work for the civil rights movement, Sinclair often dismissed the group as "squares who were like old people, only younger." Essentially, Hayden and the SDS did their best to work within the system, and, not surprisingly, the taste in music of many of them reflected that—they were into "wholesome" folk music rather than the raucous rock 'n' roll and free jazz that energized Sinclair and his Trans-Love community.

More to Sinclair's liking were the Yippies, a loose and often intentionally buffoonish confederacy of anarchists led by New York activists Abbie Hoffman and Jerry Rubin, who believed that American politics and culture had become "a fascist joke." They dismissed the Vietnam War as absurd and declared that both the Democrats and Republicans were completely bonkers. The shaggy duo—who disdained the button-down look favored by Hayden's university students and dressed more like Cheech and Chong in denim and headbands—decided that the only way to disrupt the system was through absurd behavior.

During one anti-war march in 1967 in Washington, D.C., they teamed up with legendary Beat poet Allen Ginsberg to hold a public exorcism of the Pentagon. The crowd of an estimated thirty-five thousand protesters—some dressed in witch hats—attempted to cast out the demons of war and even tried to levitate the massive Pentagon building

"300 feet in the air." Hoffman and Rubin's wild political theater generated national headlines for weeks and piqued the interest of thousands of kids who normally wouldn't give a toss about the government—which is exactly what the pair wanted.

In January of 1968 Hoffman and Rubin established the "Yippies," which was short for the Youth International Party (YIP). Conceived in a New York apartment during one cannabis-fueled evening, they started riffing on ways they could disrupt the Democratic Convention, scheduled to be held in Chicago in late August. They felt the Democratic Party had become a "National Death Party" because it supported the Vietnam War, and Rubin proposed organizing a counter-convention called the Festival of Life, to be held in nearby Lincoln Park, near the site of the Democrats' gathering at the International Amphitheatre, west of Chicago's South Side.

Rubin argued they could grab media attention with an alternative celebration filled with music, marijuana, and crowds of young people dancing through the streets of the Windy City. Then they would cap off the fun by nominating an actual pig for president.

After hearing the idea, Rubin's friend Paul Krassner, a journalist with a bent for political satire, spontaneously yelled out "Yippee!" and the word instantly stuck, as it encapsulated the buoyant spirit of the group's bizarre brand of political theater. Hoffman's wife, Anita, worried the press wouldn't take them seriously, came up with a "straighter-sounding" moniker, the Youth International Party (YIP).

The whole point of the Festival of Life was to "stick it to the man" through a massive expression of joy, and as the event began to take shape, Yippie co-founder Ed Sanders immediately thought of Sinclair and the MC5 as potential allies. Sanders's band, the Fugs, regularly played Detroit's Grande Ballroom, and he knew Sinclair and the MC5 would appreciate the serious fun that fueled the Yippie philosophy and could provide suitably potent music for the August protest.

But little did the Yippies know that by the time August rolled around, Chicago mayor Richard Daley had taken dramatic action to forestall any attempts to disrupt the convention. Daley was no sweetheart. During the Chicago riots that followed the April 4, 1968, assassination of Dr. Martin Luther King, he famously ordered the police to "shoot to kill arsonists" and "shoot to maim looters." He wasn't about to let a bunch of long-haired agitators spoil his city's nationally televised grand political convention.

Citing intelligence reports of potential violence and insurrection, Daley fortified the convention hall with a barbed-wire fence and put the 12,000 members of the Chicago Police Department on twelve-hour shifts, even as the U.S. Army placed 6,000 troops and 6,000 members of the National Guard—with an additional 5,000 on alert—in position to protect the city during the convention, not to mention 1,000 FBI and military intelligence officers and 1,000 Secret Service agents. To get an idea of the scope of Daley and the government's "preparations," consider that there were more boots on the ground in Chicago at the time than the United States had in all of Afghanistan before President Biden withdrew them in 2021.

Daley's determination to squelch the demonstrators only grew when Hoffman and Rubin announced in a press conference they were going to spike the water supply of the amphitheater with LSD and flood the convention hall with "superhot" hippie girls to seduce delegates and well-endowed hippie "studs" to do the same to their wives and daughters.

On Sunday, August 25, 1968, at 4:00 p.m., the Festival of Life began with the MC5, which turned out to be the only band with the nerve to show up. After they delivered an electrifying performance before approximately three thousand kids, all hell broke loose when the police arrived and turned what had been a peaceful gathering into a series of violent clashes between the cops and angry protesters. Sensing trouble, the band was smart enough to pack their gear just minutes before the pot smoke was overwhelmed by tear gas, and they miraculously escaped with their music equipment and skulls intact.

"We finished our show without incident, but then the shit started hitting the fan," said guitarist Wayne Kramer. "The crowd wasn't focused on us any longer and turned to the police, who had been provoking them with violence all day. It was on. The cops made sweeps through the crowd busting heads with nightsticks. Back and forth, back and forth. We packed our gear up and headed back to Detroit."

Sinclair was enraged by the chaos. He and the MC5, however, soon learned their performance in Chicago had not been the total washout it appeared to be. Shortly after the convention, Pulitzer Prize–winning journalist Norman Mailer published a riveting account of their pulse-pounding set in the park in *Harper's* magazine, lionizing the group as true counterculture heroes.

"Had the horns of the Huns ever had noise to compare?" asked Mailer, who went on to describe their music as "the sound of mountains crashing . . . [an] electric crescendo screaming as if at the electro-mechanical climax of the age."*

Mailer's over-the-top description of the MC5's performance helped the band gain national attention, contributing to a meteoric rise that ultimately landed them a major-label record deal with Elektra Records.

JOHN SINCLAIR We were determined to go and play during the Chicago Democratic Convention, which was scheduled at the end of August in 1968. It was going to be such a big break for us. We were unknown nationally, and we figured it would put us on the map. I was in touch with Ed Sanders, who was organizing the concert for the Yippies. Ed was a member of the Fugs, and we had known each other for a long time.

We didn't want our performance to be a "protest"—just an alternative example of how to live life. It could've been something special. We

---

* Norman Mailer, *Miami and the Siege of Chicago: An Informal History of the Republican and Democratic Conventions of 1968* (New York: New American Library, 1968), 97–98.

wanted the freaks to come out and dance and smoke dope, but Abbie Hoffman and Jerry Rubin issued some inflammatory statement about putting LSD in the water system and it almost totally decimated everything that we were trying to accomplish. They were more interested in causing a mass disruption.

We got a gig in Milwaukee, for $100 or something, so we could afford the trip. The Yippies were supposed to set up some lodging for us when we arrived. So, from the time I was in Wisconsin, I was calling in like every hour or every other hour to see what was happening, because the police had the city shut down, and I wanted to know if we could even get in.

We ended up sneaking in at 5:00 a.m., but we weren't supposed to play until four in the afternoon. Of course, they had no accommodations for us, so we ended up sleeping on benches. I started getting suspicious about the whole thing, but the organizers insisted that we were going to play. Another band I was managing, the Up, was coming in from Ann Arbor that afternoon, so we were in touch with them.

When we started setting up, I asked Ed, "Where's the power?" That brought him up short for a minute. He looked around and there was a hot-dog stand about fifty yards away, and fucking Sanders literally had the cord in his hand and went over to see if he could plug into their power. From that moment, it was clear they were totally unprepared.

My hallmark was preparation and production, and being able to do things right, so I was aghast. "Jesus, what the fuck is going on here?" No stage, no power. They didn't even have a PA, and luckily we had brought our own.

While we were setting up, a police officer came over and said to me, "Who's in charge here?" I told them I was the manager of the band, and that we just came to play. He then took me over to talk to a lieutenant—you know, with the white shirt and the gold braids and everything—and he said to me, "I just want to tell you one thing. This is your sound system, huh? Well, if it's used for any kind of inflammatory speeches, we can't guarantee its safety. Do you understand?"

I thought, Yes, I understand perfectly—you mean you'll smash it to smithereens! I'll never forget that. I was terrified.

As we were playing, I could see that there was some weird shit coming from the street. We were by the lake. It turned out that Hoffman was leading an invasion of people who were pulling this flatbed trailer that was supposed to be used for a stage. Well, we were already playing without a stage, right on the ground. Then I remember seeing a wave of police coming in after them. When we finished, Hoffman came up and grabbed the mic.

When he started talking, I told everyone to get the shit into the truck. We literally dismantled the PA system from around Hoffman while he spoke. We just beat it. As we left, you could literally see these waves of police entering the park with all their shit. As we were heading out, the Up's equipment people were coming in, and we frantically told them, "Turn around, turn around! We're getting the fuck out of here!"

We didn't really have much of an experience in Chicago, and what we did have was disappointing. We weren't supposed to fight with the police. Our idea was to have an alternative to the Democratic convention, to show off the alternative culture. We wanted to show kids how to put out underground newspapers, have bands, and it'd be fun—not to have them beaten up by the police. That wasn't my concept at all, but it might've been Hoffman's.

The band didn't have any real sway with the radical left. The stupidest mission I ever embarked on was trying to forge a link with these characters. We had different bases and were just a whole different class of individuals. Man, I always tried to get along with them. Finally, I had an epiphany. I realized that these people had no grasp of street-level reality at all.

By '68 I felt we had so much to offer these people, whereas they didn't really have that much to offer us. We had a band; we went out and did things, produced stuff, we made things happen. These other guys like Hoffman and Rubin just went around to college campuses and gave speeches. I felt we were on a higher level organizationally and just in terms of productivity. Instead of being anxious to be accepted by them, I always thought they should be happy that we were trying to hook up with them. We were among the most productive people in the entire counterculture.

ROB TYNER We came into Chicago the night before and slept at this place called the Straight Theatre. No food, no money, no accommodations, no nothing. The next day we woke up and went out on the street, and there were millions of people all over the place, and a tremendous amount of police. The city was like an armed camp. It's hard to imagine nowadays, but there was a police force of incredible size, and there were helicopters, dogs, horseback and riot cops of every kind everywhere. It was like a scene out of *The Road Warrior*; and they build these cops in Chicago *big*, man. There was a tremendous amount of tension. It was a disaster looking for a place to happen.

Driving in, we didn't know what was going on, and there was no way to tell. The Chicago police were standing on the corner with riot clubs. I began to get nervous when I started seeing them on every corner, with helicopters flying over. Suddenly, it felt like war. It felt like going into combat. Tense. Our attitude was that we would stick it out and see what happened.

I remember hanging out at the park and grooving with my brothers and sisters. It was real pretty during the early part of the day. I was starving to death, so I ate a couple of brownies, and they said, "Oh, wait, man, you should only eat a half of one—those are pot brownies." And I had eaten two. So, suddenly, OMMMMM! The day started to get *real* pretty.

The organizers had rented a flatbed truck for us to play on, but it was a huge bone of contention with the authorities. We could see why—the park was jam-packed full of people, and it would've taken a million years to get to us. So, we just put some blankets down, set up, and played. It was kinda muddy, which caused electronic problems and I was getting shocked like crazy, so I spent as much time as possible jumping up in the air, so I was not in contact with the ground. Because every time I hit the deck: BANG! I'd get zapped again.

Norman Mailer and the poet Allen Ginsberg were there. Mailer said that we're like "the electro-mechanical climax of the age," and little did he know, I was actually being electrocuted! Our set was curtailed in the middle by this big old demonstration of people who had come in with flags and stuff and took over. They took over the microphones while we just stood there like idiots for a while and then we just split. We tore our gear down and got it in the van *quick*, because you could see the people like human waves just surging back and forth, and the cops wading in with batons swinging. It was one of the scariest mob scenes I've ever seen in my life.

The air was full of war—you could feel it. We had to detour around to get out of town because it was so chaotic in the streets. Hey, man, it wasn't just in the park that this stuff was going on, it was all over the city.

For me, Norman Mailer's story in *Harper's* magazine was a certification on some levels. On a gut level it was extremely satisfying, because it meant that we weren't inconsequential anymore, and that the band was doing something that was significant. A vindication.

But to tell you the truth, we rarely spoke with the heavyweight counterculture people; that whole thing was taken care of by John. We were being treated on a lot of levels like artists under a quasi-Maoist regime. In Mao's China, art was to be subjugated [to] political message and propaganda, and we weren't always playing that game so good for them. In the end, there wasn't a lot of doctrinaire mumbo jumbo in our music, and I think that was resented. We didn't have a whole lot of rhetoric in the songs.

On the other hand, we were always right in the middle of it. It was a difficult education; we'd wind up playing places where bands would normally not even go in. We'd run up against problems a lot where we'd play these rallies and stuff, and the political folks would want to come up and take over the microphones right in the middle of our set. We would often stop in the midst of our show and give over our microphones to the local politicians. That was very generous of us, because we were the reason people were there—to see rock 'n' roll.

WAYNE KRAMER We'd already accepted our role as the figureheads of the youth of our day. So, when we started hearing all these plans the Yippies were making for a counterculture convention during the Democratic Convention in Chicago, we figured we're going to be there.

We took a couple of jobs out in Indiana or Illinois in the farmland up there, to pay for the trip, because we knew it was going to be a nonpaying gig. It was palatably tense. We met up with some people from the Yippies, and they turned us on to a church where we could spend the night and get off the street.

We're laying in these pews trying to sleep, but finally the promoters got us a couple of apartments where we could go and get cleaned up before the show. I took a nap and a shower, got ready, and went over to the gig. From what I could see, there were thousands of young people milling around all over the place, but I didn't see any bands or anything. That's when we found out that [rock musician] Country Joe McDonald got punched out in an elevator and left, and none of the other groups had the guts to show up. I said, "Okay, well, we're here, we'll do what we do."

The organizers had these hash cookies, and they were giving them out. They told us, "Just have one apiece, because they're real strong and we don't want you guys to get too fucked up." So naturally, being the MC5, we all ate two or three apiece and then we split a few more. When it was time for us to play, we were all really getting off on the drugs. It really made for a remarkable theater for me. In the middle of the spacey part of "Starship," helicopters started coming down on us. I was so stoned, I said, "Yeah, it's all music, it all fits." I'd hear the *wom-wom-wom* helicopter sounds and I'd go *rah-rah-rah* on the guitar. Yeah!

Unfortunately, there were these agent provocateurs in the audience that were going around starting fights and shoving people around. You could just see it. I mean, c'mon. The audience was basically in awe of us because they had never seen anything like the MC5 before. We were intense and loud, and we were talking about all the shit that was happening right then and there.

Sinclair and I decided the minute we were done playing, we'd unplug the shit, throw it in the van, and get the fuck back to Detroit, where we'd be safe. No sooner did we stop playing than the police started making these waves of attacks, and the tear gas started. We got the fuck out of there.

There was this wonderful girl, I think her name was Laura, who I had had my eye on for a long time. She was sort of loosely associated with us. She wanted a ride back to Detroit with us. So, after all those hash brownies, we did the wild thing from Chicago to Detroit in the back of the van. All the way. Stoned to the bone. Then when we got back, we got out of the van and said, "See ya, okay, bye." We went our separate ways. It was like one of those '60s things where the timing was perfect. She was exquisite.

While Sinclair hated how disorganized and undisciplined the Youth International Party was, he admired its wacky sense of humor and media savvy. His close encounter with Yippies planted the seeds from which he created the White Panthers, his own political machine.

But that would come later. First there were more important fish to fry—namely the MC5, whose success appeared to be inevitable and unstoppable. As word of their explosive performance at the Democratic Convention began spreading throughout the rock-'n'-roll underground—not to mention their reputation for regularly upstaging established acts like the Jimi Hendrix Experience and Janis Joplin—it was only a matter of time before the record labels came sniffing around.

By the end of 1968, the group and their "little brothers," the Stooges featuring singer Iggy Pop and guitarist Ron Asheton, would be signed by A&R exec Danny Fields to Elektra Records.

The MC5's remarkable debut, *Kick Out the Jams*, recorded live in front of an exuberant Grande Ballroom crowd in downtown Detroit in October 1968, remains one of the most important recordings of the era. Wild, powerful, and at times chaotic, the album is regarded as the cornerstone of punk rock, and the band's incendiary cry of "Kick out the jams, motherfuckers!" struck a blow against government censorship.

But were the kids in middle America ready for anything so raucous . . . and "obscene"? It sure seemed like it. But then again, anything seemed possible in 1968.

Even meeting the Beatles . . .

JOHN SINCLAIR We submitted a demo to the Beatles when they started their record label, Apple. We sent a package to the *motherfucking* Beatles! We thought, Wow! They're looking for us!

It turns out they were just looking to sign some pop acts that sounded like Paul McCartney. They ended up giving contracts to wimpy artists like James Taylor and Mary Hopkins, and bands like the Black Dyke Mills Brass Band. I remember how high our hopes were, because we literally felt that we were what they're looking for. All we needed was money, and we could've done so many wonderful things. We believed in the Beatles.

ROB TYNER We thought, Wow, the Beatles would be perfect, because we really liked those guys. We had this notion of "Gee, they'll sign us, and everything will be lovely and we'll all get together and have tea." But they listened to it and sent it back and said, "Hey, man, this is not suitable for *any* kind of catalog we're ever gonna have."

Then on the White Album they had songs with lyrics like "Why don't we do it in the road" and "If you go carrying pictures of Chairman Mao/ You ain't gonna make it with anyone anyhow." I don't know if they were talking about us, but it felt like it.

JOHN SINCLAIR We met Bob Rudnick and Dennis Frawley through the mail. They were the kings of the underground at the time. They wrote the music column in *East Village Other*, which was one of the biggest underground papers in the U.S. They were huge! They enjoyed our press releases, which were pretty provocative. It wasn't like what you'd get from a traditional band like Cream. We would include tales of police brutality, being busted, and shows being stopped. It was really an underground thing.

We knew that Rudnick and Frawley were always trying to meet a deadline, so we would always try to provide them with a well-written, frank, thrill-packed account of some adventure of this band in Detroit. We made it very easy for them to just write an opening paragraph, and then print the rest of the press release as if it was something they had written. When it was printed, it was all you could ever hope for—they left our ideas completely intact!

They also had a radio show called *Kokaine Karma* on WFMU in East Orange, New Jersey, which was listener supported and completely independent. Unlike WABX in Detroit, they were wild about "Looking at You," the single we cut in Ann Arbor. They invited me on their show many times. At some point, they told Danny Fields about us, who worked at Elektra Records. Eventually we met him and hit it off right away.

BOB RUDNICK I had heard of Sinclair, and I had heard the MC5 when I was in Chicago. One of my friends was a guy named John Kovachovich, who was from Detroit, and kept on telling me about them, and brought me to Michigan where I saw them at some teen club. I was really flipped out by the scene. Young girls were pinching my ass—it was great.

Dennis Frawley and I started writing a column for the *East Village Other*, and Sinclair had sent a press package, and I saw the single with John Coltrane on the cover. I just went nuts when I saw that cover, and I liked "Looking at You" and "Borderline." That was my first real contact with Sinclair.

Frawley and I wrote about the band, and John started sending us more stuff. Danny Fields was at Elektra, and I turned Danny onto the MC5.

DANNY FIELDS In the early '60s, I dropped out of Harvard Law School, and went to graduate school at NYU downtown and lived in Greenwich Village. I started getting interested in publishing and answered an ad and became the editor of a teenybop magazine called *Datebook*. This was at the height of the Beatles. I was fired after a few months and decided to move to Los Angeles during the Summer of Love. I had to do something to make money, so I presented myself as a publicist and worked for the Doors, who were on Elektra Records.

While I was working with the Doors, I met the people at the label. They were setting up a publicity department and I became their guy. I didn't really have any experience, but everything was much more casual then than it is now. It was so casual that the press department could also sign groups. I was friendly with the president of the company, so I brought him the David Peel album *Have a Marijuana*. It was my idea to do a drug album. I thought it would be funny.

We have extreme censorship now, but it's always existed. Back then there was a great panic over "Eight Miles High" by the Byrds, because it was supposed to contain veiled references to drugs. Soon, people started finding drug references *everywhere* . . . even when there weren't any, and I hated that. I said, "Let's just do a drug record, but instead of making veiled references, let's do a record of unveiled references to drugs and see what happens!" We recorded the Peel album live in Washington Square for about $1,500, and it sold hundreds of thousands of records. Elektra was impressed and thought I had my ear to the street.

At that time, I was friendly with two guys, Bob Rudnick and Dennis Frawley, who wrote a column in the *East Village Other*. And they had a radio show on WFMU in New Jersey. In early 1968, they told me about the MC5. They had put me on the band's mailing list or something, and I started getting barraged with all the MC5 propaganda, which was extensive and very impressive.

I was totally intrigued with their propaganda, and the dynamics of it. The nerviness of it. The total self-belief, and the total self-promotion. I thought, If you're working with anybody that can help themselves along this far, it's going to be a breeze and a pleasure to work with them because they're going to do most of the work for you. I loved the literature and the way it was worded, and I loved the way it was presented. You know, "Eight million people stampede . . . fall down before new gods . . . worship new deities," all that stuff. It was great.

The band had great graphic designers, and they used pretty colored paper, and Leni Sinclair did the photographs, which were fantastic. It all looked super exciting and professional. I admired any group that spent so much time and effort promoting itself. You had a feeling they had all the bases covered: rock 'n' roll, revolution, dope, fucking in the streets, and changing the world? Well, we all felt like that back then. We were anti-war revolutionary, and just starting to find out how wonderful drugs were!

Knowing what I know now, I wouldn't say drugs are wonderful, but we were innocent, and they were new, and we thought fucking was wonderful too. So, in our blissful preliterate state, we thought all this stuff the MC5 was promoting sounded like good, clean teenage fun, and what the world needed a dose of. It's certainly what American music needed a dose of. I loved the sound of L.A. bands, and it was some of my favorite music, but that midwestern energy was intriguing to me.

I'd heard about the band before I heard their music, but that didn't matter as much to me. I mean, I was in the business of making images, not music. We knew they had a big following in Detroit. They were famous, locally famous. That wasn't hype, that was fact.

JOHN SINCLAIR Danny knew what was happening, and we became good friends very quickly. He was a guy of intelligence and good taste. That's what I liked; he was just so hip.

Danny was interested in us, and he worked with Elektra. He was an important person there because he had worked with the Doors, which had turned them from a folkie label into a company that made a lot of money without diminishing their artistic credibility. Jac Holzman was the president, but he didn't really know anything about rock 'n' roll. He was a bit of a pompous ass, but he wasn't a money-grubbing record industry guy either. He was someone with a certain amount of class and certainly artistic integrity. Unusual indeed.

DANNY FIELDS I went to see the MC5 on September 22, 1968. I flew out to Detroit, and John Sinclair picked me up. I thought he was wonderful, and I never changed my mind about that for a second. His charm and his energy and his belief in what he was doing was so . . .

I came from a very jaded scene. I was in what they now call the Andy Warhol crowd; we were involved in the underground art scene and theater, loved the Velvet Underground, and we were very cool. Sinclair was the opposite of cool. He was high-energy and an imposing figure. He was a magnificent specimen of power poetry, and he liked all that intellectual jazz stuff that was meaningless to me. He was nothing like the people in New York, and I just thought he was a great guy. He was also a charismatic, wonderful speaker, and he seemed to have his finger on the pulse of what the kids in town wanted and, by extension, what kids throughout America would want.

The band filled the Grande Ballroom and played this great show. Their clothes were amazing, and the kids were screaming. They were loud and fast and spun around onstage. What else did you need to see? I mean, if you worked for a record company, you go, Wow!

It was quasi-fascist and enormously appealing for that reason. It was a glimpse of things to come. They'd say, "Wave your hand" or "Make a fist," and everyone would do it! If they'd say, "Say, 'Oh,'" everyone would say, "Oh." It was a forerunner of contemporary rock concerts, which I adored. I just thought it was fabulous. Such power.

They had a hype man named J. C. Crawford doing his speech at the beginning: "Brothers and sisters," and all that. It was a total package. The MC5 had everything, and I was overwhelmed. The show had a beginning, a middle, and an end, which is extremely important, and they had a built-in base of audience support. They had a radical political philosophy, which I thought was cute at the time, and felt it would work with the bigger cultural direction everything was going in. Anti-war sentiment was building, and we were down marching on fucking Washington three times a year. It was election time, and it was right after Chicago. Things were in a roiling state, and they just seemed to fit in with the spirit of it. I could see them placed in the forefront of the spirit of what was happening. I could see that happening.

Unfortunately, in the end, it didn't. But at the time, they seemed like a good gamble.

After the show, we went back to Sinclair's house in Ann Arbor. I had never been in a commune before. I'd been in crash pads and squats and stuff in New York, but never a whole house with four walls and a basement where all these people lived and the guys would sit at the table and pound, and all these little women with long skirts would run in and out of the kitchen. I mean, it was *so* unliberated. It was supposed to be revolutionary, but it was so oppressive to these poor girlfriends. It seemed to me that they were treated like slaves. Except for Leni Sinclair, but she was in a class by herself, because she was a German revolutionary.

The next day, Wayne Kramer said to me, "If you liked us, I've got something you're really going to like. We've got like our little brother band called the Psychedelic Stooges. You should go see them too."

I don't know how, but Wayne must've had some clue to my thinking. Because I tell you, I loved the MC5, but they didn't change my life. They were a great, straight-ahead rock-'n'-roll band, but their music didn't change my life. Kramer must've suspected that, because the Stooges *did* change my life.

The next afternoon, I saw Iggy at the Student Union at the University of Michigan. I thought everybody in the audience had to be from a record company too. I figured I'd better run up to him right away. So, I did. I said, "I'm from a record company." He said, "Yeah," and kept walking. He didn't believe me! Because nobody had ever been to see him from a record company.

Musically, I preferred the Stooges. I thought they were more advanced and modern. They were making the music I'd wanted to hear my whole life. The MC5 were full of energy and the songs were catchy. More traditional. The Stooges, on the other hand, were on the edge of the cliff of modern musical taste. That to me was art. Art to me was something I couldn't imagine in my mind. The MC5 was a well-rehearsed machine. But the Stooges were fooling around with something I thought was bigger than that. They resonated with something I was looking for. And Iggy as a performer, I don't have to tell you... Even more than Iggy as a performer, it was the sound of the band. But between both bands I thought, Wow, this is like the one-two punch.

ROB TYNER We were pals with the Stooges and played a lot of gigs together. But even as radical as we were, we were much more mainstream than the Stooges.

DANNY FIELDS So, the next day I called Jac Holzman from Ann Arbor and I said, "I've just seen two bands that changed my life." He asked what I thought the label could get them for. I said, "Well, one of them is famous, I think. It's gonna cost you about $20,000. The other one nobody's ever heard of, so you can probably have them for $5,000." He said, "Do it." I hung up the phone and shook hands with John Sinclair, and with Jimmy Silver, who managed the Stooges. I said $20,000 for the MC5 and $5,000 for the Stooges, and they flipped. It was big bucks for them. They'd never heard of so much money, and it was a major record thing. We all just hugged, and it felt great. I went back and it all began.

The next thing that happened was Jac Holzman came out to see them play, and he saw and heard the same thing I did. He was the son of a Jewish doctor from the Northeast, as I was. You can imagine, this wasn't like anything he'd seen. This wasn't Jewish at all—it was like the opposite of Jewish—so, it was *very* attractive.

Sinclair and the MC5 were very hale and hearty; big, strapping lower-middle-class working-class boys. Big boys. That was my first impression. They were big. Every one of them was bigger than me. They were bigger than life. Big boys and big bodies and big clothes. They were big guys. I remember feeling like Woody Allen, dwarfish, among them. John was the biggest of all. He was so big. Everyone was big: big men, big women, big skirts, big meals. It wasn't like my life at all.

The Hill Street commune in Ann Arbor was a big, airy, funky, college-y fraternity house. The basement was all offices, printing presses and photography labs. It was extremely organized. It was a self-contained community for the band and the dissemination of all its propaganda. I think John and Leni had the big room in front, and they slept on a mattress on the floor.

A lot of marijuana. John would use the main toilet in the hall, without closing the door. He would sit on the toilet with the door open, barking commands. I never saw anything like it. I mean, I never saw anything like that whole thing. It was not like anything I could relate to. The men and women separate, people carrying guns . . .

The men ate first, and then the women. The women, I mean we don't know what happened to the women. We presume they ate sometime, in the kitchen or something. But they weren't allowed at the table with the men; it was very traditional.

I remember waking up mornings and everything would be covered in snow and ice. If it was me, I would just go back to bed and say, "Fuck this." But they would have to drive into Detroit, and Sinclair would say, "Well, let's go." To me it was very Midwest farmer. So, it was icy? So what? You got in the car and drove through the ice. That's the way they were.

RON ASHETON Jac Holzman came down. Danny had them already draw up the contracts, so the Stooges just went to the Hill House and signed them. I don't remember any great celebrations, I just remember we smoked some dope, signed the contracts, lots of pictures were taken, and that was that. I was kinda high and tired, because we'd played a show, and I just wanted to go home. It was anticlimactic.

ROB TYNER Signing to Elektra was a dream for me. The Paul Butterfield Blues Band album came out on Elektra Records, and I said if these guys are hip enough to sign them, they were cool enough for me, man. I could picture us on Elektra Records.

WAYNE KRAMER Elektra was just a little folk label, and then they hit with the Doors and realized, "Hey, there's millions of dollars to be made in this pop-music business." When they came out to see us, they told us that they believed in what we believed in, and gave us a check for $20,000 that night, and we hadn't signed anything. Sinclair looked at that check and said, "Whoa, this is great." They said, "Yeah, and there's plenty more. If you need more money, just let us know. We're going to take care of everything. Everything's going to be great."

But where all the money was going started to become an issue when it started to become *real* money. I'd meet people in New York, and they'd ask me, "Wayne, what are you doing with the Elektra money?"

We were just hoodlums from Detroit in a band and didn't think much about it. We just knew it all went into one account, and John Sinclair paid the bills with it. The Trans-Love account. There may have been grumblings from the Rob-and-Becky faction about the money back then, but I was never that concerned with it. I always had kind of a simplistic view that there was plenty of money coming in, and as long as I stayed on my job, the money would keep rolling. I certainly trusted John, and I don't think my trust was unfounded.

He never did anything malicious; he never stole from the band. He never tried to take advantage. I'm not sure he was competent enough to handle that amount of money, but we fucked all that money up together. When we got that advance, we just paid off a bunch of old bills, and everybody in the band got $1,000 apiece, and Danny Fields got $5,000 for middling the deal. The rest of the money just went bye-bye. That was real money back then! But Sinclair did what he thought was the right thing to do. Though if I had it to do over again, I certainly would've rearranged the cash flow.

ROB TYNER I loved Danny right from the start. He literally taught me everything I know about dealing with the press. Honestly. Back then, I'd use this self-deprecating kind of thing. Somebody would use a word like "catharsis," and I'd say, "Hey, let's not get all intellectual, man." I knew perfectly well what they were talking about, but I didn't want it to get all intellectual. And Danny would say, "Let it get intellectual, for Chrissake. Deal with it. Get in there and tell them exactly what it is. They don't want to dig it out of you. You should be ready to tell them." So, if anybody can lay claim to starting my motor mouth, it was probably him.

He was brilliant, and it was fun to just listen to him talk. I looked through his Rolodex one time at Elektra, and he had Pablo Picasso's home phone number! He had everybody's fucking phone number. Marlene Dietrich's phone number—people nobody could get to, nobody in the world. The man was, is, and will always be amazing. A *lot* of people owe Danny a lot.

JOHN SINCLAIR Initially we were thinking the first album would be a double LP, which would've been idiotic, but "restraint" was not a word that would properly characterize any of our activities at the time. I thought that what we had going for us in terms of marketability was that we had this incredible live show, and a following. Our live show was also part of our myth, and the catalyst for all the other things that happened with the police.

There was also the question of what we would sound like in the studio with this material. We knew it worked in front of an audience. I wasn't worried about their competence, or the quality of what would emerge, but rather the *heat*. The heat and the intensity—that was our stock in trade. We didn't have pop tunes that were going to go to the top of the charts or anything.

DANNY FIELDS Jac made the decision to record them live on the spot. I suppose the thinking was this is where they were at their best. When they played, it was an event! It was more than just a band or songs. So, rather than go for a measured series of singles, we figured we'd do this as a live thing and capture the entire surrounding atmospherics. It was a cool idea to just record the moment. It was a little bit hard to hear the songs anyway, because of the dynamics of the whole thing—the noise and the screaming.

ROB TYNER Playing in front of an audience was what we did best. Let's face it, we had no experience to speak of in the studio, but we had a *lot* of onstage power.

JOHN SINCLAIR We also liked the shock value of making our debut a live album. We felt it would demonstrate we had a big following even before we had an album out. It showed we were already playing to packed houses of screaming fans.

ROB TYNER I know why *we* thought it was a good idea, but I think Jac Holzman liked the idea of doing a live album because of the cost factor. The budget could not have been much, even by the standards of those days.

WAYNE KRAMER We didn't understand exactly what a producer did. They said Jac Holzman and Bruce Botnick were going to produce the sessions. We were doing a sound check and they sat in the front row, and every now and again they'd say, "Ah, Wayne, your guitar might be out of tune a little bit. Will you check the tuning?" Fine, bing-bong, bing-bong. "Okay, good." That's all they ever did. We just did our show.

Recording our first album as a live album just seemed like the right idea at the time. Obviously, it was the right thing from the record company's point of view because it was cheap. All they had to do was hire recording engineer Wally Heider to come out and set up his gear. But they also lied to us.

Holzman said, "We want to do a live album, but we're not going to use the first show we record. We're going to record a lot of shows until we all agree we've captured the best one." Then they recorded the first one and put the record out. They did exactly what they said they *weren't* going to do.

I'm not thrilled with that performance. There were way better shows. We were intimidated by the recording equipment and understandably nervous. It was supposed to be our shot. I remember being terrified the night of the session. I'd borrowed a new guitar to try, and I couldn't tune it up; it wouldn't work. And Rob was fucking up. Shit wasn't tight like it usually was. Everyone was wired up out of their gourds from the pressure.

RON ASHETON The night they recorded the *Kick Out the Jams* album was a cultural event. It was the culmination of all the years of work they did to build the Detroit music and subculture, and it was a way to include the fans and the people that helped them. It was like, "Come in free and see it!"

I was very excited, and I was there both nights. It *was* a happening, but in a way, I was disappointed. For me, it was kind of anticlimactic, because it took on the atmosphere . . . there was a lot of tension in the band. I kinda felt for them. I could just feel that they knew this was it.

It's not well known, but Dennis Thompson and Wayne Kramer took acid one of the nights. They wanted to make it so special, and they thought they were so on top of it, and they thought that the acid would loosen them up. I think that was the worst of the two nights.

They told me they were tripping, and I thought, What? You took acid to record your first album? I didn't say that out loud because I didn't want to spook them. Thompson said they were tripping, and I thought he meant that they were really into it. Then somebody told me he meant it literally, that they were all on acid.

I thought they were insane. We talked about it a bunch afterwards, and they all regretted it. Wayne was out of tune, and they were the sloppiest I've ever heard them in my life.

Michael Davis told me he had to drink some beer, because he was too tripped out. I think they went back and did it the next night straight. I remember Thompson saying, "Don't ever play on acid. It took every ounce of every fiber of my being to try and play the drums. I thought my heart was going to explode. Michael said his bass strings turned into giant rubber bands. They felt—and sounded like—giant pieces of rubber.

They truly believed that acid would relax them, and they would be able to put on what they thought would be their greatest show. They had to put on a show for the crowd, which they did. Personally, I would have just attended to the task at hand, of doing the music, but the show was part of the music. They wanted to do a total "happening."

WAYNE KRAMER We were *not* chemically fueled when we recorded the album. On those two nights, we smoked plenty of weed, but, no, we didn't take any psychedelics. Still, it was not our finest hour.

I don't know about the rest of them, but after hearing the finished tapes I wanted to scrap the record. I said, "Oh, man, that can't be the record. That ain't going to work." Nobody liked it. I'm sure we expressed our displeasure, because I distinctly remember Elektra telling us they were going to record more than one show, that we would keep recording until we got one we liked. That's why I wasn't that nervous about it. When we got the tape, I said, "Well, we're not going to use that one." Then, surprise, surprise, that's the record.

JOHN SINCLAIR Over the years, Wayne has made comments that he didn't like the way it turned out, but you couldn't have a more accurate representation of how the band sounded.

DENNIS THOMPSON I was taking a lot of LSD at the time, and smoking massive quantities of "sacrament," as Sinclair would say. I played high onstage all the time. But those two nights we just calmed down. We didn't take the normal quantities of drugs that we would usually take. I think we took a little less. "Let's just low-key it tonight," we said. So instead of smoking fifteen joints, we probably smoked ten.

The night we recorded *Kick Out the Jams*, I played harder than I ever played in my life. It was so intense, like we'd been waiting for that moment to get recorded. It was like: "Finally this is it—we're making a record! This is what we've been doing this for. This is what I dropped out of college for!" I think I broke at least ten sticks each performance. I had calluses on all my fingers, and the forefingers of both hands and the index finger had blood blisters underneath them.

WAYNE KRAMER We were under a tremendous amount of pressure, and the MC5 was a mercurial band. Some nights we were just spectacular, and other nights, we could be something of a train wreck. Recording the album rattled us. I hear it every time I hear the record. I hear me making clumsy mistakes on the guitar, I hear Dennis all over the map in terms of tempo, I hear Rob not quite in the perfect voice that he was capable of. I hear all of us being affected in one way or another by the pressure. That doesn't make it a bad record, because it *isn't* a bad record, but if you're asking me from the inside, it was more imperfect than we were willing to accept. I mean, we weren't trying to make perfect music, but we knew what we were capable of, and that was well below the mark.

ROB TYNER Yeah, it's ragged, and it might not have been a great night, but it was representative of the day. And as a document, all our strengths and weaknesses are right up in your face. Of the band's three albums, it tells our story best. If you want to call it sloppy, we're fallible. We're human beings, man.

I remember listening to the early mixes of the album and I thought it sounded real tumultuous. I regretted that it might not have been a really inspired night, but to me the whole experience of it was probably just as important as whether it was a good night for us.

Jac's production was very minimal. I mean, he didn't come a month in advance to do preproduction. He just came in, and we did it that day.

Yeah, I was tense. They had me singing through two microphones, and that made me uncomfortable. But I think everybody in the band was a little tense. I wish that we could've had more time.

MICHAEL DAVIS We recorded it over two days and I don't remember much difference between them. We had our heads in the clouds. I think we probably thought that we did great and didn't really have to change much. Personally, having gotten over the first-night jitters, I came back the next night and attacked the rough spots a little stronger, because I felt more confident.

Oddly, I think the night we recorded *Kick Out the Jams* was actually the end of the band for me. Before that night, the MC5 was totally experimental. Every time we went up onstage, it was like we were making the sound up for the time. After October 31, 1968, the MC5 would forever be molded that way, because now we knew what we were supposed to sound like. We were like Play-Doh before that, and after the album, we were formed.

We stopped being so experimental, but we got better musically. We became better musicians, better writers; we were able to make recordings that were more polished. It was kind of a bittersweet victory, in a way.

DENNIS THOMPSON Our tempos were a little sloppy, but we sounded like this big, huge dinosaur going *crunch, crunch* through the jungle, and everybody's on board this dinosaur. So, the dinosaur goes a little fast or a little slow, so be it. Everybody's on board. It's more of an energy.

The personality on the first album is explosive and spontaneous. *Kick Out the Jams* is my favorite child. The firstborn. Plus, there are all the memories attached to it; how we got there and how it all happened so fast, and how it was so exciting. It was all so compressed.

But when we got the first pressing, we all sat down and listened to it and said, "Bullshit. Fuck this. This is not our album." We weren't hot that night; we wanted to do it again. And Sinclair said, "No, no, that defines it."

Jac Holzman agreed. "No, no, that's exactly what we were trying to capture, the live MC5." We said, "Close but no cigar."

JOHN SINCLAIR I liked *Kick Out the Jams* then, and I like it now. I still get excited when I hear "Now it's time to . . ."

DENNIS THOMPSON We didn't want to release it, but Sinclair was walking around, saying, "This is *it*, man, we're not going to record it again. It's really good, and it captured what you played." We told him that it sounded sloppy. Which was the truth.

WAYNE KRAMER Why has that first album lasted so long, and mean so much to so many people? I really have no idea. People always come up to me and say, "That record changed my life." I usually just laugh and say to them, "I'm sorry I can't change it back."

I'm going to say the reason that album has lasted is the purity of the spirit. It was the sound of the five of us with all our tribe—our family, John Sinclair, all our friends and allies—it became something more powerful than any of us individually, and that power is concentrated in that record in a way that you can't deny. It has the rigorous honesty of a band doing everything by principles. They were principles that were higher than any of our petty personal ideas. It's just a powerful statement of a moment in time.

ROB TYNER People always ask me why "Black to Comm" isn't on the album. Basically, we didn't think it worked those evenings. That was the experimental nature of the time. If something relies on magic to happen, sometimes the magic happens and sometimes it doesn't, and you can't force it, and there's no substitute for it.

We eventually tightened "Black to Comm" up. We had to cut back on doing that tribal-energy orgy. It became so chaotic . . . We knew we had to tighten it up. We began to tighten it up, and the band sorta went in that direction from then on.

JOHN SINCLAIR We had a very frank and open discussion about censorship with Holzman before recording the album, anticipating the reaction to using the word "motherfucker" on the record. I was willing not to put it on the record if need be. It was 1968, and I wasn't sure if people would go for that.

It didn't matter that much to me whether we did or didn't. I knew word of mouth would be enough to make it a catchphrase. I thought, Why bother to put it on a record if nobody would play it or sell it? But Holzman had a kind of New York liberal outlook at the time and told us not to worry about it.

Believe it or not, I was the one who warned them about adverse reaction in some quarters here in America. But he insisted that if there was a problem, Elektra's legal department would stand behind the record and fight for us, and the negative publicity would help sell the record.

He was positive the controversy couldn't hurt us. He continued to say that they were a record company, and probably not exactly the kind of people we had in our world, but they were sympathetic to what we were doing. I appreciated the recognition of our sincerity because we were sincere—this wasn't just a "revolutionary hype." So, with that pledge of support for what in my mind was sure to be a problem, we said, "Okay, let's go."

WAYNE KRAMER We weren't stupid. We knew that "Kick Out the Jams" was not going to be a hit single on AM radio—or FM radio, for that matter—but we recorded a version where we substituted the words "brothers and sisters" for "motherfucker" just for the radio anyway.

It was just a tactic, so were surprised when it worked. Suddenly we were everywhere. The record shot up to Number 2 in Detroit, and Number 6 in Chicago, and was on the radio in New York City, and was in the Top 10 in San Francisco, and we were in *Time*, *Newsweek*, and the *New York Times*. Unfortunately, against our instructions, Elektra Records rushed the release of the album. Our plan was to let the single descend from the charts before we put out the album, and then we would have a second wave that would eclipse the first wave.

But Elektra rushed the album out and it was a big mistake. As soon as the radio trade magazines got wind there was an obscenity on the album, they started telling the radio stations to drop the single. The trades, like the *Gavin Report*, were very powerful and started writing things like "This album release contains an obscenity. You're going to have problems with parents and teachers and it's un-American and plus we want you to start playing the new Red Skelton version of 'America the Beautiful.' And we've got the new Sgt. Barry Sadler track."

ROB TYNER I knew the record was gonna cause trouble, and people were gonna get pissed. I knew it was gonna be controversial, and there might be court battles. I could see Lenny Bruce all over the place. But we had already thought it all out.

In the early moments of the album, there was a real sense of vision. A true sense of the band working with our management, with the record company, with everybody. There was a moment in time when everything was beginning to work, and Holzman seemed to be very idealistic on some level.

JOHN SINCLAIR Immediately after we recorded the album—literally the next day—we announced the formation of the White Panther Party. We conceived it as an "arm" of the Youth International Party, who were important at the time. We had thousands of buttons made and handed them out at shows and started talking about "revolution" before each show. We wanted to show the connection between the music, culture, and politics in a more explicit way.

We were just coming from inchoate feelings of hatred and rage and frustration about the way that America was. We didn't have any formal left-wing political orientation or background at all, until we started seeing that we were all part of this political struggle. Our culture—this culture of loud music, long hair, no underwear, smoking joints, taking acid, fucking—all this kind of stuff was political, because it existed in this political world of [the] uptight white people of America who ran everything.

CHAPTER III (PART 2)

RISE, PANTHER, RISE

> Forming the White Panther Party wasn't going to be a dead serious thing. We definitely had a sense of humor! We just became more serious because we kept on getting busted.
>
> —John Sinclair

"Initially, I thought the White Panthers were a joke," said singer Rob Tyner. "I don't mean that in a negative way. I just thought they were hysterically funny. I mean, look at it—they gave our road manager, Steve "the Hawk" Harnadek, the title of Minister of Fucking in the Streets! Try and say that with a straight face. Say your name and then add "Minister of Fucking in the Streets." It's a funny line, but that was its essential coolness. The White Panther Party was a way for folks in the audience to be a part of something political without it being too heavy, and I was all for it."

While humor was an essential ingredient to the White Panthers, their intent and goals were dead serious. Launched in November 1968 by John Sinclair, his wife, Leni Sinclair, and Lawrence "Pun" Plamondon, it was initially designed to be an anti-racist political adjunct to the more business-minded Trans-Love Energies. The trio later said it was created after Huey P. Newton, co-founder of the Black Panther Party, was asked what white people could do to support the Black Panthers and he replied, "Form a White Panther Party."

The White Panthers, however, had larger aspirations than becoming what would have amounted to being a forerunner to the modern-day Black Lives Matter movement. In "The White Panther State/Meant," an essay written by Sinclair for the *Ann Arbor Sun*, he declared, "Our program of rock and roll, dope, and fucking in the streets is a program of total freedom for *everyone*. And we're totally committed to carrying out our program. We breathe revolution. We are LSD-driven total maniacs in the universe. We will do anything we can do. Drive people out of their heads into their bodies."

But what *really* separated the White Panthers from the SDS, the Yippies, and the Black Panthers was Sinclair's sincere belief that music would play an essential part in his youth revolution.

"Rock and roll music is the spearhead of our attack because it's so effective and so much fun," he wrote in the *Ann Arbor Sun*. "We have developed organic high-energy guerrilla rock and roll bands who are infiltrating the popular culture and destroying millions of minds in the process. With our music and our economic genius, we plunder the unsuspecting straight world for money and means to carry out our program and revolutionize its children at the same time.

"We don't have guns yet—not all of us anyway—because we have more powerful weapons: direct access to millions of teenagers is one of our most potent, and their belief in us is another."[*]

---

[*] John Sinclair, "White Panther State/Meant," *Ann Arbor Sun*, 1968.

Sinclair was convinced that it was art, and not politics, that would ultimately change the world. The White Panthers drafted a manifesto entitled "White Panther Party 10-Point Program," which would provide the blueprint for all of Sinclair's activities over the next few years, including his management of the MC5.

To a contemporary reader, the language and earnest, if sometimes funny, demands in the "state/meant" sound hopelessly anachronistic, but many people took it seriously, including local law enforcement and the FBI. It read as follows:

1. Full endorsement and support of Black Panther Party's 10-Point Program.
2. Total assault on the culture by any means necessary, including rock and roll, dope, and fucking in the streets.
3. Free exchange of energy and materials—we demand the end of money!
4. Free food, clothes, housing, dope, music, bodies, medical care—everything free for everybody.
5. Free access to information media—free technology from the greed creeps!
6. Free time and space for all humans—dissolve all unnatural boundaries.
7. Free all schools and all structures from corporate rule—turn the building over to the people at once!
8. Free all prisoners everywhere—they are our brothers.
9. Free all soldiers at once—no more conscripted armies.
10. Free the people from their "leaders"—leaders suck—all power to all the people—freedom means free everyone!*

Along with the formation of the White Panther Party came a new cast of characters that soon had starring roles at the Trans-Love Ann Arbor

---

* "White Panther Party 10-Point Program," *Ann Arbor Sun*, 1968.

commune. Of the dozens of new faces, perhaps the most significant was Pun Plamondon.

Given up for adoption at birth, Plamondon had a difficult childhood and left his foster home in his early teens. After hitchhiking around the country, he settled in Detroit in 1967 at the age of twenty-one, making sandals by day while living at the Trans-Love Energies commune at night. He moved with Sinclair to Ann Arbor in June 1968 only to be arrested a few days later on a charge of "sale and/or distribution of marijuana" in Traverse City, which at that time carried a twenty-years-to-life sentence. He was held in the Grand Traverse County Jail, and it was there he became radicalized.

"I made bond in Traverse City after eighty-nine days in jail and returned to Ann Arbor," he said. "Now that I was facing twenty to life, I felt some action was needed to subvert the government's criminal intent of locking me up.

"Sinclair was facing a similar charge in Detroit that carried the same penalty. To keep Sinclair and myself out of prison, I felt a political response was called for."*

It was with Plamondon that Sinclair created the White Panther Party. Initially, both men shared the same belief that the best way to change the world was through infusing music with revolutionary content, although later they would take it in a more radical direction.

"We at Trans-Love Energies did not see ourselves as political activists; rather, as cultural revolutionaries," said Plamondon. "To me the difference is significant. I tried to get involved with the politicos, but quite frankly I found them dull and narrow-minded, more interested in having the perfect position paper and being ideologically pure than in organizing and getting large numbers of people to move in the same direction.

---

* *Interim Report on the Background of Pun Plamondon and the Founding of the White Panther Party circa 1968*, Ann Arbor District Library, https://aadl.org/freeingjohnsinclair/essays/interim_report_on_the_background_of_pun_plamondon, accessed February 6, 2024.

"Upon my release on bond from [jail], I realized there was a great mass of reefer-driven rock 'n' roll outlaws who could be educated and mobilized. This mass of young and progressive people was already alienated from the dominant culture, had an antagonistic relationship to the power structure, and was eager to bring change to this decrepit country."

Joining Plamondon, who was appointed the White Panthers' Minister of Defense, was the blond-haired, bearded Jesse "J. C." Crawford, the organization's deeply eccentric Minister of Religion. A native of Cleveland who relocated to Ann Arbor in the mid-1960s, Crawford was the co-founder of a goofball religious order called the Church of Zenta, whose beliefs mirrored those of Trans-Love—namely the worship of sex, drugs, and rock 'n' roll.

Crawford became a significant part of the MC5's show, going to all their gigs, delivering "fire and brimstone" introductions designed to get the crowds riled up before the band hit the stage. His importance was such that the first thing you heard on the group's iconic debut album, *Kick Out the Jams*, was his bellowing voice:

"Brothers and sisters!" he cried like a Southern Baptist minister in the throes of spiritual ecstasy. "I wanna see a sea of hands out there! Lemme see a sea of hands! I want everyone to kick up some noise! I want to hear some revolution out there, brothers! I wanna hear a little revolution! Brothers and sisters, the time has come for each and every one of you to decide whether you are gonna be the problem or whether you are gonna be the solution! You must choose, brothers! You must choose..."

Other prominent Panthers included Skip Taube, Minister of Education, and Jerry Younkins, Minister of Survival. Sinclair was, of course, the self-appointed Minister of Information, and the members of the MC5 were ordained the Ministers of War. While the titles were meant to be tongue-in-cheek, perhaps the cleverest was reserved for David "Panther" White, Crawford's partner in their quasi-religion, Zenta.

"We made Panther White the Chairman, because it made a palindrome," said Sinclair. "We thought when we issued a press release or a statement, it always would start 'White Panther Chairman Panther White,' so everybody'd be able to tell that we weren't a group of humorless fucking college debate society radicals."

JOHN SINCLAIR We became more politically aware and active after Pun got busted for weed in his hometown, Traverse City. He had to do ninety days up there in the summer of '68. It was a drag, because it was during the same time the band really started to take off. He was an important part of Trans-Love Energies but was in jail during our gigs with Blue Cheer and Cream, and our shows at Chicago and Saugatuck.

Initially, Pun was just a hippie who tooled leather belts and sandals and shit. Then he was sent to some fucking county jail for just smoking some pot, and that made him angry. It was there that he met Skip Taube, who came from a group of people who became the Weather Underground, an organization that started blowing shit up. So, you had Pun, Skip, and me. I was in with them, because I felt the same way about the world that they did.

Pun's time in jail opened the door to our future in a way. He was introduced to the Black Panther Party, and when he got out, he wanted to hook us up.

Forming the White Panther Party wasn't going to be a dead-serious thing. Initially it was just bizarre, crazy, and fun. Everybody always misses that about the White Panther Party. We just became more serious because we kept on getting busted all the time.

We had direct contact with the Black Panther Party in the spring of '69. They realized we were totally politically naïve, and they instructed us to study. They had political education classes with the Detroit chapter. That's when we got into Mao. They turned us on to Mao and the Red Book.

ROB TYNER John had a real admiration for bad dudes. Miles Davis was a bad dude. [Writer and Black Panther leader] Eldridge Cleaver was a bad dude. The idea of the White Panthers was that they're gonna fuck with you. John knew that the authorities were gonna take issue with him. But when they did, it would not be just one guy, it would be an entire organization. This is what he told us, and I started getting nervous right then.

Sinclair was radicalized by the fact he had been persecuted by the police and narcotics people, then entrapped and sent to jail in 1966 for possession of marijuana, so his resentment toward the authorities was quite intense.

Rock 'n' roll can be political, but it's best when it's culturally motivated. When you're politically motivated, it isn't art anymore, it's propaganda. It stops being art when it becomes a slogan or a jingle. You can move people with a great rock-'n'-roll song much more effectively than you can with a speech. The MC5 often disappointed the political elements that surrounded us because we did not and would not turn our music into propaganda. People often tried to take our energy so they could use it politically.

The political situation got super hairy. The Black Panthers had seized the headlines, and they were on TV every day. Sinclair really related to it. And he always had a tremendous empathy for Black Americans and related to them because of his own political experiences. The guy really had a vast intelligence, and his frustrations motivated him to actively voice his opposition to what was going on.

So, the White Panther Party came into being. I think John was trying to fill what he saw as a need. It was an outlet for John, but also for other people with similar frustrations. The White Panther Party gave them a rallying point, and that's probably the most important thing about the movement. I mean, they didn't really do anything that earth-shattering. They didn't achieve any great victories. The main function was to serve as an outlet for a lot of people who wanted to make a positive impact on society. I think it served in a social capacity for a lot of folks.

It was kind of adolescent, but it served the purpose. It was a club for guys who held the same political beliefs, and John wanted to send out the message that you couldn't mess with us. "Mess with us, and you're not only messing with us—you're messing with a concept called the White Panthers." There was the vision, and we began adopting the White Panther outfit: long black leather coats . . . even in the summer!

There's always a danger in political circumstances to take yourself too seriously, and to be offended if somebody doesn't believe in your cause. There were moments when the politics of the White Panthers and the music of the MC5 really clicked. You could see the possibilities of moving people with the music and then enlighten them.

LENI SINCLAIR Every time John got arrested, it pushed him into a more radical direction, which scared the band. John's activities brought them more notoriety, but the band were not political revolutionaries. Cultural revolutionaries, yes.

WAYNE KRAMER It was our mandate to be the advance guard. We disrupted everything we contacted. That was part of our tactics, and our way of carrying our message.

JOHN SINCLAIR What made the MC5 political? Well, if the political apparatus of the state was trying to interrupt their music, then obviously it had some kind of political aspect.

ROB TYNER As the Panthers evolved, they became less fun and interesting. Instead of Jesse Crawford whipping the crowd up, he eventually became a drone talking about insider politics that meant nothing to our crowd. "I want to talk to Danny Wiztooki and Norman Carello and Robert Hines backstage after the set for White Panther Party business . . ." It would just drone on. I'd walked through the crowd, and you'd hear people saying, "What the fuck is all this?" They'd ask me, "How come we've gotta *sign up* for shit?" Eventually, it would really drag the tone of the evening down.

Sinclair began to take it all too seriously, but it was in perfect keeping with the Maoist view of entertainers or artists, who were always considered the worst and most useless part of the revolution. We were these fucking parasite artists. They felt we should be writing only to support the party line, and if we didn't, we were drunk, lazy dinks. If we weren't stopping the show and going, "Everybody join the White Panther Party!" we were a bunch of bourgeois scoundrels.

WAYNE KRAMER How committed were we to the White Panthers? To be honest, it varied. Not everyone in the band embraced it. Me personally, yeah, I was in it with both feet.

Ultimately, I don't think the politics hurt us. You couldn't really separate politics and music from what was happening. We were part of a whole generation that was rebelling against Nixon and the Vietnam War. These days, when you oppose government policy, people might call you patriotic. But in those days, it made us outlaws.

JOHN SINCLAIR J. C. Crawford, Panther White, the MC5, and the Stooges had the same radical outlook, but they weren't pissed off like Pun and I were. They were mostly angry when they weren't getting paid enough when they played, or when they were getting ripped off by promoters and club owners. They had that typical working-class outlook about the way government and capitalists are. They were basically determined to have a good time and fuck those people.

I'm not criticizing them for that. I often felt the same way. The things that pissed off the band might not seem like a big deal, but it would've made any sane person crazy. Typically, they'd go out and play a gig and any number of terrible things would happen. The promoters would fuck them around on the performance conditions, or the police would try to shut their power in the middle of the show. Or maybe the promoter would try to beat you out of the money they owed you, and if you protested, they'd call the police in to beat you up. This shit happened week after week. In a wide sense, they were pissed off just like the average young person that got high and listened to rock was pissed off about the government and the war and all that.

I was like both the band and the radicals, but I had been angry since 1960! I was totally alienated from the world. I didn't watch TV, read a newspaper, or listen to the radio from about 1960 to 1965. I missed John F. Kennedy altogether. I just didn't pay any attention. I thought they were all crooks. Malcolm X was the only person in public life that I could relate to at all. And Elijah Muhammad—I knew he was an idiot, but he had a good idea.

The main contradiction between me and the band was that I was single-minded, and my purpose was a revolutionary purpose. Making it to the national stage was a way to really get the program over: "Let's reach millions of kids!"

DANNY FIELDS I could go on for a long time about John's use of the band as a political instrument, and how it sowed the seeds of their destruction. I felt that very profoundly. The politics doomed them from the beginning. We signed a rock-'n'-roll band, and all that other stuff was seen as a cute promotional gimmick. No one at Elektra took it seriously. No one at all.

ROB TYNER Janis Joplin told me, "Politics? Are you crazy? I ain't gonna say *nothing* about politics. Jesus Christ, that's nuts!" And people like Country Joe McDonald took me aside in Chicago and said, "Look, don't you know what this is. Don't you know these people are just exploiting you and fucking you?" He was talking about John Sinclair and the rest of the politicos. He said, "Man, me and my band used to go to all these goddamn benefits and everything and look what it got me. We got out there and we got used and abused. And that's what's happening to you. You can't see it because you're right in the middle of it, but man, that's what's happening to you."

He said, "Do you know how many benefits I've done? Do you know how much benefit I've received, or that I have seen the people receive from it? Absolutely nothing. These people will drain you dry, and they will bleed you till you can't stand up and won't ever say thank you; they'll just throw you away like tissue paper."

And, of course, like an idiot, I gave him the party line. "Listen, man, we got solidarity. We're *together*."

MICHAEL DAVIS Rob's vision wasn't political in the traditional sense. He could relate to the White Panthers and their desire to tear down an oppressive system, but he wasn't into speaking rhetoric. Tyner was always very tuned into a kind of tribal thing. He brought that to the table, as well as his intellectualism and his art.

He was much more into the idea of spontaneity and freedom of expression. He liked to relate to people, and he thought of himself as a common person. He didn't think of himself as a rock star. He wasn't a celebrity in his own mind. He wanted us to always draw the audience members into his trip. It wasn't selfish. It wasn't ego-driven. It was about his humanity. I think he might have been more comfortable if the White Panthers never entered the picture.

ROB TYNER To me, the most important thing was the expression of freedom. I think rock 'n' roll will go down in history as one of the purest expressions of American freedom that there is. That's why there was such a tremendous negative reaction to all the stuff we tried to do. It was too free, too noisy, and it excited too many of the freedoms that people would prefer to keep stored at the back of the drawer. There was that time we played in Benton Harbor they passed an ordinance stating that we could not move onstage! In these little towns, it was very puritanical. We could bring this kind of big-city craziness to these smaller towns, and they'd get really scared and call the cops. As a band, we might not have been the greatest musicians, but we symbolized the times, and their possibilities and restriction. Our attempts at being free and expressing freedom necessitated restrictions.

JOHN SINCLAIR I was politically oriented, which wasn't true of the band. They were cool with it, but as far as they were concerned it began and ended with their performance. They weren't necessarily eager about politics, but they were certainly not loath to make a political statement in the widest sense. And again, our concept of politics, my concept of politics, was much wider than the political left per se. The stuff we did was political, but not in a sectarian way.

We didn't have much interaction with the radical politicos of the time, except for a guy like Skip. He and Pun were tight; he came out of the radical faction of Students for a Democratic Society and all those people were his comrades. But I didn't know any of them.

I kind of thought that the SDS and all them were just squares. They didn't even listen to the Beatles or Jimi Hendrix.

WAYNE KRAMER On the one hand, John's escalating political fanaticism made me nervous, but on the other hand I was proud to be a part of it. Like, I knew that when Pun eventually blew up the CIA office, the dynamite was probably paid for with MC5 money. So, I thought, Hey, this is great. But on the other hand, who wants the grief? Who wants to go to jail? Or worse.

ROB TYNER The establishment had the money, the cops, and the power. They had everything. And they had ways and means of letting you know just how far you can go . . . unless you were real sneaky. The counterculture at that time was all about thinking of different ways to get around the restrictions that were created by the Nixon administration. The '60s were probably one of the most turbulent times in American history, and the power structure was really trying to put their boot down so that they could stay in control.

But if you hem people in, you just make 'em sneakier. They'll think up some way to get around you. The Panthers were an attempt to send a message back to the power structure that "We're a unit, and you can't move us. You can't mess with us." Sinclair told me one time, if you're just a person, then they're just messing with a person. But if you're part of an organization, they're messing with all of you, and the media will look at it differently.

Our audience consisted of suburban, middle-class kids. That's why the White Panthers were important. They would have chapters in different towns all over Michigan, where people wanted to be connected to a group that was hopefully going to have a major impact on America. They wanted to be part of that excitement. I think a lot of people hung their dreams on the Panthers. I know I did for a while.

JOHN SINCLAIR If the White Panthers were the political arm, then Zenta was the joke religious arm. They were like comic relief. It was conceived as a counterculture religion by Brother J. C. Crawford and Panther White. It just seemed like a good idea to combine rock 'n' roll, politics, and religion. Zenta was cool. Anyone could blend with it conceptually, because no one really knew what the fuck it was. It was invisible, had no commander, but all powerful in its own way. Crawford and White used to take up collections, and I think they made a decent living at it for a while.

ROB TYNER We were onstage, and I heard someone yell, "Zenta!" Zenta? Yeah, cool, man. The drums are going *badadada* and somebody said, "Let us take up a collection for Zenta." Cool, man!

You remember the archetypal flimflam man in cowboy movies. He'd have this little tie and a dirty hat and this wild suit, and he'd be in this frontier town: "Oh, yeah, they got this bridge. It's in Brooklyn. I got this deed." One time I told J. C. that he should buy a flimflam outfit. He got a little pissed off at me. Because maybe it was a little too close to home. But Brother J. C. would go out there and really exhort the troops some nights, and it'd be great.

RON ASHETON The whole Zenta thing was just one more excuse to get high. Jesse would say, "Isn't it a special day today? Let's see, what's the reason we can get fucked up?" It was a bit of a joke, but then it got a little serious. Other people around the situation would make a big hoopla, and *they* made it something special. It was a Jesse Crawford joke, but then, "Oh, these guys are going for it? Okay, Zenta!" That's Jesse, he was a great kidder.

BECKY TYNER J. C. was very loud and boisterous. Real outgoing. I think he was into it for the party. I don't think he really took the revolutionary stuff seriously. He was appropriated by John Sinclair to help him control the band. But you had to ask, why bring in somebody crazier than they were to deal with their craziness?

ROB TYNER To sit with J. C. and the Panthers, you had to be able to rap down serious "zone talk." Flat-out, no prisoners, be in it and don't quit it. The horror of it is that very little of it meant anything. Whatever was said, you'd just respond, "Raht ahwn! Raht ahwn!" I had a bigger muscle on one arm in those days from giving the salute and saying "Right on!"

Much of the talk was absurd, but I liked the slang. "Killer." "Destroy." "Chumps." "Chomp punk." "Ponk." "Bogue." "Douse." It was endless.

JOHN SINCLAIR J. C.'s role was to geek the fellows up. He and Panther White were these two totally crazed individuals that would show up at a gig and ask, "Can we give a little pitch for Zenta?" They were a little crazy but very powerful, both in their presentation and their effect.

Jesse was a big fan of Brother Dave Gardner, who was a comedian that parodied a Southern Baptist minister, and he adopted elements of his persona... even though Crawford was from a wealthy family in Cleveland.

RON ASHETON Jesse was just a pot-smoking party animal, and eventually he was the guy that broke down the band's discipline. He would also later sow the seeds of discontent between the band and Sinclair's commune.

WAYNE KRAMER When J. C. arrived on the scene, we started drinking a little beer here and there. He was the instigator, because he liked to drink. None of us used to drink; it was all just reefer and acid or whatever psychedelic was around. John was against that, because he thought drinking was part of the straight culture. But J. C. couldn't stand by that. He was who he was, which was one reason we liked him, I guess. He broke up the party line with his irreverence. Where we were like good soldiers, he was [like] "Ah, fuck that."

ROB TYNER The Stooges really shied away from the White Panther Party and politics in general, and I can understand it. They were friends of ours, but they weren't "joiners." I don't think there was ever a time when Iggy was really a Panther. The Stooges thought the whole idea was humorous . . . and sorta stupid.

RON ASHETON I hate to say it, but the Stooges thought the White Panthers were a big joke. We seriously never gave it any thought. But the joke became a detriment to the MC5. We thought it was a bad move for them to be tagged with all that shit.

DENNIS THOMPSON The Stooges had the presence of mind to keep themselves separate from Trans-Love politics. Every one of the guys in that band were wary of the "hippie hoax." They wanted no part of it. They stayed away from it, and it was to their benefit that they did that.

Wayne thought the Stooges were garbage. Tyner thought they were cute, weird, and different. Sinclair hated them. He would say, "They'd never be an MC5. They don't study, they don't know." But they had the energy of youth and a certain . . . raw power.

John would say, "These jazz guys have been living and dying in poverty for years and they play the shit out of their instruments. And you guys, you're doing that, and you're going to be respected. But these Stooges assholes, they're just lunatic fringe."

Meanwhile the Stooges were picking up speed, and they were passing us. None of them could play. Ron Asheton had just picked up a guitar. Dave Alexander had just picked up a bass, and Scott Asheton had just started playing drums. But they had *that* feeling, that MC5 feel. They hung around us. They picked up on the energy, but they didn't get involved in the politics. They loved us. We were their guru band. They didn't give a shit about our politics, but they admired our playing and attitude. They knew we were the best. And we *were* the best.

JOHN SINCLAIR The Stooges were doing a lot of glue; that was their thing. I think perhaps it had something to do with why they were called Stooges. They would sit around with that bag, sniffing glue, and watch TV for eight hours in a row. Then they'd eat some cheese puffs or Diet Pepsi or something. They were just totally gone.

Personally, I thought the whole idea was disgusting. In general, the basic organizing principle of my life was consciousness and energy expansion. I smoked pot every day, [did] speed every other day, and LSD on the right occasions. Drinking, drunkenness or downers, or sniffing glue, anything that would reduce you, was not my thing. I felt "rocket reducer" was so aptly named because it was reducing these people to the dimension of idiots.

RON ASHETON Jesse was the guy that introduced everyone to "rocket reducer," which is basically sniffing glue. I remember going to the house one day, and Crawford and the band were passing around the rocket reducer. They're passing around this rag and getting all geeked out. Geeked out!

Rob and I abstained. John hated it too. He thought it was decadent and made people lazy. Ironically, one of John's guys, Jesse Crawford, started the whole thing. On glue, they were incapacitated. Out of their minds. Have you ever been around a bunch of guys that have sniffed paint remover? They laugh and get very silly, but then they just pass out and mumble. I saw a circle of friends become blithering idiots in a matter of moments. It's a very quick high, so you continue to want to have more of it. You just get dumb and dumber.

I did it one time and didn't like it, because you completely lose your motor control and just become a zombie. John was absolutely right—it was decadent. But it was also part of MC5's eventual revolt against Sinclair—they wanted to fight for their right to be blithering fucking idiots. It was almost a fuck-you to John. It was their way of saying they didn't want to be a part of his hippie shit anymore.

CHAPTER IV

MOTHERFUCKERS!

> They say you've got free speech, but try it and you'll see how fast they put a piece of tape over your mouth.
>
> —Rob Tyner

For a brief and shining moment it appeared that the MC5 and John Sinclair were going to prevail over the cops, club owners, and other "straights" who regularly beat and busted them for playing too loud, looking too weird, and coloring outside the lines with their communist-leaning politics.

Between their riotous concerts, major-label record deal with Elektra, and John Sinclair's formation of the White Panther Party, they seized the national media by the scruff of their necks and left an impression that they were a lasting force to be reckoned with. Both the *New York Times* and *Rolling Stone* dutifully sent reporters to Detroit to cover this hot new rock-'n'-roll revolution happening, and the latter printed an impassioned cover story on the band weeks before the release of their debut album, a move that was unprecedented at the time.

And when the "Kick Out the Jams" single, with its problematic "motherfucker" changed to the more radio-friendly "brothers and sisters," was unleashed in early 1969, it further cemented the band's potential as a genuine phenomenon when it shot to the top of the charts in Detroit and Cleveland and looked set to spread well beyond the band's midwestern base.

Yes, the MC5 and their rowdy rock 'n' roll, dope, and fucking-in-the-streets agenda were improbably speeding towards the American mainstream, and within the band's communal bubble, their giddy utopian dreams of hippie insurgency—which six months earlier seemed as remote as their getting a private audience with Chairman Mao—suddenly appeared to be within their grasp.

"I knew all along in the MC5 that we were never going to be the Beatles," said Rob Tyner in 1989. "But as John Sinclair made me very aware, you're only given this time and place, and if people try to restrict you from doing things, you gotta fight—if only to set an example for the next generation of fighters."

Little did the band realize just how fragile their bubble was, and how difficult their battle would be. Just as they appeared to be on the brink of success, they were suddenly attacked from all sides—the conservative right, the radical left, and even their own record company. Worse yet, many of their most significant wounds were self-inflicted.

If their climb to the top had been long and hazardous, their downhill slide was shockingly rapid and twice as painful. Much of it was due to one word: "motherfuckers."

The Five's initial fall from grace began innocently enough. The band's label, Elektra, decided to introduce its new discovery to New York with a free concert at the Fillmore East on December 26, 1968. The idea was simple enough and sure to generate publicity and holiday goodwill during the lull between Christmas and New Year's Eve. But there was an unpleasant snap in the Manhattan air. Legendary promoter Bill Graham had been feuding with a radical street group called Up Against the Wall Motherfucker, to whom he'd granted a weekly "free night" at the Fillmore but then canceled after damage was done to the theater during one of their gatherings.

The Motherfuckers were furious with Graham. The group of extremists grew out of a Dada-influenced art consortium called Black Mask that consisted of shit-stirrers of every stripe, including people involved in the anti–Vietnam War movement. Until the formation of the White Panthers, they were reputedly one of the only white organizations taken seriously by the Black Panther Party. In May 1968, Black Mask changed its name and went underground, reemerging with a provocative new moniker, Up Against the Wall Motherfucker, taken from "Black People," a poem by controversial Black writer LeRoi Jones (later known as Amiri Baraka). Abbie Hoffman characterized the former Black Mask as "the middle-class nightmare ... an anti-media phenomenon simply because their name could not be printed."*

Skilled rabble-rousers, the Motherfuckers had fought their way into the Pentagon during an anti-war protest, cut the fences at the Woodstock Music and Art Festival in 1969—thereby allowing thousands to enter for free—and counted radical feminist and would-be Andy Warhol assassin Valerie Solanas among their ranks.

They were intense, wild, and fearless, which gave them considerable credibility with other late-'60s provocateurs like the notorious Weathermen. For those reasons—and over vehement objections by Elektra and Graham—the MC5 decided to invite the Motherfuckers to their free show at the Fillmore East. It turned out to be a remarkably bad decision, especially given that a few days earlier, MC5 permitted one of the Motherfuckers' spokesmen to make an appeal for funds during their set opening for the Velvet Underground at the Boston Tea Party. He used the occasion to urge the crowd to burn the building to the ground,

---

* Marty Jezer, *Abbie Hoffman: American Rebel* (New Brunswick, NJ: Rutgers University Press, 1993), 131–132.

thereby earning the Five the permanent enmity of Don Law, the club's powerful East Coast promoter.

The Five's refusal to play unless the Motherfuckers were granted admittance to their Fillmore show was the first of many self-hammered nails in their coffin. Almost predictably, the Motherfuckers used the MC5's night at the Fillmore to exact their revenge on Graham by engaging in pitched, bloody battle with his staff. Not only was the legendary rock promoter beaten with a chain in the ruckus, but he almost lost an eye in the process. And when the MC5 finally arrived in a limousine rented by Elektra to ferry them to the Fillmore, they were accused by the Motherfuckers of being tools of the capitalist oppressors.

In approximately one short week, the Five had managed to alienate two of the biggest promoters in the music business *and* were now regarded with suspicion by the radical political establishment. They were well and truly fucked on both ends, though they wouldn't feel the full effect of it until later. At the moment it appeared to them to be nothing more than a minor speed bump on their road to world domination.

The band hit another bad patch a few weeks later, in February 1969, when the *Kick Out the Jams* album was released. The record flew off Detroit shelves in breathtaking numbers and was picking up steam nationally when an influential radio programmer abruptly advised his stations to drop "Kick Out the Jams" from their playlists, asserting that the "clean" single was being used to promote an "obscene" album that dared to include the word "motherfucker" in a song.

That stopped the single cold. But even more influential was the verdict of the rock intelligentsia. When many finally heard the group they'd been reading so much about, they were appalled. Typical of this turnabout was *Rolling Stone*, which, perhaps to atone for putting these rude, crude Motor City barbarians on their cover, printed a scathing review from a first-time contributor named Lester Bangs. The writer—who would later be hailed as "America's greatest rock critic"—wrote them off as overamped and overhyped "bozos" who couldn't play and compared them to amateurish groups like the Seeds and Question Mark and the Mysterians. In today's garage-rock climate, such comparisons would constitute high praise, but in 1969 few insults could be more cutting.

To add to the growing hue and cry, record store clerks across the country were being threatened with jail time for selling *Kick Out the Jams*. Additionally, the *Berkeley Barb*, perhaps the country's most radical underground paper, printed a photo of multiple members of the Five having consensual sex with a female admirer. When the powerful Detroit retail chain Hudson's finally refused to carry the album, Sinclair stirred up even more trouble for the band when he took out a newspaper ad headlined "Fuck Hudson's!" In retaliation, Hudson's responded by promptly pulling Elektra's entire catalog.

This all proved too much for the label. On April 16, 1969, with *Kick Out the Jams* bulleted inside the American Top 30, it took the shocking step of terminating the band's contract.

According to Danny Fields, the Elektra publicist who'd convinced label head Jac Holzman to sign the band, corporate forces had been aligning against the MC5 from the start: "Jac liked the idea of people with divergent tastes working for him, but there were power centers at Elektra that loathed [MC5] from day one. Hated it. *Hated it*. Elektra had been the well-mannered label of folk musicians like Judy Collins and Theodore Bikel. It was bad enough when they started signing Sunset Strip thugs like Love, but with the Doors at Number 1 they couldn't complain. It was enough to have this monster called Jim Morrison, but then I come along with this band of five monsters, and a monster manager, and a monster political agenda as well. The more conservative element in the company wanted us gone, all of us, and they ultimately got what they wanted."

JOHN SINCLAIR The Up Against the Wall Motherfuckers [*sic*] were an anarchist political organization based in New York City. They were Marxist kind of dudes who were way more radical than the White Panthers, but we were friendly and brothers in the revolution.

In December of '68, the MC5 were scheduled to play the Tea Party in Boston, which was sort of like the Fillmore or the Grande, and the Motherfuckers wanted to give a fundraising speech at our show. It wasn't unusual for us to allow political activists to speak at our gigs, so we invited them.

The underground was such a beautiful thing at that time, and that was where our base of support was. That's who we could count on, regardless of the vagaries of the record industry, or the radio, or any of that stuff. I was eager to do anything we could to tie in with the scene at street level. It was a signal of our authenticity.

We were part of an entire network. I had been hooked up with all the underground papers via my syndicated column for *Fifth Estate*. As an outgrowth of that, everywhere we went we'd support them by playing benefits. This was part of my plan all along. The Motherfuckers were just a part of that.

But after we played the Tea Party, they got up and started directing the audience to burn the club down and take to the streets. Don Law, who was the club manager and one of the biggest concert promoters in the Northeast, was understandably pissed. He banned us after that. As far as he was concerned, it was entirely our fault.

ROB TYNER To be "right on" in the revolution, sometimes you had to let the people have the microphone. It was part of the bit, but sometimes it got to be too much. The Motherfuckers were too much. Way too much.

JOHN SINCLAIR Once we started touring outside of Detroit, contradictions between the band and my messianic political outlook stood out in sharper contrast. The incident in Boston really angered the band, and I can't really blame them. They were getting their big chance, and there I was inviting these crazy geeks up onstage to cause problems. It worked somehow in Detroit, but everywhere else the audiences were just annoyed and confused.

RON ASHETON I remember having discussions about why the MC5 didn't translate to the rest of the United States. It was a big shock to the band because they felt so confident coming out of Detroit. They thought their music and politics would snowball to the rest of America. Not true. Not so. They found that the response was a lot different out of Detroit.

This is terrible to say, but I loved that they were struggling. I found some sort of satisfaction that those arrogant monsters discovered that the rest of the world wasn't going to automatically bow down when they left their Midwest dominion.

JOHN SINCLAIR We planned to release the album in February, so a month before the record was released Elektra wanted to introduce us to New York with a free concert at the Fillmore East on the day after Christmas. We were going to give away a single of "Kick Out the Jams," backed with "Motor City's Burning," and it was going to be great.

Our timing was weird, though. We walked into the middle of a big fight between Bill Graham and the Motherfuckers. Graham had tried to make peace with them in previous weeks by letting them have a series of free shows, but they totally abused the Fillmore East and police threatened to revoke the hall's license. So Graham threw them out.

We had supported the Motherfuckers the week before in Boston and they expected us to do the same in New York. They wanted to use our concert as their platform to get back at Graham. They were furious with us when we hesitated. They thought we were siding with Graham and the record company, who wanted nothing to do with them.

I had to tell Holzman that we weren't going to play unless the Motherfuckers could be involved. It was ugly. Eventually they made some accommodation, but Holzman wasn't happy.

DANNY FIELDS The idea was to establish them as a "people's band." There was all this shit about "people's this" and "people's that," whatever the fuck that meant. It was just an obtrusive, stultifying, Stalinist kind of label to put on anything. When you label something a "people's park," what the fuck does that mean? Basically, it means that you can't take your children there because it'll be filled with winos and junkies.

There'd be all these people walking around with Mao's *Little Red Book*. They believed this stuff, and they were spouting things like "Power comes out of the barrel of a gun."

So, okay, the MC5 were going to do a free night at the Fillmore. I don't really know what was going on between Graham and the Motherfuckers, but they had a disagreement and the Motherfuckers lived to make trouble. They were occasionally charming, but they were also agitators—some would call them agents provocateurs.

As luck would have it, the night we booked the MC5 into the Fillmore was a night the "community" forces were planning to stage a demonstration there.

Elektra rented the theater from Graham and did radio promotions on WNEW, giving away free tickets. As part of the deal, we had to appease the Motherfuckers by also giving them five hundred tickets to give away for free as they saw fit.

It turned out later that Kip Cohen, who was managing the Fillmore, locked those tickets in his drawer and never gave them away. He didn't want those people in the theater. So the Motherfuckers were all wondering where their free tickets were. On the night of the show they were given maybe twenty or thirty free tickets but not the hundreds they were promised, so they were storming and raging.

And me . . . I lit the spark that started the fireworks. I did the dumbest thing you could possibly, possibly, possibly do. To this day I can't believe that I did it, but I was so stupid and naïve that I didn't know what the consequences would be. Can you guess what I did?

I decided to rent a limo to take the band to the Fillmore. The streets are full of these ranting Stalinists, anarchists, and Trotskyites, and a limousine pulls up with "the people's band" enthroned in the back seat. Well, everything went wild at that point and there was a riot. The band were seen as traitors to community values because they arrived in a limousine. And I'd always say, "Well, what did you want me to bring them in . . . a Jeep? A tank?" What else were we supposed to do? When you need to get ten people around town, you hire a limousine. I always hired limousines for everything. I should've known better.

Politically, I didn't see it as a flagrantly provocative gesture, but I didn't stop and think. So there was a riot, and Bill Graham himself was out there trying to defend the theater and keep the doors closed while people were trying to storm in. Graham was hit across the face by someone swinging a chain and he almost lost both of his eyes. The show went on, but it was very tense. There were screams from the streets and sounds of things going on, doors breaking down. It was a total disaster.

And after that, if anyone even mentioned the MC5 to Bill Graham he would go apoplectic. He blamed them for everything. He claimed that he saw someone in the band swinging the chain that hit him in the face.

Of course they didn't, but he thought he saw it, and that perception was his reality; after that, he wouldn't book them. To get booked from then on, they had to carve out their own circuit of theaters and venues across the country, which was an extremely difficult thing to do under the best of circumstances. I mean, I know because I did it again years later with the Ramones. It's hard when no one wants you. You can get a record, but if no one wants to put you on, no one's ever going to see you.

That was in December of that year, and it was a great disaster in the career of the band, and in my career. It was quite a story! The Motherfuckers versus Bill Graham versus the MC5 all colliding on this one night, and all we were trying to do is give the people of New York a free concert.

ROB TYNER The night was total chaos. It was like the movie *Escape from New York*. Real scary. I was upstairs in the office, and when I came back down, the whole place had exploded. There was all this commotion. I saw a knife blade come through the curtain—slash, slash, slash! Then this guy sticks his head through, leering like Freddy Krueger. And the gear was flying all over the place. It was completely *destructo*.

JOHN SINCLAIR Talk about nuts, man. Somebody physically attacked Graham and hit him with a chain, and that was the end of us with him, right there. Nice start, huh? First you piss off Don Law and then you alienate Bill Graham, two of the biggest rock concert promoters in the U.S. It could be argued that the shows in Boston and New York had as much of a hand in derailing the MC5's career as Lester Bangs's negative review in *Rolling Stone* a couple months later.

It was galling. What did the Motherfuckers want? We'd already laid our whole fucking career on the line for these people by refusing to go on until they'd been accommodated. It was a free concert and we gave everyone a record. What more could you do for a Motherfucker? What did they want, a blowjob? Their behavior was totally unreasonable. It was a turning point in the MC5's career. Bill Graham wouldn't touch them with a ten-foot pole after that. They were completely ostracized.

For most revolutionaries, record companies were capitalist pigs. But to me a record company was a medium through which you reached a lot of people. I was one of the few people who could see both sides of the coin.

From our perspective, an organization like the Motherfuckers should've appreciated that we were ripping off the establishment. There was no contradiction for us. Being flown in to talk about a record deal. Great! Can we go first-class? Can you have somebody pick us up at the airport? How much can we get away with [with] these chumps? The limo didn't represent any contradiction to me at all.

Of course, if there had been another limousine for the Motherfuckers, they would have been very happy to have jumped in and gone wherever we were going. So that was the other side of it too. That was disgusting to me.

We played a free concert for them and made the record company pay for it. Please! Our reward was to get blacklisted by the biggest fucking promoter in the business.

They were pissed because we were traveling in a limo, but that was just the most efficient means of transportation for a large party of people. What did they want us to do, take the subway? After the show, with our equipment? What the fuck? You want us to walk back to our hotel? We're staying in a hotel! What do you think of that? Should we be sleeping in the park? What do you want? I was disgusted. They were just macho guys with an attitude problem.

ROB TYNER After I escaped the building, I went out into the street and saw a limo being showered with what looked like *our* record, and it was leaving. I thought, How the fuck am I gonna get out of here?! That's probably the band. Suddenly, this car comes along and stops next to me. Bzzz . . . window down. "Are you Robin Tyner? The record company sent me over. What's going on here?" I was like, "I don't know, man, take me to [New York nightclub] Max's Kansas City."

It was a little frightening, but on another level it didn't faze us. The band was becoming very seasoned about living with chaos.

WAYNE KRAMER The kids that were there for the show seemed to dig it. The place was packed. Sold out. The people that were there all saw a great show. As near as they could figure, everything was fine. There was some trouble down in front, but when we finished and brought the curtain down, the Motherfuckers just went wild and trashed the stage and our equipment.

So, J. C., Dennis, and I got the hell out of there and jumped into a limousine that was waiting for us out in front of the building. Then I saw the Motherfucker women—a bunch of their girlfriends and wives and shit—and they were crying and screaming in the street that we had sold them out. They started yelling that we were pigs and capitalist tools.

We'd given away free records and they smashed them on the limousine. It was like, what's wrong with this picture? We're giving away free records and they're smashing them. The rest of the band got in the limo and basically said, "Fuck this noise," and went to the hotel to chase women or something. But I felt like we were really being called out. So J. C. and I stayed behind and stood in the street, trying to talk to these Motherfuckers, and a mob scene developed.

I had a couple of the leaders there, and I was trying to explain our position and what had happened, and told them, "We're from out of town. This thing with you and Bill Graham doesn't necessarily have anything to do with us. We're righteous." But they weren't going for it.

Then I saw another fucking knife in the crowd. A couple of Motherfuckers also saw that the situation was getting out of hand and that I was in serious danger of getting hurt. To their credit, they physically picked me up and carried me back into the Fillmore. After a while I realized it was pointless, that there was nothing else to say. I hung around and we talked a little bit more. Then they escorted me out and walked me a couple blocks up off Third Avenue so I could get a cab back to the hotel. They wanted to take care of me after I showed them that I had some heart.

But we didn't come out of that situation smelling good. Our constituency was turning on us, and the businesspeople didn't like us either. Shit like that was starting to take an effect on me, and I was starting to have this feeling of impending doom.

JOHN SINCLAIR After the debacles in Boston and New York, we caught a break when *Rolling Stone* decided to do a cover story on the band a month before the album came out. I don't know how Eric Ehrmann was chosen to write the piece. He was a college student from Ohio. I didn't question it. To me, *Rolling Stone* was sending someone to do a big story. Great! And the guy was totally sympathetic. Great!

Unfortunately, I've never seen worse reporting in my life. He didn't take one note or make one tape. Everything was reconstructed. Everything. It was all his impressions, which is why it was so awful. For good or bad, he wrote about the spirit of what he saw. There's no getting around that. The exuberance, the arrogance, the macho. The spirit was close, but *every* paragraph was literally riddled with errors. The details didn't make that much difference, but God, it was hard to read.

ROB TYNER It was getting difficult to back all of John and Danny's rhetoric when we were interviewed. We could sound real lame because the truth wasn't being said: that basically we were a kick-ass hard-rock band from Detroit and didn't give a shit about anything. That was our line. More than "power to the people" or "free everything for everybody."

The *Rolling Stone* story is just dripping with romantic adventurism. It was an irresponsible statement, politically, but for the moment it made us look like Errol Flynn, with our scarves blowing in the wind while we threw Molotov cocktails.

We weren't dealing with reality. But with the rhetoric that was happening at the time; it was easy to just slide down into that whole "I'm Che Guevara" Marxist revolutionary thing. And many people paid a price for that kind of talk, including ourselves. I saw it and paid the price for it, but I'm not putting down the revolution, because I believe that it was a fantastic moment in history whose repercussions are still being felt.

WAYNE KRAMER My worst fears were realized after I read the *Rolling Stone* piece. I had a full-blown panic attack. I said, "Goddamn, man, if people believe this shit that this guy's written and think that's who we really are . . . I mean, nobody in their right mind would believe it. Or could believe it. It was just too outlandish." I don't think the writer had ever smoked reefer before, and we, of course, forced him to smoke reefer nonstop for three days. Then he went back and reconstructed the whole thing.

RON ASHETON Let's face it, the band fell for the dogma. John Sinclair is a mighty good preacher. We called him the Pharaoh. That was an MC5 joke, but to this day I still call him the Pharaoh in an affectionate way. But the MC5 believed it for a while.

ROB TYNER One thing I found amusing about the *Rolling Stone* cover was that they added a whole bunch more hair than I had! There was definitely some enhancement happening there. I was into big hair, but they enlarged it even more, which was sorta like making Johnny Rotten's face . . . *greener*.

JOHN SINCLAIR When the record came out, Elektra immediately started getting flak. K-Mart refused to sell it. Hudson's in Detroit refused to sell it. Big department chains like E. J. Korvette refused to sell it. It was having a hell of an impact, so we had a discussion by phone. Elektra said, "All these things are happening, what should we do? We want to pull the record out of the stores; it's too much."

I asked the record company about their lawyers that had promised to defend us. "Well, the lawyers just say this is beyond anything we'd envisioned. People are getting arrested for selling it in stores; people are getting arrested for buying it."

The response was exactly what *I* had envisioned. At first I wasn't even worried when the big chains refused to sell the album, because I knew the kids would just go to the mom-and-pop record stores and buy it. In my scheme of things, as long as the album was available somewhere, things were fine.

WAYNE KRAMER Elektra sent us some proofs of the record artwork, and the quality was terrible. They had sent Xerox copies but no one told me that then, and it didn't help that I was on acid at the time. The initial proofs were so shoddy and cheap, I thought, Oh man, this is all going wrong. We're losing control here.

When the actual cover arrived, it wasn't so bad. One weird thing was that they altered all the kids' faces in the picture so none of them could sue, since they didn't have releases from anybody. The crowd looks like somebody airbrushed them—because they did!

When the first record came out, John and I went to New York for a meeting with Elektra's ad people about how their campaign was going to work. The ad agency's ideas were, of course, asinine. Their radio commercials were like "Haven't you heard? It's the new sound. The MC5!"

John and I looked at each other like *Are these people crazy?* We countered by playing them a radio ad we had written and produced. John had created this very clever spot that was a parody of the kind of ad you'd hear promoting a horror film: "Shocking! Scandalous! Murderous!

Witness this bizarre testimonial as thousands of drug-crazed American youth scream for their heroes, Detroit's MC5. Live!"

We had another one John and I came up with, which was of a bunch of guys sitting around getting high when someone comes in and says, "Hey, man, did you hear that stuff about that band the MC5? What's that? You mean the ones that are all on drugs? Didn't they kill a cat onstage? No, that ain't true. Well, that's what I heard. Well here, here's the record. Check it out yourself." Then the tagline: "MC5, available on Elektra Records."

The ad agency loved it, but by that time Elektra had pretty much crossed us out of the picture.

DANNY FIELDS What irked the MC5 the most was when Hudson's, a department store in their own city of Detroit, refused to carry the uncensored version of the album. So the band took out their own ad that said, "Fuck Hudson's," and put the Elektra logo on it. When Hudson's saw it, they refused to carry any Elektra product, including harmless stuff like Theodore Bikel's recordings of Yiddish folk songs.

In response, the record company wanted to get rid of them. This was all happening at the same time they had the cover of *Rolling Stone*! If you fire a band that was just on the cover of *Rolling Stone*, you must *really* not want to be involved. The truth is, the record got to Number 30 on the *Billboard* charts on the basis of the hype and publicity. They should've been happy.

Jac Holzman was radical. He was in the flush of "Hey, I've discovered the Doors. I'm far-out. I'm a far-seeing, visionary record-company executive; it's time the American people learned what was happening."

He knew that using the word "motherfucker" in "Kick Out the Jams" was going to be controversial, but he thought he could get away with it. He was shocked when people started refusing to carry the album.

WAYNE KRAMER Jac Holzman told us that he would back us up from the fallout of putting the word "motherfucker" on the album. The plan was to release "Kick Out the Jams" as the first single, replacing "motherfucker" with "brothers and sisters" because we knew it was going to be a hit. And once it got huge all over the country, we'd come out with the album and blow everybody's mind because they'd hear the real version.

It'll be controversial, but they wouldn't be able to do anything about it because people would have already bought the single. It's like inviting a guy over to dinner and not finding out he's an axe murderer until he's already in your house. But Elektra fucked it up. Jac got greedy because the single was doing well, and he rushed out the album to capitalize on it. Once Middle America heard us use "motherfucker," it was over.

Jac said he was still going to stand behind us, but then they came out to see us and said, "Can we put out a clean version of the album? We'll do whatever you tell us to do." We said absolutely not. It'll look like we sold out to the establishment. This is the single and this is the album; that's the way it works. You said you were going to be behind us, now you have to *be* behind us.

They agreed and did what they wanted to do anyway.

JOHN SINCLAIR The label came out to Ann Arbor and we had a serious discussion about the use of the word "motherfucker." They wanted to pull it off and change it, and we said, "Man, to us, that's the worst possible thing. We'd rather eat the record."

We argued that it had probably already paid for itself. And even if it hadn't, we'd pay for it out of the next one. I felt it was pivotal to our career. If they couldn't stand behind it, let's eat it. If we changed it, we would lose all our credibility.

We planned this little press tour on the West Coast that we were going to pay for by lining up gigs. We also wanted to record some new material with Bruce Botnick at the new Elektra studios on La Cienega Boulevard while we were there. We wanted to start right in on the next record.

We had all the great material that Jon Landau would eventually butcher on *Back in the USA*. It sounded eight hundred times better at that point than what came out on the record. I said, "Look, we'll just start on that right away, we'll work fast, we'll get it done and get it out." If we had to swallow this one, so be it. And they agreed . . . or so we thought.

DENNIS THOMPSON It's not like everybody in every tool shop, factory, and office in the U.S.A. didn't say "fuck" or "motherfucker" every other word. But the government started thinking that "these guys might be dangerous," especially in light of our White Panther politics. I think Jac Holzman just got chickenshit. He was worried about getting sued and would get the kind of attention that he didn't want.

We were rallying against injustice, greed, the war, racism, and the way the country was being mismanaged. *Time* and *Newsweek* called us the vanguard of the revolution, so suddenly we were the focal point for a whole movement. But when the shit did finally hit the fan, Holzman was like a turtle and he hid in his shell.

WAYNE KRAMER "Kick Out the Jams" was just a catchphrase at first. If we played with a band that was not getting the job done, we'd heckle them with "Kick out the jams or get the fuck off the stage! Kick out the jams, motherfucker! Get down or get out!" We'd all do it, harass and try to intimidate these groups that would dare to play with us at the Grande. We were more like a hockey team than a group of sensitive artists. We'd harass people if we didn't think they were righteous.

ROB TYNER "Kick Out the Jams" was my birthright, my challenge, and my warning. It's not a song—it's a way of life and a way of death. It was the battle cry of the White Panther Party. It was also ambiguous, so it could be whatever you wanted it to mean. That's the beauty of rock 'n' roll: people can hear the sound that you make and they interpret it however they want because it is open-ended. We consciously tried to write songs that were open-ended so people could use them to insert their own dream.

However, the actual definition of "Kick Out the Jams" is all about a way of playing music. It was originally a verb in the Black and jazz communities—"to jam" referred to the act of playing music. When I would go to jazz clubs with my friend who was a tenor saxophonist, the musicians had this bit where they would let people go up onstage and improvise. The players would say things like "Kick out the jams or get offstage"—in other words, "Kick ass or go home." Years later I started saying it again, because you'd go to the Grande Ballroom and they'd have these bands playing that were so wimpy and lame that it made sense again.

On another level, what we wanted to do was loosen up society a little bit. Our underlying goal was to try and let people know that it was okay to kick ass—that you could let your hair down and enjoy yourself. That whole idea of "Kick out the jams, motherfuckers!" really attracted people, and we began to get radicalized by the situation.

We would go play a gig somewhere and the cops would come to the people putting on the show and say, "Hey look, we can't allow the band to say 'motherfucker,' and if they do, we're gonna shut *you* down." So the promoter would come to me and go, "Don't say it, or they'll shut us down—they really will." We'd get out there on the stage, and the people are all screaming for it. What are you gonna do?

There'd be a big mob scene and the cops would get pissed off and the promoter would get pissed off, and then the club owner wouldn't pay us! It started becoming an issue of free speech. "Do we have free speech in this country or don't we?" No! They say you've got free speech, but try it and you'll see how fast they put the tape over your mouth. So they forced us to be sneaky, to cook up some way of getting around it. It became a pain. That's when the White Panthers really started to make sense to me.

But let's face it, fun is fun. "Kick out the jams, motherfuckers"—one joke. It was something that just started out as this *little* thing, but it became sort of a gimmick. And that really did lessen the possibility of saying anything more. Sometimes the crowd was just waiting for you to do *that*. It was a trap on some levels, and it did make the music appear more superficial.

The problem is that we were serious about it, we kept doing it, and people began to groove behind it. These guys at the record company were like, "Okay, all right, well, this is a bizarre time in the history of America, and we'll just do our best to deal with this because these guys are on a roll and lots and lots of street people all over the country are behind it."

We started getting cocky once we got signed to the record company. Then all the rest of the craziness happened, it kept getting crazier and crazier, and the guys at the record company were shaking their heads more and more. But they had bought into the idea on a lot of levels. They put the record out but had no idea how much trouble it was going to cause because of its First Amendment aspect, as well as the cultural aspect. It became more and more complex, and more and more difficult for Elektra to stand behind us.

Sinclair put out a statement at one point that we stood for "rock 'n' roll, dope, and fucking in the streets," so Hudson's, the retail chain, refused to sell our records. When Elektra saw our response, which was to take out an ad that said, "Fuck Hudson's," they drew a line because Hudson's was a major outlet for their records. And for an act of theirs to use obscenities to put down their major outlet, and then to put the Elektra logo on the ad . . . that's three insults! So they said, "Forget it," and started talking about booting us off the label.

DANNY FIELDS There were power centers at Elektra that didn't like what I was bringing into the company. When I got there, Elektra's roster consisted of safe performers. And then I came along.

It was disconcerting enough for many of the executives that the Doors were selling millions of records, but who could complain? And then I came in with MC5 and the Stooges, who stood for "drugs and sex, revolution, and fucking in the streets," and that was overwhelming for many of the conservative record businesspeople that worked at the label. They reflected the thinking of a large part of the American communications and retail establishment, so the MC5 and the Stooges were a great test! Albeit one that failed.

John Sinclair and the guys in the band eventually came out to our offices in Los Angeles to record demos for their next album. They would close the door of the publicity department and take out giant joints and start smoking away in the middle of the afternoon. That didn't go over too well with the vice presidents of sales and marketing.

But hey, it was the MC5. There was nothing that they didn't do—they were beyond the law. They even had something called "the landscaping budget," which was money allocated to buy hash and grass for the band while they recorded in our studios on La Cienega. It wasn't a big surprise when Larry Harris, who was Elektra's director of business affairs, called me in one day after they'd come and gone, and said, "This has got to stop; no more drugs in the office. No grass, no hash."

I said, "Jac says it's okay to smoke hash in the recording studio," and Larry started screaming, "No hash, no LSD!" With a straight face I responded, "Larry, if I can't smoke my LSD every morning with my coffee, I'm no good for the day."

He became enraged, slammed his hand on the table, and said, "Smoke your LSD at home." He didn't really know anything about drugs other than that they were evil and could get you in trouble. Eventually, Elektra started to perceive that the MC5 were indeed going to get them in trouble, and they weren't completely wrong.

WAYNE KRAMER Elektra Records didn't know how to market the revolution. But we did feel that we knew how. We felt that we had a connection with our generation, and that we knew how to talk to them because we *were* them.

JOHN SINCLAIR Before the band's March 1969 tour of the West Coast, Dennis Frawley and I flew out to Elektra in Los Angeles in advance, and we went straight to the warehouse to get our records for us to give to the radio stations and *Rolling Stone* magazine. Unbelievably, they didn't have any! Then I discovered that they'd recalled the album and that they'd changed it—they had removed the word "motherfuckers" without our permission.

I've never seen an account of this episode that's accurate. Everything we had strived to get across about the MC5 was totally undercut. It looked like we had collaborated in all this when in fact we hadn't, and in fact they'd lied to us. Before they censored the album, we'd sold about ninety thousand copies and were Number 30 on the *Billboard* charts with a bullet. The shit was happening. We were poised to take off and Elektra just pulled the rug out from under everything.

If they would've done it our way, the public sympathy would have been incredible. But because the record was changed everybody thought we had backed down, and we lost our base of support. I was so sick. I discovered that not only couldn't I trust Elektra, I *hated* them.

After going to the distributor, Frawley and I went to *Rolling Stone*. Their "American Revolution '69" issue was about to come out, and our record was going to be the giveaway with the subscription. Even though they had done a cover story on us, their newest reviewer, Lester Bangs, filed a vitriolic review of the album that was going to appear in an upcoming issue, so they decided not to do the promotion. I didn't know any of this.

As far as I knew, everything was great between us and *Rolling Stone*. So I came bounding into their offices to go and see Jann Wenner, and everyone was kinda chilly. No warmth was exuded.

Adding to that, we quickly discovered that the rock establishment on the West Coast couldn't stand us. Those first few days were a nightmare.

Despite the incredible errors in Eric Ehrmann's story, you couldn't beat the fact that we had a cover story in *Rolling Stone* before our record came out. But when the record did come out and they printed the Lester Bangs review that said the band wasn't at a level of second-rate garage bands like the Seeds—that we were incompetent and a hype—it really hurt us.

WAYNE KRAMER When I first saw the *Rolling Stone* review, my heart sank. Lester didn't really like the band, but what really burned my ass about it was that he said that Fred and I couldn't play and we couldn't tune our guitars. That got me where I lived. He crushed us with that one.

JOHN SINCLAIR Following the lead of young Lester, all the critics attacked the first record. Lester eventually recanted and admitted that it was one of his favorite records—and that made me even more angry. For him it was just a few paragraphs that got him into a big magazine for the first time, but it ruined our career.

As far as I'm concerned, things really began to splinter in rock culture when *Rolling Stone* set themselves up as the arbiter of what's supposed to be hip. Before then, a new Otis Redding record, a Donovan record, a Who record were all part of the same thing. Then *Rolling Stone* started telling people, "This is hip and this is not."

ROB TYNER When we arrived in San Francisco to play some shows, I looked at those people and immediately understood that they were not gonna get the Detroit groove.

We played the Straight Theater. Nobody came, so we just did our show. That's one thing about the band: we just went ahead and did our show no matter who was out there—no matter what, no matter who, no matter how many.

But Detroit moves didn't work out there. People didn't understand the attitude at all. Don't forget, they had this whole big West Coast hippie-dippy insider's club, and we were shocked that we were not included. That's when I began to realize that maybe we weren't hippies after all.

We may have been on the cutting edge of rejecting the hippie ethos, because shortly after that Quaaludes began to hit, and that was the death knell of the entire movement. From '66 to '68 there was a time of real idealism, and there had been an intellectual underside to it. I had put in my time with the Kerouac books and the John Coltrane records. You could see the younger Grande kids didn't have that background, and they didn't have to search or fight for their right to be freaky. I'm not putting them down for it, because it was just part of the change in youth culture, but they didn't have the training, they hadn't gone to the intellectual boot camp.

DENNIS THOMPSON Having a tight show didn't make a difference when we played out West. They were too low-energy. They ignored us. California had always been our nemesis, our archenemy. You put the MC5 anywhere else in the country—South, East, Midwest—it worked. That energy worked. But California was laid-back. If the music was raw, on the cutting edge like ours was, they were afraid of it. They saw you as being too extroverted, too overbearing. They told us, "You people don't understand love." We said, "Yeah, we do. You ought to live in Detroit, though. You gotta be tough to love in Detroit. Otherwise, you get your nuts busted."

JOHN SINCLAIR Frawley and I went to meet our West Coast comrades and made sure they had a record, but we became a kind of a laughingstock to the laid-back West Coasters. MC5? All that leaping around? They weren't looking for that at all!

We were kind of down in the dumps, and then we went over to Berkeley and took the city by storm. There was this maniac who was running for mayor, and by the end of our week there he had adopted the White Panther banner and was the White Panther candidate for mayor. We wanted to do a free concert, but they had outlawed them in Provo Park, so we just went and did one there anyway, right across the street from the police station. That was big fun.

We also played this benefit for the Black Panthers at Berkeley's Finnish Kaleva Hall. They were showing pornographic films and newsreels in this little room that was packed wall to wall. It was the ultimate type of MC5 event. Incredible. We had finally found some people on the West Coast that liked us! We just really rocked and worked our nuts off. All the revolutionary guys like Tom Hayden were there, and they *loved* us. It was a high point.

It was the opposite in San Francisco. We played two nights and both times the hall was empty. I think the free night was even worse! We were not welcome in San Francisco, even among the scumbags of Haight Street. People who were old friends of mine suddenly weren't home. The party line was "Get them out of here!" In a sense, Lester Bangs's sneering review was the voice of that whole community; that's the way they all felt.

We were supposed to go to Miami after San Francisco, but the promoter, Mike Quatro, called and warned us not to go because they were planning to arrest us as soon as we got off the plane. They had just busted Jim Morrison for exposing himself, and the police knew that if the Doors were trouble, then we were *definitely* trouble.

GREIL MARCUS [music journalist] In the wake of their *Rolling Stone* cover story, I decided to attend the MC5's ludicrous Berkeley show. It was at the Finnish Kaleva Hall, which was an unusual venue. I had never been to a concert there. It wasn't a full house and the audience seemed to be there more out of curiosity.

I recall the show was chaotic. First, J. C. Crawford introduced himself as the White Panthers Minister of Information and gave a pretentious introduction. He went on about how there might be cops in the audience, so "know your neighbor." And how the concert was about "kicking out the jams." And that to be there "was a revolutionary act."

As for the band, there was a lot of shouting and running around and attempts at very loud jazz. The audience was not responding. After what seemed like twenty minutes, Crawford came back and announced, "WE ARE BEING SHUT DOWN! THE PIGS ARE SHUTTING US DOWN! THEY DON'T WANT YOU TO HEAR THE MESSAGE! BUT WE'RE NOT LEAVING!"

Then there was more chaos on the stage. Finally, the band ran off the stage with raised clenched fists. The crowd was disgusted because they knew the cops in Berkeley didn't shut down shows. Everyone left and there was no sign of the police. It felt like a parody of the '60s.

Everybody in the audience had probably at one time gone up against the police and been tear-gassed or worse. They were hip—they knew this was not real.

WAYNE KRAMER The Straight Theater gig [in San Francisco] was a fiasco. There was nobody there. I think we played there a number of nights. It was empty. That was an experience—go out there and play a show like the MC5's, on acid, to an empty house. We did the whole show, though. That's the only thing I knew how to do. What else could I do?

From my point of view, San Francisco was really just about rampant sex. We met these girls that had a house over by the motel we were staying at. They had an orgy/birthday party for one of their girlfriends. The birthday-cake icing was laced with acid. It was wild. All kinds of freaky-deaky stuff going on. There'd be ten people in the shower together, all jumping up and down.

Later, I met this attractive redhead at somebody's house and I was on the serious make. I was in a rock band, so things were looking good. We were leaving somebody's house and going to go to the Winterland concert hall or someplace to hear a band, and I asked her if she wanted to come with us. She said sure. As she was getting in the truck I goosed her. She goosed me back. Yeah! It was going to work.

She turned out to be such an incredible freak that before we got across the bridge, everybody in the band was having some kind of sex with her simultaneously. She was just wild and insatiable. We went back to the motel, and it just turned into this nonstop orgy. Emil Bacilla was there and took some pictures. The girl basically fucked the band to death. A few days later, I ran into her and I said, "Hey, whatcha been doing?" And she looked at me and said, "Fucking."

JOHN SINCLAIR Yeah, when they ran the photos of the band having sex in the *Berkeley Barb* newspaper, that was a problem for me. I didn't have anything to do with it, but I was already in trouble for the original

White Panther Statement, in which I'd proposed the following: Fuck God in the ass and fuck your woman till she can't stand up. That created some controversy. I was so out of it that I couldn't even understand why anyone would be upset.

But that kind of macho behavior was finally beginning to be challenged. In our little midwestern teenage frames of mind, things like gang bangs were rebellious acts, until the women's movement ended up calling for a revolution within the revolution. Many of the men in the revolution felt, "We're revolutionaries. How dare you attack us?"

ROB TYNER We also played in Seattle on our West Coast swing, and it was shocking how much they hated us. But hey, I'd had plenty of experience where people did not like the band. My tactic was to fight back, attack more. Counterattack. Our problem was that we were rowdy and snotty, and we were coming on too strong for some punk band from Detroit that nobody on the West Coast knew about. And didn't want to know about us after that.

JOHN SINCLAIR They really hated us in Seattle, I'll tell ya. That's the one I remember the most vividly. We opened for Jethro Tull, the worst group in the world. Oh, they hated us!

DENNIS THOMPSON I think being from Detroit was essential to who we were, which didn't work that well once we got to the West Coast. We were there to try and win some fans, sell some records. We played with Jethro Tull in Seattle, and the band's lead singer, Ian Anderson, was making fun of us when we were onstage. He dressed like a wood nymph, and he was making fun of our leather jackets? C'mon. One of the mornings we were with them, Ian and Fred got into a philosophical debate about music, and Ian called Fred a stupid fucking bloody colonialist. Fred took his orange juice and threw it in Ian's face and walked away. That's pretty much what we were up against.

IAN ANDERSON Memorably, we played in Seattle with the MC5 and were warned not to go anywhere near them because they were very violent and aggressive and scary. Quite nervously, we did our sound check and waited to go on. They were actually pretty scary onstage, but a couple of months later we were playing again in the U.S.A., and some of the guys from the band came to see us in Detroit and were real pussycats, really friendly.

WAYNE KRAMER I remember meeting Ian Anderson a couple times, and I thought the guy was about as intelligent as a mailbox. He was telling me something about how he didn't do anything political because he didn't know who he was, politically. To me that was such an absurd point of view. Well, how could you not know where you're at?

All I ever got from fans was love until we went to someplace like Seattle. Somebody threw an egg at me and I was forced to say, "Please don't throw eggs at me, or I'm going to come down there and beat your ass."

The crowd would go, "Oh, no, get them with your music, brother," and I'd say, "Yeah, the music is fine, but if he throws another egg I'm going to beat his ass." And we did. Outside of the West Coast I never sensed any antagonism from an audience. We were a band and came from the school of honoring the audience. We weren't there to antagonize them, we were there to inspire them.

We played a few more shows on the West Coast. We did a gig in San Bernardino with Janis Joplin. She wanted to take me to her hotel and ingest narcotic drugs together, which I probably should have done, but the gig was just another one of those blank things. They didn't hate us, but they didn't love us either. There was nothing there they could grab on to. We did a teen fair thing that was even more disconnected. The MC5 at that point had about as much to do with a teen fair as... We came from the counterculture. It didn't work. It was really bizarre, like playing in another time and place.

JOHN SINCLAIR We were pretty relieved to get back home. We headlined an all-Detroit show at Olympia Stadium and drew more people than when the Beatles played there! To me, that was the ultimate landmark of what this scene meant.

WAYNE KRAMER I remember the gig at Olympia as being like one big fucking orgasm from the beginning to the end. It was just total energy, flat-out, tear-it-up. We just rocked the house. It was perfect. There were fifteen thousand people there, and they were all into it. We couldn't do anything wrong. The equipment worked and we didn't blow anything. That was one of the first times that I was so into the performing that the music wasn't an issue. I don't remember anything about the music, I just remember the leaping around and the dancing. At that time I knew that the music probably suffered, but under the circumstances, it didn't matter.

JOHN SINCLAIR Holzman finally faced the fact that the MC5 were a genuinely revolutionary group. We weren't just making this stuff up to sell records, and they decided we were just too big of a headache to deal with. It was a mutual parting. They made us look like idiots, and the only thing we could do was fire them. Then they were happy to fire us. It was a somewhat honorable solution for both sides.

CHAPTER V

FULL-ON DESTRUCTO

> Think about Aristotle's theory of tragedy. It's the tragic flaw that always gets you in the end.
>
> —Becky Tyner

In May of 1969, the MC5 had reached a critical juncture in their career. Their reputation as a fierce live act had earned them a devoted following, but their association with the White Panther Party and the explicit language on their debut album, *Kick Out the Jams*, stirred up controversies that hurt them. As their relationship with Elektra Records soured, the band faced an uncertain future.

But fate had something else in store for the MC5. In an unexpected turn of events, they caught the attention of Atlantic Records, a label known for its willingness to embrace experimental and progressive rock acts like the Velvet Underground and Emerson, Lake & Palmer. An offer from the label presented a new opportunity for the band, and with it came both excitement and trepidation.

Two weeks after being dropped by Elektra, John Sinclair and Danny Fields found themselves in the New York offices of Atlantic, sitting across from label honcho and legend Jerry Wexler. They were recommended to Wexler by *Rolling Stone* critic Jon Landau, who had an uncanny knack for recognizing what young audiences were thinking and, more important, music that would appeal to them.

The label, already home to iconic bands like Led Zeppelin, Crosby, Stills & Nash, and the Allman Brothers, recognized the potential in the MC5's fearless, high-energy sound. Impressed with their revolutionary spirit, Wexler offered the band a record deal with a substantial $50,000 advance. It seemed too good to be true.

Bassist Michael Davis recalled the moment: "It just seemed too easy." The advance was a significant step up from the $20,000 they had received from Elektra a year and a half earlier. Still, the band was far from rolling in dough. They were burdened with debts from buying equipment and supporting the thirty-seven people living communally in their three-story Ann Arbor hippie complex.

On the bright side, the Atlantic advance allowed the MC5 to move out of the commune and rent a six-bedroom house on ten acres of wooded terrain in Hamburg, Michigan, located seventeen miles northeast of Ann Arbor and fifty miles southwest of Detroit. This newfound autonomy provided them with a fresh start, away from the growing social and financial entanglements of the White Panther commune.

The first studio album they produced for Atlantic, *Back in the USA*, represented a radical departure from their earlier work. Produced by the twenty-one-year-old Landau, the album aimed to showcase the band's instrumental precision and songwriting skills. Still smarting from Lester Bangs's scathing dismissal of their debut album in *Rolling Stone*, Sinclair hoped that hiring Landau, a music writer who was held in greater esteem than Bangs, would buy the band some much-needed credibility in the rock-'n'-roll journalism community.

"John Sinclair may have thought I'd bring a certain profile to the project that would be useful," Landau recalled. "And perhaps it would influence the way the music press would look at the band. But I wasn't there to influence writers—I was there to make a great record. Being a producer was my dream, and this was my chance."

Landau moved into the library of the band's Hamburg house, where he remained for the next four months, putting the five musicians through rigorous rehearsals, improving their work ethic, and tightening their playing skills. Some believed that the producer also began sowing seeds of discontent with their manager, Sinclair, questioning his ability to handle their finances. The individual band accounts were conflicting on some points, but one thing was for sure—by the time their second album, *Back in the USA*, was finished, so was Sinclair.

JOHN SINCLAIR In May of '69 we went up to Atlantic and made a deal with Jerry Wexler, a lifetime idol of mine. I'd cut my musical teeth when I was eleven years old on rhythm-and-blues records he produced by the Clovers, the Drifters, Ruth Brown, and Ray Charles. It was the greatest music in the world to me. Even today, I'd consider those productions by Jerry Wexler and Ahmet Ertegun as top-shelf.

Danny Fields had connections there and brought us over. We were so grateful that we cut Danny in on the deal, and I gave him a piece of my percentage of the band. I was only too glad to do it. We did the Atlantic deal together and everything felt very positive.

ROB TYNER I was honored to sign with Atlantic Records. Some of the greatest jazz and R&B records of all time were made on Atlantic. To have Jerry Wexler involved was an honor.

JOHN SINCLAIR The vibes were so good, Atlantic even took out a full-page ad welcoming us to the label [see page 15 of photo section], which was kind of a radical thing. Wexler was just a mensch, and a down-to-earth, street-level type of guy. We talked things over and his response was, "Just make good records."

The $50,000 from Atlantic was the first money we really had, because the $20,000 we got from Elektra was spent in an hour. I had used it to pay for the equipment and transportation that we needed. We were still scuffling when we got that fifty grand from Atlantic.

ROB TYNER But this is what you might find a little unbelievable: money was considered evil, and only certain people could handle it without being contaminated by it . . . meaning John Sinclair!

After we got signed for all this money from Atlantic Records, it all went to John to manage. I was excited and I went to Sinclair to get fifteen dollars for a pair of boots, and he gave me a list of stuff he was paying for. He lectured me, so I shrugged and took some cardboard and put it in my shoes to cover the holes.

RON ASHETON The band was a major component of everything Sinclair was doing, but they were souring on the whole commune situation in Ann Arbor with "Papa John," as they used to call him. They basically went, "Fuck it, man, we're important, we're entertainers." And that was the gist of their bitch. We're entertainers, and hey, why do we have to do chores in the house and all this other mundane crap that comes from living communally?

They wanted to live the life that they really wanted for themselves. What's so wrong about a guy busting ass practicing, playing, and wanting to lay back after doing a bunch of work? For a long time, the guys would have set hours to go in the practice room and play and write. But sometimes you're creatively quiet. So what's so wrong with a guy wanting to be by themselves or alone, and not have to participate in this . . . it was like being in the army. They didn't want to be in the army anymore.

I like to be alone a lot, and imagine being in a house of thirty people where the next person that walks in the bathroom is gonna smell your shit. You get tired of that. On occasion, they just wanted to hole up and heal up their wounds, man, and re-psych and recharge. I think basically that's where they were at the time. They were trying to come to grips with themselves and what was happening to them, and I think they were very unhappy.

The other people in the house were also starting to have problems with the band. The White Panthers were basically street people. Many were transient and would do menial tasks in the hope that they would work their way up to something better. They resented the fact that here's this band who had their own sanctuary and that the women were catering to them. I thought it was fantastic! But the peons, the servants, resented it.

It got very exclusive. "Hey, don't go on the second floor at two in the afternoon; the guys are sleeping. Don't wake 'em up, they worked last night." So, the guys that scrubbed the toilets had their mini revolutions. To protect themselves from the bad vibes, the band eventually created their own little universe in their own little corner of the house.

BECKY TYNER When we moved to Ann Arbor with John into that big house, a serious divide developed between the band and the Panthers. And it deepened the longer we lived there. It was the band versus the revolution.

LENI SINCLAIR My memories of the time in Ann Arbor are vague because I was so caught up the whole time with the business of the commune, the business of the children, and the business of keeping John happy. I have little recollection of anything I did personally. While we were in exile in Ann Arbor for those seven years I almost didn't exist. I was caught up in the whole whirlwind of the MC5/White Panther Party/Rainbow People's Party/Free John Now/Human Rights Party. When you're in a group, you go along with the program. You even help write the program. But after it stopped being a group, after the commune broke up, we just realized how far out there it was as a way of life. We were pioneers of a new lifestyle, but it did not last.

RON ASHETON The women were smarter than the guys. The women saw what was going on clearly and fended for their boyfriends. They were always in the front lines, fighting in the trenches with the hippie-dippies in the house. And the hippie-dippies sort of resented the women because "they're queens; we can't get the bitches to wash the dishes and shit." The girls put their time in, but most of it was spent looking out after their men.

There was also some fighting between Wayne and Rob's girlfriends, but they did have one thing in common—looking out for their men. They wanted their men to be treated properly.

I think the women were right on. They said, "Hey, man, you guys are making this happen. And they're taking all your money. You don't need this; you need to be treated special."

Are you kidding—Becky? Rob's wife? She never even came out of the bedroom, man. She was so intimidated by the whole freak show. The commune showed that no matter what utopian situation you set up, it comes right back to the real world. There's a pecking order and the tops get the top. There are executives, middle management, and the peons. And that place became that.

But you have to understand how bad those guys felt. They'd put in their time, kicked ass, and brought in most of the money to support that whole situation . . . and had no privacy. That's why the guys would come over and hang at my place. I fully empathized and agreed. That's why they finally made the second floor a band floor.

BECKY TYNER I've always liked the early Detroit badass version of the MC5 more than the Ann Arbor White Panther version of the band. John's political and legal problems ended up taking precedence over everything.

You've heard this before, but living in the commune eventually became difficult. Any money that the band made went to John, and we would have to go to him to ask for money or to buy groceries. Chris, Sigrid, and I moved into the house in Ann Arbor and we'd grocery shop.

We would have things for breakfast and make a meal every day. In the beginning it was kind of fun, but it really became a pain.

I will tell you this—and John will probably have a fit if he ever hears it: We started scamming money. He would give us money to go to the laundromat to wash clothes, and because we were there so often, we worked out a deal with the laundromat guy. We'd take thirty dollars from John, he would charge us twenty dollars, and we'd keep the extra ten dollars. It's funny, but how sad is that?

After a while it felt like we were living in a police state. There were a lot of rules. And probably more than anyone, I had problems with most of them. My mother and father were not as strict as John was. How could that be?

We had rules like no women were allowed to wear makeup. My classic story is I got busted for sneaking eyeliner into the commune. You've got to have your eyeliner, and I would get busted for that. No television was allowed. But I had a television in my bedroom, I loved *Star Trek*, and we'd watch it. But it was not an addiction. Everyone would come to our room and watch television until John pulled in the driveway, and then they'd all run. Then John would get down on Rob. "Yeah, look at your old lady up there watching television all the time." Whatever. John and I were on conflicting paths; we were always at odds a bit. The Hill House commune was not my dream.

You had to clean the house, you had to cook the meals. It was a reversion back to pre-suffrage times. I always crack up at the whole women's lib thing that we supposedly embraced. Instead, it was, "You are a woman. This is your job. This is what you do." Rob, however, was not like that. He was very, very enlightened. So, it'd be hard for him, and he took crap for me. You know, that whole chauvinist "Get your old lady in line" kind of thing.

CHRIS HOVNANIAN When we moved to Hill Street, we started dividing up the cooking chores. 'Course, it was only the women; the *men* didn't work, the *men* didn't clean. But just dividing that up took a lot of the stress off.

BECKY TYNER I can remember Sigrid getting into a huge fight with Leni because she didn't want to wash the windows on the outside.

JOHN SINCLAIR I was just involved in so many different things at the same time and all were major commitments. We'd go to a gig somewhere out of state, get back at God knows what time, and then Fred, due to a 1968 arrest, would have to get up at eight in the morning to drive to Pontiac to go to court all through April. Stuff like that. The White Panthers were also becoming more active, so I had to do things related to that.

ROB TYNER During one period, John began to believe his own publicity and became, in his mind, the "Pharaoh of the Hippies." People said it was a joke. I want to go on record as saying that I believe he believed it. I think he wanted to have all these minions that would follow his thing.

John wouldn't beat us or anything of the kind, but you would be reprimanded and ostracized on a bunch of levels for *any* kind of uncoolness. You'd get yours.

JOHN SINCLAIR After the *Kick Out the Jams* album I started thinking, Okay, the critics think the MC5 is a hype and that we're just a garage band, so to win them over, on the next album we'll use one of their own. Jon Landau was one of the most respected rock writers in America, and he wanted to be a producer. He had studied the group from a production point of view, and I thought it would be a stroke of genius to use him. If we brought in the big enchilada to be the producer, the critics would have to deal with it. They wouldn't be able to dismiss us as a garage band.

I was strictly trying to manipulate the situation to our advantage. I wasn't that worried because I thought, frankly, that the MC5 had their direction, and we had these great tunes for the second record which were even better than the first. We'd bring in Landau, take his two cents' worth, make our record, and put his name on it. I mean, that was how utterly cynical I was. And it backfired on me 100 percent. Perhaps rightfully so.

JON LANDAU Danny Fields called me at the end of my senior year at Brandeis College in 1969 and informed me that Elektra had dropped MC5 because of all the controversy. He stayed loyal to the band and asked me whether I thought any other record company would be interested. I believed in the band, so I reached out to my friend and mentor, the great Atlantic records producer Jerry Wexler.

The MC5 had made themselves famous but just weren't selling records. Jerry said, "What am I going to do with fucking MC5? What do I know from what they do?"

I told Jerry I thought they were a phenomenal band. They had recorded only one live album, and I felt they had the potential to do much better. He saw that I really believed in them, and he respected my opinion, so he said, "Okay. I'll tell you what. I'll sign them, but you have to produce them, because I have no idea what to do with them."

I called Danny to tell him what Jerry had said. I don't know what kind of discussion took place, but he called me and said, "It's fine with the guys." So Jerry signed them and I became their producer.

MICHAEL DAVIS Lester Bangs wrote that contemptuous review of *Kick Out the Jams* for *Rolling Stone*, but when I met him, he was so apologetic about it. I had forgotten how hurtful it was, because *Kick Out the Jams* didn't sound like a *real* record to me either. I thought Lester's review was funny. I didn't really see the destructiveness in it. But he wrote that we couldn't play, and some of that was why we wound up with Jon Landau, which was the beginning of the end.

I met Lester again later in New York when I was in Destroy All Monsters [a post-MC5 band with Stooges guitarist Ron Asheton] in the '70s, and we hung out and got drunk together and stuff, and he was just so apologetic about that again. He was "Sorry, man. I'm so sorry about that." And I said, "Look, don't worry. I liked it."

JOHN SINCLAIR Russ Gibb had gotten into a bind. He had booked a festival at the Michigan State Fairgrounds for the end of May in 1969 but didn't have any acts, so he asked me to be the creative director. My concept was that it would be a rock-'n'-roll revival that would go backward and forward, so I got Chuck Berry, the MC5, and Sun Ra to headline. It was the first major appearances in the East for Dr. John and Johnny Winter. And I think Grand Funk Railroad made their debut as the replacement for another band.

I remember being pissed off at the band at the Rock 'n' Roll Revival. I just felt they were degenerating. It was one of the first times they started wearing glam. They were like a preview of the kind of glitter rock that the New York Dolls would make popular a few years later. My stomach was rotated when I saw them. Fred wore a kind of bizarre space costume. I liked it when Sun Ra would do it, but it made sense in context with his music. It didn't go with anything the MC5 were doing. I was such a relentless ideologue at the time, I felt it was sort of a move away from our vigor and virtue.

Maybe it went back to when we were in New York and started to move into a more national profile. I felt that they were just starting to degenerate into the outlook and comportment of the burgeoning rock-star subclass rather than being committed in any way to the lofty, high-principled outlook of the White Panthers, the revolution, and all that shit.

DENNIS THOMPSON The outfits were just too *Star Trek* for Sinclair, who didn't get it. And that's what it was. Fred had a full-length cape, and he had this black cowl on and a mask. It was all black and silver lamé, with an "SS" across his chest for Sonic Smith. It was the funniest thing . . . he was way ahead of his time. He beat Bowie to the punch on that one.

We were all glitzed out and I don't think Sinclair appreciated it. We were always wearing spangles and bangles when it wasn't fashionable to do. Mainly, I think John was ticked off with Fred because he was no longer Clark Kent, he was Superman. And here was this comic-book character playing guitar. It might not have been in keeping with our image, but it was in keeping with Fred Smith. He was just being different.

I'm not sure Fred's appearance was prompted by Sun Ra's stay on Hill Street. It might have. Fred got along with the boys in Sun Ra's band surprisingly well. They were pretty spaced out and claimed to be astral walkers in distant galaxies. To be in Sun Ra's band, you had to be dedicated. You didn't make any money. They were all hellaciously avant-gronk players, and where else were they going to play? It was a rough life. But they were really far-out thinkers. Fred was like that too.

BECKY TYNER The sonic suit was Fred's idea, and Sigrid made it. I remember John Sinclair saying, "I was their manager, and I didn't know anything about it." But that's what was going on in Fred's head. It was telling that John had become that out of touch with the band.

RON ASHETON Shortly after the first album, the MC5 really started to become a caricature of themselves. I loved them—they were my favorite band. They were originally guys that just dressed and acted like regular guys, but then they started wearing clown clothes and people began calling Wayne Kramer "the Brother" and all that stuff. Dennis Thompson started playing so fast that nobody in the band could play with him, and then Michael Davis started getting high and that's when it really started coming apart.

JOHN SINCLAIR Whenever the band talks about it, it's like, "These White Panthers threw everybody out and started taking all the MC5's money." Isn't that kind of the way the story appears to you? The official writ. That's the story that always grinds my motherfucking ass. Because it was the same people that had carried them through with selfless dedication for a long period of time and had helped them get over. And then once they got over, instead of turning around and saying, "Yeah, man, thanks, we're gonna do this now," it was like, these people from New York came and they told them, "These people aren't cool." To me it was sick.

ROB TYNER We had pumped so much money into the White Panthers, but it was not being handled properly. It was being spent in all these ways that, by today's standards, would be absolutely insane. And we were supposed to keep supporting this? I think if we *had* kept supporting it, people would look upon it and say, "God, what a bunch of fools. Fucking fools."

MICHAEL DAVIS We never made a lot of money; it was just hand-to-mouth. It's expensive to run a business, which is what we were doing but didn't realize it. Any money we made from gigs wasn't just supporting us, it was supporting lots of people, two houses, a bunch of vehicles . . . you name it. One of the reasons we wanted independence from John's activities was that we just could no longer support all of it. The game completely changed after we made the first album, which is what we wanted. We wanted to branch out and become bigger, but we just didn't have the correct handle on how to do that.

JOHN SINCLAIR Every gig would require a dozen sets of drumsticks, repairs for the amps and, many times, the whole PA system. The speakers would blow out and somebody would have to drive to Kalamazoo and wait there while the guy fixed them, and then drive back for the gig that night. It was totally nuts.

And a lot of the gear would be smashed by the band on purpose. You couldn't say no to that because it was so exciting. The deep thing was that it was *all* of us: it was the equipment men, the guys who did the lights, the poster artists. Nobody ever got paid anything. Nobody ever had more than five dollars in his pocket at any time, for *years*. Individual economic existence was not a factor at all. That's deep.

We went through a lot together. It was a hell of a trip. Then everything changed. I understand it as something that was inevitable. Then they said, "Well, we're getting over, now we're going to be rock stars, which is why we started this."

My motivation was totally the opposite. When we started to get over, I thought, Now we're gonna be an influence. We're going to be able to do all kinds of shit. We're going to be able to get our own record company, buy radio stations, take over the world. The idea of buying a Cadillac for my mother and a new house was totally foreign to my mental landscape.

My whole vision was trying to bring that consciousness that was associated with jazz to rock 'n' roll, particularly the high consciousness of the jazz artists of the '60s.

LENI SINCLAIR The way John dealt with this band's finances was that for two years we got by just by stretching things, borrowing money, and getting things on credit. John just hoped his labors would pay off before the band would leave him, because he knew that if the money went away, the arrangement wouldn't last. There were some band meetings after the album came out and before John went to jail that were not all that amicable. John tried to not let it come to a confrontation just yet, because he knew that once they signed with Atlantic and got some money, all these problems would be over, and they'd feel much better. They could have everything they wanted: big cars, big houses, whatever . . . But he didn't count on having to go to jail.

JOHN SINCLAIR We brought in these two geeks from the East into our world. First Jon Landau, and then this guy David Newman that Danny thought would help with our finances. He was a friend of Danny's, and he was supposed to be a hip accountant. One of the cats. We thought he would help me by taking over as business manager for the band. I welcomed this and accepted him with open arms, as I did with Landau. I had the ridiculous outlook that we were all in this together. It was an outlook that killed me over and over. I was too trusting. Rudnick told me it was Landau who started asking things like, "Well, what's Sinclair doing with all the money?"

Our situation had to be taken in context. It had started two years previously, when these guys were hoping to scratch out $125 a night. It was a period where they were supported in so many ways by all these people who were part of Trans-Love Energies. They were carried and buoyed by this. They'd helped them get over, and now it was just beginning to enter the period of the big payback, where all the work was going to be made worthwhile. I was in a mode where I was taking care of this house and these different people, all of whom were pretty much involved in one way or another with supporting the MC5.

Then, when they started to get over and got the place in the country in Hamburg, the MC5 suddenly became a separate entity, whereas I thought we were all on this trip together.

They had never had any money until we got the advance from Atlantic. The economics of the MC5 are a whole fascinating side trip. Nobody *ever* had any personal money. There was never enough money for everything that we were doing. So, when we'd get some money, it would always go for regenerative activities like getting equipment fixed, paying a printing bill from something you'd put out a month earlier. Whatever charges they make about me ripping them off, I can say the same thing about them. I never took a commission. I never got anything out of it personally.

For example, when we got the $20,000 from Elektra we all went to Louis the Hatter's in Detroit and got leather coats, and the guys got a thousand dollars. That was our dream, a three-quarter-length leather. We loved those coats—they were like the kind the Black Panthers used to wear.

BECKY TYNER We were thousandaires. We used some of it, and I bought a nice sewing machine. Other people bought their own sewing machine or whatever, but the bottom line, John got everything.

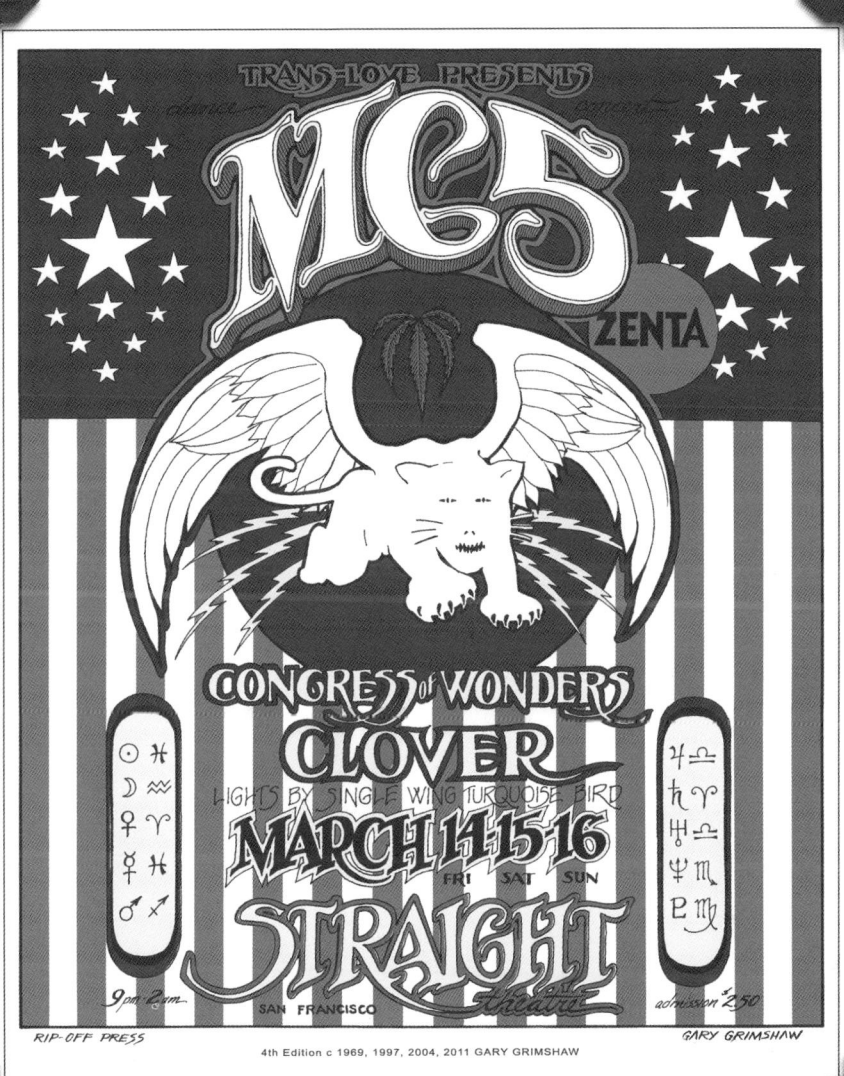

Another Gary Grimshaw masterwork promoting three March 1969 MC5 shows in San Francisco. It's got it all: the American flag, astrological symbols, a pot leaf, Zenta, and an incredible rendering of the White Panthers logo. *Courtesy of Laura Grimshaw*

The MC5 and the Stooges pose for a photo with friends and record executives as they both sign contracts with Elektra Records. (From left top) Jac Holzman, Danny Fields, John Sinclair, Fred "Sonic" Smith, Ron Asheton, Steve Harnadek, Iggy Pop, Dave Alexander, Scott Asheton, Ron Levine, Wayne Kramer, unidentified, Emil Bacilla, Jimmy Silver, Susan Silver, Barbara Holiday, and Bill Harvey. (From left middle) Michael Davis, Dennis Thompson, Rob Tyner, and Jesse Crawford. (From left bottom) Sigrid Dobat, Chris Hovnanian, and Becky Tyner, October 1968, Ann Arbor, Michigan. *Leni Sinclair/Michael Ochs Archive/Getty Images*

Recording the first of two shows at the Grande Ballroom for the *Kick Out the Jams* album. Brother J. C. Crawford is center stage, hyping the crowd and delivering the album's immortal rabble-rousing introduction, October 30, 1968. *Leni Sinclair/Michael Ochs Archive/Getty Images*

The MC5 making the best of the Ballroom's narrow stage. "There was barely any room to move at the Grande at all. No room whatsoever. What it made you do was jam-pack as much movement into whatever space you had," said Wayne Kramer. *Charles Auringer*

After the release of Kick Out the Jams in February 1969, the band reputation exploded, landing them on the cover of two of the biggest American music magazines of the era—*Rolling Stone* and *Creem*. Author's collection

A sweaty and elated MC5 celebrate backstage after another high-energy sold-out show, September 8, 1969. During this period, they are also busy working with producer Jon Landau on their second album, *Back in the USA*. *Michael Ochs Archives*

One of the most influential figures in the history of punk rock, Danny Fields signed the MC5 as well as Iggy and the Stooges, managed the Ramones, and worked with the Doors, the Velvet Underground, and the Modern Lovers. In 2014, the *New York Times* said, "Without Danny Fields, punk rock would not have happened." *Danny Fields*

Stooges guitarist Scott Asheton and Rob Tyner backstage at the Birmingham Palladium, Birmingham, Michigan, 1969. Asheton later said, "[The MC5] certainly paved the way for the Stooges." *Leni Sinclair/Michael Ochs Archive/Getty Images*

MC5 hype man and the White Panther's Minister of Religion, Jesse "J. C." Crawford, whips up the crowd at Ford Auditorium, Detroit, Michigan, 1969. *Leni Sinclair/Michael Ochs Archive/Getty Images*

After the MC5 were kicked off Elektra Records in April 1969, they found a more welcoming home at Atlantic Records. Unfortunately, it didn't last long—they were dropped two years later. *Author's collection*

Arrested for possession of marijuana, MC5 manager John Sinclair was given ten years in prison on July 25, 1969. The sentence was criticized by many as unduly harsh. This special supplement printed by the underground newspaper *Ann Arbor Sun* helped fuel the outrage. *Author's collection*

John Lennon and Yoko Ono perform at the "Free John Now" rally at the Crisler Arena, Ann Arbor, Michigan, on December 10, 1971. Over fifteen thousand people attend, but the MC5 are not invited. As Lennon explained, "We don't mind helping get Sinclair out of prison because it's a man who is in prison for pot. But count me out if it's for violence. Don't expect me to be on the barricades unless it's with flowers." *David Fenton/Getty Images*

The MC5 being interviewed by *Rolling Stone* writer Ben Fong-Torres in February 1972. The story is printed in June under the headline "Shattered Dreams in Motor City: The Demise of the MC5." The depressing story goes on to say, "They wanted to be bigger than the Beatles. Manager John Sinclair wanted them to be bigger than Mao. How a revolution fizzled." *Charles Auringer*

The MC5 at the Detroit Metro Airport before embarking on a 1972 tour of Europe. They were hoping for a fresh start, but it was the beginning of the end for the group who had been fragmenting due to hard drugs. *Charles Auringer*

ROB TYNER We tried to make the transition from being a band of the people to being a professional rock-'n'-roll unit that would be worthy of handling business with a major corporation.

Jon Landau was a rock critic and a close friend of the people who ran Atlantic. He wanted to produce, so they figured that they would give him this very difficult group of people to work with. I think he was really appalled at first. He came in and saw us live, and I think that one of his early quotes about us was that our music was "like man's inhumanity to man."

On *Back in the USA* we went through a musical transformation. Sinclair had a heavy influence on the first album, but he was no longer much of a musical mentor for us because we had grown quite a bit. At the same time, we were headed in a direction we didn't feel was right. Our songs tended to be real long with long solos. Jon Landau helped us discover a different sort of thrust. He really put the magnifying glass on everything and questioned why we would play a song for fifteen minutes when we could say the same thing more powerfully in three. We had the energy, and his goal was to help us focus it so the songs were shorter and faster. We attempted to create shorter pieces with real velocity—like the music was going right past you. And on some levels I think it worked. It was good for us and a healthy learning experience.

Back in the USA was Landau's first production project, and we were like his laboratory guinea pigs. He had a way of pointing out problems to us and tried to make certain that our situation was translated to the record company. He was very good at that. A lot of people said that he exerted too much influence on us and turned us into something that we never intended to be, but I disagree. We had always intended to be a very tight hard-rock band, and he got us closer to that, for which he deserves thanks.

JON LANDAU I thought *Kick Out the Jams* was not creatively successful. It suggested some of the power of the group, but at the time I thought it fell short. If you had seen them, you'd understand the album only captured a fraction of their power live.

My vision for their second album was largely what the record ended up being. My idea was just to make each sound as concise and explosive as it could be. I'm a born editor. I immediately crossed out the idea of any kind of long jams or psychedelia. My model was the early records of the Rolling Stones, which were three and a half minutes of dynamite. I just loved that kind of pacing. I was also thinking more about creating something for the Top 40 than free-form FM radio.

During one of our first meetings at their house in Hamburg, I brought a bunch of singles with me as examples of what I had in mind for their album. So, we're all sitting there and I put on "Ramblin' Gamblin' Man" by Bob Seger, not even considering that they knew each other. I mean, I knew that Bob was from Detroit but just thought it was a fantastic single. To this day, I think it's one of Bob's greatest songs—I just loved the drive on that single, the way it just keeps coming at you. I waited for a reaction and they were like, "You're playing us this? Bob Seger? This local guy? You come all the way from New York to play us Bob Seger?"

They just laughed at me for not making the connection, I guess. But I loved "Ramblin' Gamblin' Man." I knew that the guys all had different ideas about it, but I loved it.

This was my first production, so I was making it up as I was going along. I just had a few touchstones. Fortunately, the guys happened to be writing short, tight songs that were very much in sync with what I was thinking. I mean, take "Human Being Lawnmower"—what a masterpiece that is. You show me another recording that creatively says as much as that record does in a little over two minutes. That was a high point for me.

ROB TYNER "Human Being Lawnmower" was a metaphor for what was going on in Vietnam. A metaphor for the horror. The song starts out in ancient times with a group of killer apes who, as they become more advanced, create a huge machine that kills people. With all their potential for greatness, this is what they create. Their final accomplishment is creating a machine big enough to destroy the entire world.

WAYNE KRAMER Landau loved "Human Being Lawnmower," and that was all Rob Tyner. He brought the song in, and I started to say, "This is how the first verse will go and then..." Rob kept saying, "No, no, I don't want to do it that way. I don't want to do a first verse and then a chorus and then do the second verse the same way. Every one'll be different." It may have taken days to learn the song the way he wanted it, but it was brilliant, and Landau could appreciate that. Even though it was totally bizarre, Jon could appreciate how it was crafted and wanted to record the most condensed and powerful version of the song possible.

We knew Landau was a guy who'd never produced anything before, but we picked him just because he was smart. He understood how things get to be how they are, especially in the music business. And he was knowledgeable about music itself—who played on what record, what group sang what song—he was a walking encyclopedia. But Jon also helped me articulate the problems in the band. Whether they were actually problems or not is speculation. If we hadn't tried to fix Michael and fix Dennis, we might've made a different record. The thing was, Landau could analyze the situation and explain in a coherent fashion his view of what was happening. Then he was able to give me options: "Well, whaddya think? How do you want to handle this?"

DENNIS THOMPSON Enter the infamous Jon Landau, the Hitler who came in and reduced the powerful MC5 into a goddamn wedding band. I called him a fascist dictator.

WAYNE KRAMER Because I was still stinging from Lester Bangs's review in *Rolling Stone* and all the other negativity around the band, I wanted to make a perfect record. I wanted to answer all the criticism. The guitars are going to be in tune. The tempos are going to be right. No excuses for anything to go wrong. It was like a make it or break it.

Our local popularity had peaked, and we needed to make a strong statement on a national and international level. Landau felt the primary problem was our rhythm section.

In retrospect, if this is worth anything, he should have just turned the recorder on and let us record, but he got all involved with us in the process. He made Dennis play to a click track, and we started recording in a manner that was foreign to us.

JON LANDAU In the studio, one of my biggest hurdles was getting Dennis to simplify his playing. Dennis tended to be very busy, and my role model for a drummer was early Charlie Watts or the Stax drummer Al Jackson. If you listen to the Rolling Stones' version of "Can I Get a Witness" from their first album, the groove is incredible and Charlie does not play one single fill, but the groove is astonishing.

So, I was trying to radically simplify Dennis's style, and he *had* a style. We did our best to sort it out, and what you hear on the record is what we wound up with. The funny thing is, "Human Being Lawnmower" is one of the few songs where Dennis is in full flight, and it is admittedly one of the best tracks on the album. He is really clicking on all cylinders there, so it's hard to say whether I was right. God bless him, he did his best to deliver what I wanted, and he is very economical on the album. It was an interesting time, but I do not remember it as difficult or negative at all. I remember it as a creative thing.

Michael was another story. I don't want to be hurtful, but Michael is not on the record. He was just not in shape to deliver the necessary discipline. He tried it. After a few sessions, I finally had to say, "Wayne, you're playing bass."

DENNIS THOMPSON *Back in the USA* exemplified everything we weren't because it was trying to be so perfect. It was only half of what it should've been. The production needed more of that big, fat boom, like Led Zeppelin. We sacrificed power for perfection. It would've been better if we dropped a beat here or there and focused on capturing the energy, even if that meant a bad note in the solo, or if an instrument was a little out of tune.

Fred didn't like how the album was being recorded, but he wasn't vocal. I'd say, "Let's call a band meeting and bring it to a head." But when it came right down to it, Fred wouldn't speak up. Tyner was indecisive and Michael Davis was being shunted out of the group. Fred was vehemently against what we were doing in the studio. He didn't want Michael to be excluded. But it had gotten to the point where Landau had this power over the group.

WAYNE KRAMER There was a lot of controversy within the band over what was going down. The band thought it was another case of "Wayne forcing the issue, Wayne taking over, Wayne making all the decisions." That's when they had the big revolt regarding my authority.

We had this big meeting with Landau, who conducted it like a group therapy session. Everyone said, "We think Fred's right and Wayne's wrong." Okay, my loyal troops had all deserted me. They believed that I was the problem, and that I was the whole reason that everything was fucked up, because I didn't want to let Michael play the way he wanted to play, or I was forcing Dennis to play to a dumb click track.

Maybe they were just criticizing Landau through me, I don't know. If they really thought it was the wrong thing to do, they could've just revolted and not played. But they recorded the whole album before they said anything.

I guess it was just a real confusing time because there was so much going on. There was a lot of pressure on us to come up with a good record, and we had to think about things in a new way because Sinclair wasn't around. The old answers to problems didn't work anymore. I know that Landau liked to think that he taught us how to record, which was not unreasonable considering that everything we did was based on his dogma.

And Landau made sense. Everything he said to me made sense. The way he broke it down, the way he described it. He said things like, "You know this guy Carlos Santana that's out now? Everybody's talking about how he's such a rave guitar player. They haven't heard guys like you and Fred. You're the ones that they should be hearing about, because you're the guys that are really playing something. This other stuff is all lightweight." That sounded good to us!

Like everybody else, we wanted a hit. But in those days albums were really your statements. It didn't really have to do with any one song. And we felt all our songs were strong. But in retrospect, the production . . . admittedly, it was pretty stiff.

We were having to learn how to make records at the wrong time. If we'd done it with the first album, we would've already gone through all that so by the second album we would've hit the ground flying. But now we're in there trying to figure out what the fuck we're doing at a real crucial point, where we've got to do the right thing. And we didn't.

DENNIS THOMPSON I sat down with Landau at our table in Hamburg many times. I'd tell him, "Jon, we can't release a second album where all the instruments are recorded separately like this. Let us try and play the music as a group."

He told me, "You guys can't do it, you just can't do it. When you do it that way, we wind up making fifty takes of everything and it's not right." I said, "It can't be perfect, Jon. This is the MC5, we're a live band, not a studio band. We write music to be performed in front of an audience. How do you expect me to get the feeling of 'Human Being Lawnmower' by playing it by myself? Where do I get the energy from? How do I chase the solo if there's no solo?" "Well," he said, "you're just going to have to deal with that."

He had to sell Jerry Wexler, his boss at Atlantic, on the album, and he was insecure because it was his first production: "I'm going to deliver a perfect album. Jerry won't be able to pick out a bad note." Now, for the sake of the bad note, he'd forsaken the energy and took away the chemistry. That was the death of the MC5, as far as I'm concerned.

JOHN SINCLAIR I can see in retrospect that they just got on a program of disengagement from me and from my orbit, but I didn't really have any sense of that at the time. I thought it was great that they could afford to get their house in the country with the money they got from Atlantic. It was a good thing. I mean, I arranged it. We got the money from Atlantic, and our top priority was to hook that up. So I didn't have any problem. I didn't realize it would sever our relationship.

DANNY FIELDS I started losing track of the MC5. They became Jon Landau's project, and the revolutionary fervor was gone; it was depressing to see all it come to naught. In retrospect, you can see what happened. John Sinclair was their lifeline and their spirit, and the philosophy that motivated and energized them. I also realized that in this business of music and entertainment there really wasn't... people didn't want too much politics. People didn't want to see people carrying guns.

You saw the same thing later with the rap group Public Enemy and how they got slapped back. I mean, there are lines that you just don't cross. No one wanted to hear about the possibility of a *real* revolution. It was okay if you kept it on a very show-biz level. As soon as there was the faintest likelihood that these guys might be serious—and when John Sinclair was around, it seemed that these guys were serious—it was all over.

JOHN SINCLAIR In the spring of '68 the band started to really gel, and then it just got better until the summer of '69, which is when we began to develop differences. I felt that the band was becoming complacent and smug, and even bizarre.

The end of my relationship with the band either happened while I was on trial or when I was about to begin my trial—and then, when I was sentenced to ten years in prison after offering two joints to an undercover narcotics officer, they were gone. But the MC5 were just one part of a lot of unfinished affairs that I couldn't attend to for, as it turned out, two and a half years when the Michigan Supreme Court ruled that the state's marijuana statutes were unconstitutional and they set me free.

Man, I went into court for the last day of my trial, the jury went out, and they came back after lunch and found me guilty. And then the judge remanded me to Wayne County Jail and there I stayed.

I had made no provisions—it was so totally out of the question that they would lock me up. There were *no* grounds. The real injustice in my case was the denial of bail. The deep thing was that my appeal was successful and that my conviction was reversed, and I shouldn't have spent *any* time inside. That's the sick part. Until then, I had been tearing along at eight thousand miles per hour, and then, bam, I was gone.

DANNY FIELDS I'd rather not talk about the MC5 at Atlantic. You know why? The glamour was gone. John was out of the picture. They weren't my babies anymore. I was more involved with the Stooges.

I was at Atlantic, but I was useless. I didn't really take any interest in almost any of their music except the Velvet Underground *Loaded* album. I loved the Allman Brothers, but I couldn't get anybody there to believe that they had a shot. Can you imagine? I said, "I just saw this great band at Ungano's and they're signed to you via Capricorn. We've got to get this band. They could be real big. Great guitar sound. The Allman Brothers. I know they're just a bunch of hillbillies, but they're fabulous." Atlantic said, "Naw, who the hell wants that kind of music? It'll never do anything. Just go out there and sell Emerson, Lake & Palmer."

It was terrible because I hated ELP more than anything in the world. I was barely working there. I came in at noon, shut the door of my office, did air force exercises, and conducted Stooges business.

RON ASHETON Michael Davis was a thief. He had sticky fingers and he liked sunglasses. He didn't need them, but he wanted some shades. But the one place you do not steal them from is Campus Corner [party store in Ann Arbor], and he got popped on a day that the band had to play.

The Stooges were the opening act that night, and they thought he might still show up. But when we finished playing, Wayne came up to me and asked, "How would you like to fill in on bass?" I was so excited. I didn't have a bass, so I took Michael's bass and his monster Marshalls too.

We played a couple of songs, and we did a long blues thing. But seriously, playing with those guys scared me. They were so loud, when I walked offstage I couldn't hear *anything*. Still, I was very excited to play with those guys, and I was very happy even though I was deaf for a day after that. Wayne's piercing treble somehow wiped my ear out. But boy, that was fun.

It was also my first experience playing with Dennis Thompson, who I think was the greatest drummer in rock 'n' roll. I love my brother [Stooges drummer Scott Asheton]; he's rock hard, rock steady. But that was my first experience with Dennis, who I call the "sports car" because he will go anywhere and everywhere. His energy was boundless. He was the greatest, most underestimated drummer in rock 'n' roll. I'm not gonna say the Stooges were a Volkswagen, but playing with the MC5 was an exhilarating experience.

DENNIS THOMPSON After we left the Hill House in Ann Arbor, we rented this beautiful home for the band in Hamburg, Michigan. It was a six-bedroom, $100,000 house, which is good for a half million these days. Beautiful place. We had ten acres, we had trees, we had a little swamp, we had woods. It was nice. We got away from Sinclair and all that hippie fucking commune shit, and we got away from the cops bugging us. It was good for us.

CHRIS HOVNANIAN The owners of the Hamburg house didn't want to rent it to us, but I convinced them. They trusted me, but they didn't trust *them*. The Atlantic money was supposed to be the down payment toward buying the house, but it ended up being monthly rent. Everybody had gorgeous rooms. We even had a balcony off ours. Michael and Dennis shared a room, but it was huge. It had a sliding thing so that you could divide the room for privacy. The second floor you got to by this narrow spiral staircase. It was on ten acres of woods, and next to that was ten acres of meadowland with a little lake. Beautiful.

But the record was not going well, so there was a lot of tension. Everybody was blaming everybody else. Wayne backed Jon Landau on everything, including Landau's feeling that Michael could not play bass. I felt bad for Michael. It's one thing to be criticized, but they could be very brutal.

WAYNE KRAMER I remember Sinclair coming out and seeing it, and he was so impressed with it that he said, "Man, I need to make Jerry Wexler give you enough money to buy this house."

J. C. brought out an oversized replica of a Browning automatic rifle used for training purposes. We hung that over the fireplace so if people looked in the window, they'd see this gigantic Browning automatic rifle that looked like you'd shoot down an airplane with it.

When we first moved out to the new house, the Black Panthers and the White Panthers wanted to come out and test their guns. Target practice. They heard that we had the land. We said, "Yeah, come on out." So here comes Pun Plamondon with all these Black Panthers and carloads full of automatic weapons. We went in the woods and just shot the shit out of everything.

One of the neighbors, a priest from the town, came out to meet with us, to make sure everything was okay: "Speaking for the townspeople, we were a little concerned after we heard all the gunfire." It sounded like a firefight. It only took the one target-shooting episode to convince everyone in the area that we were heavily armed. Nobody fucked with us!

RON ASHETON Jon Landau was Lucifer who came from hell to destroy the MC5. He took away their balls. So what if they couldn't play like studio musicians? That wasn't the point of the MC5. Jon Landau was the devil, and he shit out a crown of thorns and put it on the heads of the MC5. He made a mockery of what MC5 was. It's outrageous that Michael Davis did not play bass.

ROB TYNER *Back in the USA* was almost like a bizarre New Wave album six years ahead of its time. Our hair got shorter and the pants got tighter. The songs were a minute and twenty-eight seconds long, and they zoomed along at fifty thousand miles an hour. Everything was *compact*. Really clean and right to the point.

I learned a lot about everything in the studio from Jon. He was very, very tough on me, and the band was very, very tough on me. They wanted me to lock these vocals down and make them exact, and I learned a tremendous amount just from the discipline of doing it. See, all the vocals on *Back in the USA* are double-tracked—every single vocal, and they are exact. Back in those days they didn't have Simul-Sync, so it became this insane torture game, where they'd say, "No, that one wasn't right; do it again." It was like Chinese water torture.

But I got much better at double-tracking. The guys in the band started calling me "One-Take Tyner" because they would always use up all the studio money tuning guitars and farting around, and then there would be like five minutes left over for the vocals. You got one take and that was pretty much it.

But the thing that was weird and is still weird about recording for me, you'll do a take and then there's the silence. And you can see these people in the booth, through the windows, talking. And you're sitting there with the headphones on, and you're waiting for that click when the talkback comes. I learned to kind of dread that. It was like waiting for a verdict on your performance.

People can say whatever they want about the second album, but there is a million years of experience between the first album and the second album. Better or worse, doesn't matter. There was a discipline and a return to the basics. We returned to the type of band we were in the early days, when we flat-out went for it. We went back to being a tight band, which was good. Not that we didn't know how to do that. We had done it already, but then our souls got psychedelicized there for a long while. It felt good to be back in the groove, back in the pocket.

We also created this new rock-'em-sock-'em, high-intensity live show. We rehearsed in New York in front of mirrors and got our legs all in synchronization. We choreographed real tight onstage moves and stuff. There'd be times when both guitarists would have their guitars in the air, and I'd have the microphone up and then fall to my knees, and these real tight segs between songs. Zap! Pow! Boom! At first it kinda threw people. We went out to [Michigan suburb] Benton Harbor and did this, and they went, "Rob, you're wearing a suit, what happened to you, man?"

RON ASHETON I was surprised when they moved to that upper-middle-class house in Hamburg. The MC motherfucking 5 living in an upper-middle-class house, with all the accoutrements and all the comforts that John Sinclair and his people had been bitching about! And Landau put them on a very strict diet ... steaks and salads.

Landau just came in there and took over their lives, and he tried to train them like a sports team. He was like, "Let's have the steak and salad, some exercise, and then some intense practice." Then he took them in the studio and just sterilized them.

They were very secretive about it. They felt it was gonna be their big premiere—finally, an album that's going to be kick-ass, top-notch, and filled with hits. All Landau did was take everything out of it. Not that I dislike the album, but it's not something that I put on either. I can tell you that the Stooges were all very disappointed with that record. Where's the sky, man? Where's the reaching for the stars? It was so compressed, it made you want to hunch your shoulders over and go "Uhhhhh."

Landau went in there with a mission. He—and the band—wanted to prove they could play. They accomplished that, but it had no balls. It isn't really the MC5.

DENNIS THOMPSON When we recorded the first album, we were much too high at those performances on those two nights. There was no one there to tell us we should record our first album sober. Instead, John Sinclair was saying, "Hey, light a joint up. Have some acid." Here's our fucking manager telling us to get high to record an album! Outrageous. When we met Landau, he told us, "Your manager is full of shit. You don't make it in this business by being a bunch of dope fiends." Bless Landau for that. It was a good period for us because he did clean us up. In Hamburg we wound up running and eating yogurt, reading books, and [we] started to become intelligent people again. We got off the damn drugs.

There was no alcohol. No LSD. We started to lose weight because we had gained a few pounds here and there. Some of the unity was back, even though it was a little forced.

BECKY TYNER Jon came to our house to produce that second album, and what everybody always remembers is that he made them eat yogurt. He had this whole regimen for them. He had them running laps. He said to Rob, "Rob, you have to take voice lessons." He told Michael, "Michael, you're not good enough to play."

JON LANDAU I love Becky Tyner. She's a wonderful person. She was always so nice to me. And while it was true that I was working hard to tighten up the band in the studio, I was not the person pushing them into getting them in physical shape. That was Danny Fields and his friend David Newman.

The band were already on this yogurt diet by the time I got there. I'd go to the refrigerator to make a sandwich and all there'd be was yogurt. I remember Wayne trying to explain the benefits of it. Becky's right, someone had them running laps and exercising, but it wasn't me!

DENNIS THOMPSON I would have to say that Landau's approach and higher goals were correct. He wanted to tighten up the band. He said, "I know from everyone I've spoken to that you guys were A-100 tight and crisp, a hot band. I want to get you back to that." Which was 100 percent right and anti-Sinclair. It was about time! Sinclair was a good puppy, a great mascot, but not our business manager! We needed to get an accountant, a lawyer, and a business manager. Landau sort of took over as our manager then. But he took it too far. He took all the piss and vinegar out of us and had us playing like robots.

I would say to Michael [during the Landau era], "Goddammit, Michael, would you please rehearse your part. Because if you don't rehearse this part to this song, you're not going to play on the goddamn album." He had no discipline whatsoever. Zero. The man would not practice. We'd get in the practice room in our garage and we'd practice and we'd practice . . . except for Michael.

I told him if he didn't get it right, Kramer was going to play his parts. It didn't even seem to matter to him. But if you don't have Michael Davis playing bass, you don't have the MC5 anymore. You were selling everybody a lie. You had the MC4.

JOHN SINCLAIR Michael was a competent bass player at best. I mean, there was never a hole in the bottom. The bottom was a big, wide, deep motherfucker, always. It was Landau's opinion that he wasn't good based on the genres of music that he enjoyed and appreciated, which were different from those inhabited by the MC5.

DENNIS THOMPSON At times, Michael's bass playing was brilliant. He was like Bill Wyman of the Rolling Stones—he had his own style and it fit us. You can't play the standard Stax-Volt bass parts to MC5 music; it doesn't work. He wasn't Duck Dunn, and he wasn't like Motown's Bob Babbitt, but he didn't have to be. MC5 music required a certain type of sound.

The situation could have been resolved and saved if Landau had backed off from his super-race music, where every note had to be perfectly in place. But you can't blame Landau for everything. No, Michael got his own ass in the jam.

JOHN SINCLAIR Landau couldn't accept who they were. He wanted them to sound like Booker T. & the MG's, which was absurd. Landau produced Bruce Springsteen, and Bruce and he were perfectly matched because Springsteen doesn't sound anything like rock 'n' roll. The public couldn't have been any happier with that match. Seriously. But by the same token, the public completely rejected his effort with the MC5 because they weren't a match. When he finished with them, they didn't sound like the MC5. They sounded like the Monkees.

I can't get inside the band's heads, and I don't really care to. But I can see them embracing what Landau had to offer, because at that moment they wanted to get as far away as possible from what the MC5 had come to stand for.

Landau took the arrangements and stripped them down, which I didn't agree with. The power of the MC5 was more akin to Phil Spector. They were at their best when they created a wall of sound, and he made them strip those powerful, huge, full arrangements down into *parts*. And that's when he decided they couldn't play.

He broke down their self-confidence, and in a way, he paved [the way for] their internal self-destruction because their whole identity was destroyed by him. He also convinced them that they needed to dismantle their affiliation with the movement and the White Panthers.

DENNIS THOMPSON Granted, there was *too* much sloppiness on the first album. But to go from one extreme to the other was also bizarre. I was screaming the whole time.

That's probably why I wound up doing junk. There were so many things that happened to me in that band that I should've had control over, but here I was, I was just the drummer, so what did I know? I couldn't get a quorum. I couldn't even get Smith. Behind closed doors he agreed with what I said: "We're both going to do this together, right? We're going to get rid of Landau. This fucker's not producing this album." But when it came time to face the band and Landau and say, "This isn't going to work. We're on strike. Fuck you. Until you leave, we're not going to do it," Fred wouldn't be with me. I'd say, "Right, Fred?" And Fred would be gone. He'd be in his room with Sigrid. That was the support I got from that dickhead.

CHRIS HOVNANIAN Becky would speak up. She'd get mad, and she would try to get Rob to say something about how things were going with the second album. Then the band would say Rob was being controlled by her. But Wayne was being controlled by Landau or Sinclair, although he never saw it that way.

Wayne was Landau's mouthpiece. Landau used him to control the band, and the band yelled at him because they didn't want to be controlled. But Wayne really, *really* wanted the band to make it. He wanted to play music, that's all he was going to do, so he wanted to be a successful musician. The idea of being rich and famous was fine too. He was single-minded when it came to the band. I think he probably *was* too easily influenced by Sinclair, and then Landau. If he trusted them and felt like they were going to help him do what he wanted to do, he'd give himself over to them and be like clay and be molded, and then take that back to the band and try and mold them. But nobody else was quite so easily molded.

WAYNE KRAMER There was a lot of factionalism and lobbying going on, and differing opinions about John Sinclair. I bore the brunt of most of it because I was trying to drive the ship. But the crew was starting to ignore me. Once we were meeting expenses and real money was starting to happen, people started getting more concerned about it because none of us had any. Nobody had any personal money. Fred smoked cigarettes, and he would have to go beg change to go buy a pack of cigarettes. "This is ridiculous," Fred would say. "We're making money here, and I have go beg for change from John for cigarettes?"

BECKY TYNER When Jon Landau came to work with the band in Hamburg, he demanded to know what was up with John Sinclair: "What the hell is the matter with you? You're giving all your money to this guy? You're crazy."

DENNIS THOMPSON Almost from the beginning, I was Sinclair's worst enemy. I did not like him because he tried to foist his vision of the MC5 on us. Bullshit, buddy boy. It wasn't what this band was all about. This band *was* the Rolling Stones. Leave us alone. We did not want to deal with all the politics, and we didn't want his politics least of all, because he was stupid. He got busted by the same narc twice, the dumb shit! He used to bitch, "You guys busted up your equipment and we don't have the money to replace it." But we were supporting fifteen of his people, his comrades. We were supporting forty-seven people with the money that we made playing shows. That was John Sinclair's political party. Excuse me, John. If we wanted to smash our equipment up because it worked for our show, we would do it. We had all these heated arguments over that. If the money went towards anything, it should have been the show. Sorry, buddy.

JOHN SINCLAIR I remember people pitching us on playing Woodstock. I said, Well, who's going to play? And they listed all these superstars of rock. And I said, "Eh, too mainstream. Pass."

DENNIS THOMPSON Honestly, the split [with Sinclair] happened before the second album. Two factions had developed in the band. Fred and I wanted Sinclair out and Wayne and Rob wanted him in. Michael didn't count; he went wherever the power was at the time. Fred and I wanted to get rid of Sinclair because we didn't like the direction he wanted to take us in, and because Sinclair's philosophy seemed to be overtaking *our* philosophy.

Our philosophy was just to be a rock-'n'-roll band: "Let's just go out and have fun and play the music." That's all we wanted to do. We didn't want to carry this burden that we were the philosophers of the vanguard of political thought. Bullshit! We worked our butts off and supported a regime of fifty fucking hippies. Fred told me, "I'm with ya, Den," but when push came to shove and argument time, he was in the background. Then all the guys would gang up on me. "Hey, shut up, Dennis, you're a fucking square."

Sinclair would say, "We represent the change in the world." He'd tell us the White Panthers were going to form affiliations with the Black Panthers and SDS, and this and that. "It's very important that we do this," he'd say. "We need a political consciousness here. Like [civil rights leader] H. Rap Brown says . . ."

I started hating that stupid hippie. It was all John, John, John all the time. John's game. John as the radical left guru. John as the man who wanted to be in *Time* and *Newsweek*. His vehicle just happened to be the MC5. If it wasn't for the MC5 and our music, he would never have gotten out of the Warren-Forest neighborhood. But his philosophy started to become ours. I remember Wayne and Rob doing interviews where they'd espouse Sinclair's rhetoric. Wait a minute, man! I'd think, You're not Wayne and Rob anymore. You don't believe this bullshit, not for a minute. We just got through talking half an hour ago about how you're getting tired of these hippies leeching off us the whole goddamn time. And suddenly here you are espousing the formation of White Panthers. It was all horseshit.

John Sinclair was good up to a point, but he had to be eliminated sooner or later—and I wanted to get rid of Sinclair sooner. I didn't like his blatant pot use. I didn't like the fact that we were promoting drug use. That should've been clandestine. It wasn't the smart thing to do. "Oh, we do drugs. Bust us, we dare ya. Here, I'm smoking a joint in your face, pig!"

I thought John's methods were amateurish. There was no reason we should have been promoting drug use. If you smoked and if you got high, fine, but we didn't try to turn everybody on.

Everyone was after us because of Sinclair. He made himself such a visible, easy target. "You fucking pig!" he would say, and he'd take his joint and—poof—blow it right in a cop's face! I was like, "Are you crazy? You don't walk up to a sleeping bull and kick him in the shins with your baseball spikes." John would say, "I dare you to bust us! We're the people!"

The dumbest thing we did was we ride around in a van with "MC5" painted on the side. It was like we were screaming, "Here we are! Come and get us! Bull's-eye!" All we really wanted to do was be a band. We didn't believe in the political bullshit for a minute. I don't care what any one of the guys in the band said, we did *not* believe the political bullshit. We were a rock-'n'-roll band. Period.

LENI SINCLAIR On one level it was beyond the MC5's control and beyond John's control, and they shouldn't have blamed each other for what happened. I don't even want to put it in any kind of philosophical context. Because when John went to jail, they lost their manager and nobody replaced him. Sometimes a band is held together by the manager. And another manager would mean that the band would change in some way, and it did.

JOHN SINCLAIR I didn't see any of it coming. But then I realized these guys from New York were putting shit in their ears. I could tell this just from the things the band was saying, and I was just aghast. I was crushed. The thing was that everything that they did from then on was totally wrong.

Bob Rudnick [Sinclair's friend and underground radio DJ] knows more about it than I do. I blocked the whole thing out of my mind, quite frankly. He had to tell me step-by-step what happened, kinda walk me back through it, and now I remember it. It was a very painful experience for me, and I obviously blocked it out. Couldn't remember anything about it.

I couldn't really believe they meant it when they fired me. I didn't regard it as final; I just thought it was something they were going through. Maybe I just never accepted it. It was so wrong.

JON LANDAU The band had exhausted how far they could go with their affiliation with the White Panther Party, which was John's entity. They were demonstrating their independence by getting their own place in Hamburg. They had gotten themselves into so many jams, including the one that caused Elektra to drop them, and when I came into the picture, they just wanted to be successful. They wanted what everyone who picks up a guitar, looks at themselves in the mirror, and dreams about being Elvis or the Beatles wanted. They wanted all those material things. But that doesn't mean they wanted to completely bail on John either. They were genuinely political, and they were very strong in some of the beliefs that they shared with John. But they also needed a certain amount of success to keep playing music and keep a roof over their heads.

I told John that what he was missing was that the MC5 wanted to make a great rock record. They wanted to be tremendously successful, as did I. And they wanted to express their point of view, which they did on the album, but they didn't want to be limited to being messengers for the White Panther Party. There was no doubt in anybody's mind that they had benefitted tremendously from their interactions with John. He is a brilliant man. But some of the politics were becoming counterproductive to the band's survival.

I saw the band from a different angle. And you could say I saw it from a more conventional angle. But I think that there was a lot of validity to what I was saying.

JOHN SINCLAIR Tyner and I were tight. That's what hurts me so much about the fucking shit he said later. We were tight, man. I was as inspired by him as he ever was or might've been by me.

I'm used to being slandered. Iggy slandered the shit out of me in his book *I Need More*. He made up this fucking story that I was a gangster telling him he had to do this and that. Kiss my ass, motherfucker! But Rob—that was difficult.

LENI SINCLAIR John had tons of chips on his shoulders because he knew that what we were doing then was important. And now nobody wants to even know about it. It's like everything has been swept under the rug, forgotten. Our own kids don't want to know; they don't even want to see pictures of their dad with long hair.

CHAPTER V (PART 2)

FREE JOHN NOW!

> One of my biggest accomplishments was beating the government on the marijuana issue and getting out of prison.
>
> —John Sinclair

In early 1967 John Sinclair was busted for allegedly offering two free joints to undercover police officers and was charged with unlawful possession of cannabis [revisit Chapter II for details]. His lawyers did their best to keep him out of jail by arguing against the constitutionality of Michigan's marijuana statutes, but the arrest finally caught up with Sinclair two years later.

On July 24, 1969, he was convicted and sentenced to serve a staggering ten-year prison term. The charges and the severity of the sentence for something many regarded as trivial sent shock waves throughout the counterculture movement, galvanizing activists, musicians, and artists across the country. It was clear to them that Sinclair's original "crime" provided authorities with an opportunity to silence a vocal and influential advocate for radical political change.

During his imprisonment, the rallying cry of "Free John Sinclair" began to echo across America, and his cause garnered widespread attention and support, with musicians like former Beatle John Lennon leading the charge for his release. Lennon's involvement was particularly significant, as he saw Sinclair's case as emblematic of broader issues of freedom and government oppression.

On December 10, 1971, Lennon and his wife, Yoko Ono, put their money where their peace signs were and headlined a benefit concert for Sinclair at the Crisler Center in Ann Arbor in front of fifteen thousand people, joined by prominent musicians like Stevie Wonder, Bob Seger, and jazzman Archie Shepp. The event not only raised awareness about Sinclair's situation but also served as a profound statement about the power of music as a force for social change.

The concert was scheduled to end at midnight but lasted until 3:30 a.m., with Lennon and Ono appearing at about 3:00 a.m. It was Lennon's first major public appearance in the United States in two years, and he and Ono performed four new politically charged songs, including "Attica State," "The Luck of the Irish," "Sisters, O Sisters," and finishing with "John Sinclair," a song he wrote specifically for the event.

The duo's set was impassioned, but the emotional highlight of the evening came when Sinclair spoke by phone to the thousands in attendance through the arena's massive PA system. Sinclair, his voice filled with emotion, told the audience, "What they try to do is isolate us... make us feel alone. Make us think we're *all* alone." Then, after a dramatic pause he pleaded, "Say something to me," to which the crowd roared, "Free John now!"

Just three days after the concert, the Michigan Supreme Court issued a landmark ruling, declaring Michigan's marijuana laws unconstitutional. Sinclair's case was overturned, and he was released from prison on December 13, 1971.

Conspicuously absent that evening were Sinclair's longtime protégés, the MC5. It was almost unimaginable that the band was not invited to perform, but it demonstrated just how estranged the group had become from their former manager.

To some degree, one could not blame the MC5 for wanting to create some distance between themselves and Sinclair and the White Panther Party. The Panthers had started out as a relatively benign organization that didn't take themselves too seriously, existing primarily to support the Black Panthers and other leftist groups like the Yippies. But very quickly Sinclair and his "Minister of Defense," Pun Plamondon, began taking their roles in the counterculture movement more seriously.

The twenty-four-year-old Plamondon was particularly instrumental in pushing the White Panther Party in a more radical direction. But it was clear things had gone too far when, on October 7, 1969, a grand jury indicted Plamondon, Sinclair, and Jack Forrest, the White Panthers' "Minister of Education." The latter two were charged with conspiring to destroy government property in the dynamite bombing of the CIA office the previous July, while Pun was charged for the actual bombing.

Sinclair was already in jail for his marijuana conviction. Plamondon, however, had just finished serving time for a drug bust, and he had no interest in returning to prison. As soon as the indictment was made public, Pun cut off his shoulder-length hair, shaved his beard, and went underground for eleven months, leading to his becoming the "first hippie" to make the FBI's Ten Most Wanted List. In July 1970, homesick, he went back to Michigan and was stopped for littering by police, who immediately recognized and arrested him. He spent thirty-two months in federal prison awaiting his trial.

Fortunately for the three men, during the subsequent trial, federal government officials admitted to wiretapping Plamondon's conversations without a warrant. The case went to the U.S. Supreme Court, where the judges held that the wiretaps were an unconstitutional violation of the Fourth Amendment and as such must be disclosed to the defense. This established the precedent that a warrant had to be obtained by law enforcement before they could undertake electronic surveillance even where domestic security was involved.

Plamondon returned to Ann Arbor to join Sinclair and Forrest, who were released on bond while appeals were heard. Ultimately, the Justice Department dropped the case.

Getting busted for smoking pot or yelling "motherfucker" in a crowded room was one thing, but being accused of bombing the CIA was a whole other ball of hash. Understandably, the Five wanted no part of it.

Still, despite their differences, the band steadfastly maintained that they made sincere efforts to support Sinclair during his time in prison. Their former manager claimed the opposite. Truth is, as in many divorces, they had grown apart and both parties wanted different things. Each had legitimate issues with the other, and there was plenty of bitterness and hard feelings to go around.

JOHN SINCLAIR You can imagine how I felt going to prison [for the marijuana bust] and being abandoned by those guys. I didn't even have ten dollars in my account to buy cigarettes. Nothing. My wife was pregnant. The phone got cut off. They just said, "Whew! We don't have to worry about them anymore."

I felt, "Fuck them." Then to see what happened to them while I was gone was heartbreaking. I wouldn't, *couldn't* wish it on them. It was so ugly, and they meant so much to so many people on a real direct, one-to-one basis—people that supported them and helped them get over. People who even today will tell you that they were the biggest thing that ever happened in their lives. Fans. And then to degenerate into a purely financial bunch of dope fiends and cynics, whose performances were basically designed to get them some money to buy drugs with and pay for their sports cars. It was just a whole ugly thing to me.

For all that, I wish they would've gone on to be Led Zeppelin, because they deserved that.

DENNIS THOMPSON Forget all the games and all the kiddie ploys, we had to get back to what we originally were: a goddamn rock-'n'-roll band.

ROB TYNER When you read [John Sinclair's memoir] *Guitar Army*, you have to remember that it's all propaganda to make John look good and the MC5 look like traitors. He needed a scapegoat so he could hang on to that audience that we had built up. There is a tremendous bitterness because of what could have been, but for the last third of his management of the MC5, we had very little contact with him. He was spending most of his time attending to his own politics.

We were certainly not as politically motivated as John wanted us to be. But we did our part. We had pumped a tremendous amount of money into the White Panthers. For a period, we were supporting the entire thing ourselves with money we brought from gigs and record-company advances. John would fly people in with band funds to talk about the revolution.

We tried our best to stay sympathetic, but John maintained that we left him, stranded him in jail. This was truly not the case. Sinclair had divorced himself from the band for a long time and left us with no real managerial assistance. He put most of his efforts into his political agenda, which wasn't turning a buck. But the band was turning a buck. Eventually we felt like we were just being used on a lot of levels and abused on top of that. That was a consequence of the fact that a lot of his political ideology was based on the writings of Chairman Mao.

Maoist thought was that people who were politically motivated were superior to people who were artistically motivated, and the best thing to do with artists is to send 'em out into the countryside to shovel shit. And this is pretty much exactly what happened with the MC5. They looked upon us as being naïve tools of the record company, even though we were paying for the house! There were definite reasons for the growing rift between the MC5 and the White Panthers.

WAYNE KRAMER Did we feel some hostility from the audience due to our split with Sinclair? Sure, we felt it. There wasn't that communal spirit that we had in the beginning, where everybody loved everybody. Now we heard these shouts of "sellout" and "rock star" at shows.

ROB TYNER There were a lot of people who were really trying to alienate the MC5 from our fan base. The White Panthers were engaging in total character assassination, and the band chose not to respond because initially we felt that it might give the whole thing too much credibility. But it was probably a miscalculation. The party line was being bought. As a matter of fact, that party line was chiseled in John's book, *Guitar Army*.

WAYNE KRAMER We started to develop our ideological break with the White Panthers right around the *USA* period. That's when we started to develop our own political ideas that were contradictory to what the White Panthers were talking about. We discovered that the violent rhetoric and posturing that we'd all been doing, the militant "going to die in a shootout with the pigs" was bullshit. It was around the time John and his people came up with the concept of "armed love," meaning "I love you, brother, but if you fuck with me, I'll blow your head off."

DENNIS THOMPSON We were the bad guys for dumping Sinclair. We disassociated ourselves from another chunk of our audience with that move. The PR was all negative at that point because John was in jail. We abandoned him, and he was the scapegoat for our shenanigans! Ha! That was not the way to go out and perform. You can't perform in a defensive posture. You must be aggressive.

WAYNE KRAMER You could point out a few things that broke the MC5's back. The censored version of the first album with no liner notes was a huge blow to our credibility. Losing John Sinclair, when he went to jail, was another blow. He was the only one who could communicate to the outside world for us. We were on our own without him. That was fucked up.

Contrary to what many people thought, we weren't trying to cut him out, we were trying to cut him *in*. We said, "If you go to jail, and it looks like you might, what do we do? Do we take 10 percent and give it to Leni? Do we take 5 percent and put it in the bank? We didn't know. Do we take 20 percent? Talk to us." Sincerely, we weren't trying to cut him out of anything, we were trying to include him. But he was getting very bitter, looking at doing all that time. It happens to a lot of people when they're getting ready to go to jail—they alienate people around them because they're angry. It's understandable. It's not a pleasant prospect. But I think at that point he was just so upset with culture, the band, society... everything. It was all just turning to shit for him because he thought he might end up in Jackson [Prison] for ten years. At that moment he couldn't've cared less about this fucking band. What did that have to do with him? He was going to jail.

JOHN SINCLAIR Lester Bangs would tell me years later that *Kick Out the Jams* had become his favorite record. And I always felt that just added insult to injury. He thought it would ameliorate my feelings, but it made it worse!

That fucking asshole! Couldn't he see? He ruined their whole career! He *killed* this music that became his favorite. It was his fault that we hired Landau. And it was because of Landau that they reduced themselves. They voluntarily surrendered their power.

They wanted to get over, which is commendable. Don't we all? But they got over with the White Panthers. One thing you have to say is, under my management they got over.

WAYNE KRAMER About that time I wanted Landau to manage the band. That was the obvious next step to take. I knew he was the m-a-n for the j-o-b. I knew he could do it. He was perfect. He understood the whole dynamic of the group. But he just didn't have the confidence. He was a young cat, and he had just made his first record and wasn't sure he could do it.

I think getting Dee Anthony to manage us was Landau's idea. Dee managed a bunch of huge British bands and was a big deal in the music business. Our first meeting with him was at a hotel in Detroit. We went over and met him and his lawyer, and we talked about our career and our business, and the possibilities of working together. Joe Cocker, who he managed at the time, came into the room with a bag of a leafy substance. We all said, "Reefer! Great!" Everybody rolled a joint, and Dee began telling us these stories about back when he used to manage Tony Bennett and how they used to smoke reefer and would get the munchies and would eat ravioli they would bring with them.

While Dee was talking, I noticed a funny taste in my mouth. Then I realized we weren't just smoking marijuana; it was marijuana dosed with "angel dust" [a highly dangerous drug developed as an anesthetic]. It had that metallic taste. Then everyone started getting quiet. Dee was just going on and on and on about himself and Tony Bennett, and he looked over at Joe Cocker and said, "Joe, you know what I mean? Joe? You know?" Joe said, "Dee, I haven't the faintest idea what you're talking about." Then we all looked at each other like "Whoa, this shit is strong." Then we awkwardly said goodbye and drove home in the station wagon stoned on this angel dust. "What do you think?" "I don't know what to think." "Well, do you think he should be our manager?" "I don't know, man, is this car flying or are we in a submarine?"

We met with Dee one other time, and we just agreed that he was going to be the manager. We were impressed by the obvious power he had in New York City. He had Joe Cocker, he had Ten Years After, he had Savoy Brown. He was what he called an American service manager for all these British bands, because his company was based in

Bermuda, a tax-free kind of deal. And to be honest, it wasn't like we knew anybody else.

DENNIS THOMPSON Dee Anthony was this Italian mafioso manager who came to see us with Champagne and roses. I think we saw his face only once or twice. That was our new manager . . .

We thought, Oh boy, we're saved! He's got Jethro Tull, Joe Cocker . . . everybody. He actually would've been good for us—he was a professional man—if the record had sold. It was the old catch-22. If the record had sold, he would have been great. But he wasn't set up to nursemaid a group that was not selling records, and when the record company pulled their promotional support, we got fewer and fewer calls from Dee. The phone calls we'd gotten once a day were now coming once a month. He still booked gigs for us, but he wasn't nearly as enthusiastic.

JON LANDAU Dee Anthony had been Tony Bennett's manager in the 1950s and was a friend of the booking agent Frank Barsalona, and Frank was fantastic. He was the new wave in that field. I can't even start to describe all the improvements Frank made in the touring world, and he and Dee were pals.

When people needed a manager, Frank would often recommend his friend Dee. Towards the end of the album, looking ahead, I said to Frank, they're going to need a professional manager. Somebody real. They want to go on a real tour, and they want somebody who can talk to Atlantic. And that's not me.

Since I knew both Frank and Dee, I facilitated a meeting. Dee was classic show business. He had stories about the old days that went on and on. Many of them were hilarious.

So, the guys briefly hired him to be their manager, which I was okay with. They needed a pro. The album was finished, so they called a meeting to strategize about how to promote it.

I was back home in Boston and the band invited me to the meeting because they wanted my input. They decided to meet at Dee's office on

Park Avenue and Eighty-Sixth Street, and we had a great conversation. Unfortunately, I had to leave early to catch a plane back to Boston. But before I left the building, I was standing outside of Dee's office talking to his assistant when I heard him—he had this big, deep voice—start talking about the next record. He was telling the band, "I'm going to get you somebody great. You don't need Jon for your next record."

He was talking about me! I could hear him say they didn't need me as clear as day. "I'm going to get you [Rolling Stones producer] Jimmy Miller." It was very painful to hear that, but it was also a good educational moment in Show Business 101.

I don't remember hearing how the band responded, but when it came time to do the next album, they asked me to fly out to meet with them at the Hamburg house, and I did. They asked me what I thought the strengths and weaknesses of *Back in the USA* were. We seemed to be having a preparatory discussion to start talking about the third album. Then I think it was Wayne who said to me, "Jon, the MC5 has decided to go in a different direction on the third album, so you won't be working on it." They flew me out to Hamburg, Michigan, to tell me I wasn't going to be producing the third album! I didn't like that; I really thought that I was going to be producing the album.

Recording *Back in the USA* was a great time in my life. I was only twenty-one years old, and it was very meaningful to me. In many ways it set the course of the rest of my life.

WAYNE KRAMER Contractually, a manager is supposed to function as a counselor and adviser. When we started doing press for *Back in the USA*, I was trying to consider the political criticism we might receive for firing Sinclair. When a writer from, say, the *Village Voice* asks a smart question, you needed a smart answer. I wanted to know what our position should be on the Panthers and where our money was going. We were at a point then where the old "power to the people" thing wasn't working anymore, but we couldn't dodge those issues either. I said, "Dee, what do I tell these people when they ask me about the revolution?" He said, "Well,

Wayne, tell them ooga-booga. Tell them ooga-booga about your money." I thought, Aw shit, Dee doesn't understand how serious the question is. He thinks it's like Elvis and the Colonel, where the Colonel tells Elvis to tell people, "The Colonel's handling it." But that wouldn't work for us.

In the end, it didn't work with Dee because we were like square pegs in a round hole with him. He was like a traditional music-business gangster kind of guy, and we were anything but traditional. Everything about us was unconventional.

ROB TYNER In October of '69 we played with Led Zeppelin in Boston. I had borrowed Wayne's boots that night, and the soles were real slippery onstage. I started to dance around a little bit . . . and I could slide! It was like skating. It was really fun, so by the time the night was over I was doing pirouettes all across the stage really fast. People were freaking out; they didn't realize it was possible for the MC5 to perform without any pretenses, without any politics, without any of that stuff and just have fun. It was exhilarating. When you're onstage in front of that many people, the air is so full of life and vitality and their energy. One human being can't help but be overwhelmed by it. Especially a Zeppelin crowd.

We were not Zeppelin, but we played similar music. We really got 'em warmed up well. The people of Boston were very kind to us that night. At that point we were really trying to do something on a level that we never had been able to achieve before. And I think our belief in ourselves was really peaking at that point.

DENNIS THOMPSON Playing with Led Zeppelin at the Boston Garden was hot stuff. Super concise, very precise. We did "Human Being Lawnmower," and it never felt so good because we built it right. It was egoless. No drugs. We weren't getting high. We had this thing then: "Anybody gets high, we're going to kick your ass." It was time to get serious.

CHAPTER V (PART 3)

END TIMES

> Boys, in the music business we have a concept called sending good money after bad, and we're not going to do that with you guys anymore.
>
> **—Ahmet Ertegun, president of Atlantic Records**

The MC5's second album, *Back in the USA*, released on January 15, 1970, triggered diverse reactions from critics and fans alike. Produced by Jon Landau, the record reflected the band's efforts to refine their arrangements and create more concise, punchy songs. But rock critics and fans alike felt that this approach sacrificed the grit and spark that had initially made them one of rock's most exciting groups. While the album foundered on the U.S. *Billboard* charts, reaching a modest Number 137, it did excite the band's European fans.

Rolling Stone was indifferent to *Back in the USA*, damning it with faint praise by calling it a "partly excellent MC5 album." In England, however, it was hailed as a minor masterpiece. Critics from *Melody Maker* praised it as "unbelievably tight" and "perfectly structured."

A European tour in the early 1970s proved to be a transformative experience for the band. An explosive performance at Phun City, one of England's first large-scale music festivals, resonated profoundly with a new generation that included such future punk and metal icons as Billy Idol, Mick Jones of the Clash, and Motörhead's Lemmy Kilmister.

Their third album, *High Time*, released on July 6, 1971, reflected the band's ambition and growing command of the recording studio but fell short on a commercial level. The disappointing sales led Atlantic Records to part ways with the band, leaving them without a label or managerial support. "No sales and enormous debt," Atlantic exec Wexler told *Rolling Stone* in June 1972. "[The MC5] cost us $128,000 we'll never see again." Their dream of achieving widespread recognition in the ever-changing music industry was fading fast.

Ronan O'Rahilly, the prominent Irish businessman and mastermind behind Radio Caroline, a popular offshore U.K. radio station, made an ambitious effort to keep the MC5 alive. He flew them to England and enrolled them in a self-actualizing course called "Ourselves," hoping to reignite their focus and passion. But despite his best intentions, the band started to self-destruct due to excessive drug use and internal bickering.

The MC5's final performance, on December 31, 1972, at the Grande Ballroom was a symbolic end to an era in rock marked by musical innovation and political fervor. As the band struggled through their set, tensions boiled over, and Wayne Kramer abruptly left the stage, punctuating the disbandment of the MC5. Their once-burning dream of revolutionizing rock music and igniting social change had been snuffed out.

WAYNE KRAMER We received almost no publicity from the record company for *Back in the USA*. Nobody at Atlantic seemed to give a shit about it. I remember trying to be on top of things, like asking whether were getting an ad in the *Detroit Free Press*. Where *are* we getting ads? What's the deal? "We haven't allocated any money for that," they said. We didn't have the White Panther machine anymore or [artist] Gary Grimshaw and John Sinclair to draw up ads and do layouts and send the stuff out.

On top of it, our local following hated *Back in the USA*. We achieved what we set out to achieve, which was to make a tight, solid album, but in retrospect, if it was looser, it would have been a more successful rock record.

JOHN SINCLAIR Landau enervated and deboned some great tunes. "Human Being Lawnmower" was great in performance. "Teenage Lust" and "Call Me Animal" were amazing fucking tunes; Landau made them sound like Paul Revere & the Raiders. "Back in the USA" was a great, funny, powerful, ironic tribute to Chuck Berry. "Tutti Frutti" was a throwaway, but live it was still powerful.

I remember going to the studio and having conversations with Landau. I'll never forget one thing he said. He maintained that James Brown couldn't shine Otis Redding's shoes. James Brown was the god of rock 'n' roll in our world. The MC5 would learn each new James Brown record and play it so they could learn from it and feed off its energy. They learned "There Was a Time" the week it came out.

But the band was not going to go in and back up [mellow R&B singer] Roberta Flack. I mean, this was the MC5! That was the *last* thing they were. They were thugs! Fucking thugs, man, not professional musicians. When we went into the musicians' union, the "professionals" all ran into their offices and locked the doors. Seriously! That's what he didn't appreciate or understand—what the MC5 was about.

I thought it was just a temporary thing, that soon the band would see that these guys were a bunch of charlatans. If you would've told me at that time that the band would eventually turn into heroin addicts, I would've hit you right between the eyes. It's really sad what happened to them. That's why I can't feel any hatred or anger, because what happened to them was just such an ugly thing.

WAYNE KRAMER It's funny. The people in Michigan loved the first album. It was more like a memento of an MC5 show—a souvenir or artifact. The second one they couldn't relate to. Whereas to Europeans, the first one was a little too rough, while the second one was right on the money.

We were contacted by this British journalist, Mick Farren, who wanted us to come to the U.K. and play the Phun City festival. It was going to be one of the first major music festivals in England. The band was thrilled to death to be going overseas. It was going to be one of the real payoffs. We knew what we were doing too. We were going to go over there and play American rock 'n' roll and blow their socks off. Because we already knew at that point that we were the real thing. We were from the land of cheeseburgers, hot-rod cars, and American rock 'n' roll, which is what the U.K. loved, and we were ready for them.

We flew in and we did some press. They took our pictures with headlines that read "Bad Boys from Detroit Arrive in London." The gig was in the south of England. We drove down and discovered it was in this big field of mud filled with dirty hippies. It was revolting! But William Burroughs was there and they fed us and took good care of us. I went over to meet this guy, Mick Farren, to see about the money. I wanted to get paid before we played. He said, "Money? Uh . . . There is no money." I said, "We're four thousand miles from home and you tell me there isn't any money?" He said, "No, no money. It's a free festival."

I guess the hippies had broken down the fence, and they had a hard time collecting money so they just made it a free festival. I went back to the band and said, "Look, it's the same old story. We're getting it again." We decided to go on and do our show anyway, and it turned out to be one of the real high points of the whole MC5 story. It was all English Hells Angels and all these muddy hippies, and I don't think any of them knew what to expect. We pulled out all our best shit. I remember it as just a whirling, spinning performance.

The following week we had a press party in London, where they played the record and invited journalists. Atlantic said the press party was going to be at like two in the afternoon; we met up with their publicity guy, and he said, "Listen, I've written this press release, but I don't want you guys to see it." We just physically picked him up and threw him out of the office. We looked at the press release and started taking stuff out. It was absurd and wasn't written with any degree of style or humor, or what we used to say in Trans-Love, "purity and accuracy." We told Atlantic not to give it out to anybody, but they did anyway.

Then the party started. They had a record player going and played the album over and over and over, and all the press came. I invited Farren from the Phun City festival and all his gang of leather-jacketed hoodlums. When they arrived, I had more fun with them than I did with the press. We went out on the stairs there and took some pictures with Ahmet Ertegun. I think it was the same stairs the Beatles looked down from, you know, the early Beatles pictures on a stairwell that looks like a fire escape. Later, we got thrown out of our own press party. I ripped my trousers accidentally, and we were really drunk and obnoxious. It was fun.

The rest of the week, Mick really rose to the occasion. "Since you're here, I'll take you around to some booking agents and we'll see if somebody can find you some jobs." We just walked around [London's hip neighborhood] Ladbroke Grove, from this booking agent to that booking agent: "Hey, I got this band over here." "Oh, yeah, we heard about you." They put together a little itinerary.

We played the Speakeasy, and it was something of a disaster because I had been drinking during the day. The gig came so late at night that I don't even remember playing the job. Apparently, Charlie Watts and Mick Jagger had come to see the band and we really sucked. Didn't help our legend much around London. I sunk to the occasion. But we came back from England with high hopes, because the audiences really seemed to love us.

Dee Anthony didn't really extend himself to us at all after a while. He used to send his secretary out to our jobs to collect the money and take it back to New York. Then we'd have to wait until after he deducted all his costs and send us the difference. Our relationship started to unravel pretty quickly. He wouldn't return our phone calls. We'd have pressing business, and he wouldn't answer.

It reached a point where Fred and I were running things, so we decided to go to New York and see Dee in person and see the record company at the same time. We were broke—again—and needed money. We hadn't been playing. I think we were having some tax pressure too. We went out and sat outside Dee's office and he wouldn't see us. He had his secretary strong-arm us out the door.

We said, "Look, we've come all the way from Detroit. He's supposed to be our manager." He was just hiding in his office. Then we went to see Ahmet Ertegun, who said, "Boys, in the music business we have a concept called sending good money after bad, and we're not going to do that with you guys anymore."

Fred and I went home the next day with our tails between our legs. We found out months later that Dee had already gone to the arbitration commission, got a judgment against us, and kept all our money. We didn't have a legal leg to stand on. We didn't even know the fight was over. We're standing there with our gloves on, ready to get into the ring, and the fight had already been decided.

DENNIS THOMPSON After Dee Anthony "fired" us, I wound up managing the band with my dad's credit cards for the next six to eight months. Dee sued us for thirty-five or forty grand—money he claimed he had advanced to us, plus his fees and commissions. Naturally he tried to recover that. It wasn't anybody's fault. It was all strictly business. A dollar's a dollar, and if a man was owed a certain amount of money, let him take it. We just didn't have it. We were too busy trying to survive.

WAYNE KRAMER Atlantic finally gave us an advance on the next album, but we had to use it to pay taxes and there wasn't anything left, so we were broke.

The band was in some turmoil then. We gave up the house in Hamburg. Everybody wanted to live by themselves and get their own apartment, houses, and cars. Bourgeois capitalist symbols. It *looks* like you're still in it when you have one of those: "Hey, I'm still here. Look, I've got a Jaguar." We all had to borrow the money for them from our parents, promise to pay them back. We had this accountant named Bill Rowe. Bill told us that we could probably buy them, probably afford them, but we couldn't afford the down payments. It was a thousand dollars apiece or something, so he went with us to each of our parents. We had a meeting and Bill explained to them how we would be able to pay for it if they would go for the down payment. My mother cashed in an insurance policy. Yeah, those were great cars.

CHRIS HOVNANIAN They all got cars. Wayne got a Jaguar. He got his down payment from his mother. I'm not sure that he ever paid her back. The thing was, he wanted a Jaguar. But there was no way he could get a new Jag, so he got this secondhand Jaguar, which cost a *fortune* to fix. It never ran well; for a while it was driven with no brakes; you practically had to put your foot out the door to stop it. It had all kinds of things wrong with it, and even changing the oil cost a lot of money. It was a total joke, a rip-off. The guy who sold it to him even said, "Don't buy this car." But no, he had to have his Jaguar. The guy did everything he could to try to talk him out of it. Fred got his Corvette.

WAYNE KRAMER When we were kids, Fred and I used to write together. But during *Back in the USA* he started finding his own voice and decided that he had things he wanted to say and didn't need to collaborate.

DENNIS THOMPSON Fred started to blossom creatively when we left Hamburg. He finally started living on his own. He just stayed at home and cranked out the tunes.

I was a midwife to some of his songs, like "Thunder Express." He would bounce things off me, I would give him some beats, and he'd go back and finish them off. When he presented songs to the band, they were usually finished pieces of music. Wayne was more of a showman than a composer. Fred was more creative; he had his own things to say.

WAYNE KRAMER Fred started finding his songwriting feet with "Shakin' Street" and "Tonight" on *Back in the USA*, which were his first couple of real songs. I think he just realized that he could do more and rose to the occasion. I thought it was great. I never felt threatened by Fred because his songs were good.

ROB TYNER I was restricted to only one song on *High Time*, so it was not a very creative situation for me. Other people were growing artistically, and we were waiting to see what was gonna happen with it. There were a lot of good ideas on *High Time*, but there really wasn't the spearhead tune—the one we needed to take the band to the next level.

DENNIS THOMPSON Atlantic assigned Geoffrey Haslam, who had worked with the Velvet Underground and the J. Geils Band, to produce our third album, *High Time*.

He wasn't a force of nature like Sinclair or Landau, but that was a good thing. Everyone seemed to work well with him, and it was the first album we enjoyed making. Finally, we were having fun playing music. We were smiling and laughing at the sessions. That's the way it should have been on the second album. *High Time* sounded like we always wanted to sound. Another album and we would've been killing it.

WAYNE KRAMER Atlantic suggested Geoff, and we all liked him a lot. He was low-key; he didn't try to make us do anything. He just wanted to help us develop our ideas. He listened to three songs and was beside himself with excitement. He'd say, "Well, the third one, in the middle maybe something different should happen." But he was a real Zen nonproducer, which was just exactly what we needed. That allowed us to start being creative in the studio, as opposed to being intimidated by the process.

High Time was a genuinely good record because we were finally comfortable. We knew that we needed the energy of our live show, and we started figuring out how to capture that in a recording environment. We were confident enough to not allow some engineer to bully us out of doing something we wanted to do.

For example, we had Charles Moore, a respected Detroit jazz musician, compose some horn charts for our song "Skunk." Some of the stuff that Charles had written was a bit wild and dissonant, and he brought his guys in who were used to playing an avant-garde kind of way to perform what he had written. We loved it and it worked fabulously, but the engineer on the session was a trumpet player, and between takes he was complaining, "You know, these guys aren't playing this thing right. If you want, I can get four horn players in here that'll play it correctly." I said, "No, this is *exactly* what we want them to do. We want it to be 'BREEEEEEAAAHH!'" A couple years earlier, we all would have gone "Oh God, what are we going to do? It isn't right." Now we knew enough about who we were and what our sound was.

And Michael wasn't an issue on the album either; his sound was important to what we're doing. We came to terms with the idea that the wild shit that he played sounded good. It was the kind of sound that people had come to expect from us. It's partially what made us different from everyone else.

JOHN SINCLAIR Although I felt *High Time* was lyrically suspect, musically it was really a great album. That was the MC5 that I hear when I think of the MC5. Strong.

DENNIS THOMPSON The only real problem with *High Time* was there wasn't a strong single, so sales weren't great, which meant the record company wasn't going to support it and being on the road was going to be hard. And it was. We often didn't even have gas money to get us from job to job.

WAYNE KRAMER We started acquiring a bad reputation with a lot of the important bookers. Most of it was our fault. We would often show up late and fuck up a promoter's whole concert, so a certain amount of our pay would get docked. When that happened, we wouldn't have enough money to get to the next gig and it became a domino effect. Everything was cracking. Dee was out of the picture, and we were on our own. I think a lot of the promoters started deciding we weren't worth the headaches.

A final blow came when Atlantic dropped us, leaving the band with no record company, no manager, and no Jon Landau or Danny Fields to support us. But when everything was at its worst, Ronan O'Rahilly, the owner of U.K. pirate station Radio Caroline, took an interest in us.

Ronan was the guy who was behind the muddy Phun City festival we played when we went to the U.K. in 1970. The band really liked him, especially Fred. Fred and Ronan really got along well because they would get "cosmic" together. Where my interests were in the day-to-day operation of how we got from point A to point B, Fred and Ronan would go off into an ultra-theoretic, ethereal, spacey, gaseous plane. Fred yelled at me one time when I walked in the office and he and Ronan were on another level, and I said, "Hey, the amps have blown up" or "Where are the roadies?" It was like Crash! Back to Earth. And Fred said, "Don't do that, man, when I'm talking to Ronan. Just let me finish what I'm doing."

Ronan, like Sinclair—he saw a chance to change the world with the MC5. His idea was that we should be prepared to be like Jesus. That if we had to go the road that Jesus went, then that's what we had to do, but we had to be committed enough to do that. He had this theory called "Loving Awareness," a set of principles he came up with that combined psychic phenomena, hypnosis, and past-lives shit with the modern political theory of Gandhi and Martin Luther King. If we could just get everyone into his Loving Awareness idea, then everyone in the world would have a beautiful creative existence. All that fit in fine with the wild political stuff we were already familiar with. To me, this was just, Yeah, right, okay, I'm down with it. Unfortunately, it didn't mesh well with heroin.

DENNIS THOMPSON Heroin was a bad thing to happen to the MC5, but it happened because there was so much pressure on us. The stresses came from so many angles, and we were juggling all these demons.

We had this bravado. Hell, we were the MC5, and we could conquer any drug. But smack is stronger than any person. It overcame everything. It obliterated and took over. We started off just doing these little things called "penny caps" that came in these little red gel caps. If you hung out with Michael, you would sniff a little bit of it maybe once in a weekend. Before you knew it, you were doing it twice, then three and four times a week, and then you had a habit. You can't touch heroin and not get addicted to it! You could believe you can handle it, but it's impossible. Before anyone knew it, the bad, belligerent, and dangerous MC5 were reduced to becoming a bunch of damn junkies. It stopped us cold and cooked everyone's nuts.

I don't exempt myself from any of it. We controlled every other chemical, but not smack. It can't be done.

WAYNE KRAMER Michael knew about dope way back. That's where he first got his Bob Dylan persona: the artistic troubadour. He thought he was from another time, like the Elizabethan period or something. He felt more comfortable there.

Michael was the hookup. When we were in Hamburg, we were rehearsing at this little place in Ypsilanti, and I asked Mike to bring a bag to rehearsal.

I don't think Michael was into dope during the USA sessions, but who knows what he was doing when nobody else was around? I know on the next record we were deep into it because we would leave the studio and cop right around the corner in an after-hours club. Penny caps.

We had a lot of time on our hands, and we started doing a lot of experimentation with drugs. We always took drugs, but now we were getting into Quaaludes and dope. Dope was the big one, and it all came from gangsters in Detroit. We got it from Italians on the East Side who were all Vietnam vets. Trench coats and slicked-back hair. They'd show up, drop off the package, and pick up the money.

They even promoted a couple of shows that we played and paid us in dope. We did one show and they wanted us to also get a jazz band. It was funny, the jazz guys all wanted cocaine and the rock guys wanted heroin.

DENNIS THOMPSON If I would have just snorted it, I would have been fine. But once I started mainlining, that's when I became a literal junkie. It's an overwhelming high, and I'm here to tell you there's nothing stronger than that. Nothing.

Wayne and Fred had a problem with smack too. They had it more under control, but nonetheless they still had the problem. If you didn't want to look at all the pain, heroin washed it away. We were all tired of the pain.

WAYNE KRAMER The dope began to affect the performances. Michael was outrageous with the shit. We'd go to pick him up, and the last thing he'd do before leaving the house was get off. Then he had to get off in the car while we're driving. And then Dennis would want some too. All the time. So, by the time it came to play . . .

We went up to Buffalo to play on a bill with Mitch Ryder and Brownsville Station, and Michael and Dennis shot dope all the way. Then we went to a gay bar across the street and started drinking whiskey before the show. Michael was so stoned that when we started tuning before the show, I looked over and he was holding his bass up, but his eyes are closed, and he was sort of oscillating. "Michael!" "Unnh. Yeah." "You're flat." "Okay." "Michael!" "What, what, what?" We went up there to try and do our set and of course Michael was incapable of playing. Cub Koda from the Brownsville Station pulled me aside at one point from the wings and asked, "Do you want me to play bass? I'll help. I'll play bass if you want. I know all the songs."

Towards the end, we'd go out and play three or four concerts and come home with maybe $60 apiece for the week. The travel just ate it up. We'd be making $5,000 a week and have $50 or $60 to show for it, so we said, "Fuck this." We all owned cars or rented cars, so we just started driving ourselves everywhere. But we got into trouble a lot with that, being on our own driving to the gigs. When we had tour managers it was way better. But left to our own devices, it wasn't. We'd leave Detroit and stop to get an ounce of reefer, a bottle of whiskey, a case of beer, and whatever else we could find, some Quaaludes or something. And then we'd just party off down the expressway.

I fucked up a couple of times driving after taking Quaaludes. One time I was in Arkansas somewhere, and the first thing I did was get lost. I turned a corner and went uphill on a curve, and a dog came out and started barking at me. I yelled at the dog, and next thing I knew I went off the hill into a cornfield, which woke everybody up. I said, "It's okay, guys, it's okay. I was just yelling at a dog. Everything's under control. Go back to sleep." Everyone was grumbling, "Kramer, you fucking asshole. Jesus Christ." "Relax, relax, go to sleep," I told them.

Then I started driving again, continuing up this hill. I'd started seeing traffic coming my way, it was raining, and I thought, Gee, I might be a little altered, I better really pay attention here, because I didn't want to go head-on into these cars. With my Quaalude-addled brain I started riding the guardrail all the way around the curve! So, SCRRREEECHHH all the way around. The noise was horrendous, so I stopped the car. Now everybody was *really* mad—plus we had a flat tire. We changed the tire, and I got it back together and said, "I'll drive, it's okay." I think they'd had enough, and someone mercifully said, "No, Wayne, you've done your part for today."

ROB TYNER Sinclair's harsh prison sentence inspired Abbie Hoffman to jump on the stage during the Who's performance at Woodstock to protest the penalty imposed. It also sparked the John Sinclair Freedom Rally at Ann Arbor's Crisler Arena, held on December 10, 1971.

The event brought together all sorts of people, including John Lennon, Yoko Ono, David Peel, Stevie Wonder, Phil Ochs, Pete Seeger, Archie Shepp, and Roswell Rudd; and speakers like Allen Ginsberg, Abbie Hoffman, Rennie Davis, David Dellinger, Jerry Rubin, and Bobby Seale.

And miraculously, three days after the rally, John was freed from prison when the Michigan Supreme Court, on the court's own motion, ordered that he be released from incarceration. Three months later, on March 9, 1972, the Michigan Supreme Court would declare the state's marijuana laws unconstitutional. We couldn't believe it.

JOHN SINCLAIR I imagine one of my biggest accomplishments was beating the government on the marijuana issue and getting out of prison, thanks to John Lennon and everybody else. The promoter, Pete Andrews, was about to cancel the concert—we had all these people like Commander Cody and Archie Shepp, and I think Phil Ochs was the biggest name. Pete said to everybody, "Man, you're never going to get a thousand people to show up with that lineup. It's going to be a flop and everybody's just going to laugh at you, and Sinclair's not going to get out." That's when Jerry Rubin stepped in and talked John and Yoko into coming to Ann Arbor. Three days later I was out of prison.

The point is that it was just part of a huge strategy that we had been playing for two and a half years—or, more accurately, five years since I first got charged. I wanted to overthrow the law. I challenged it for five years, and two and a half of those I had to spend locked up. But finally, we got our arguments in, we also lobbied in the legislature, and we got them to change the laws. The day before the concert, they did just that. By then I had already done more time than the new law called for, and so they were going to let me out on appeal bond.

It was already in the works before John and Yoko showed up. The mechanics of this are interesting in their own way, but we never promoted them too much because the myth that John and Yoko were responsible for my release was so powerful. Our preachment was that this music could do things and make things happen, and it's ours, and we can do it for ourselves. And here it was, they got me out of prison. You see, it does work! John Lennon showed up because it coincided with a change that he was going through in his own life. Which was heavy in itself.

LENI SINCLAIR The MC5 wanted to play the event, but I think the leadership of the Rainbow People's Party, the Central Committee or whatever, felt that it was an opportunistic move on their part to get on the show just because John Lennon was coming. But to me, they were still people. If it had been up to me, I would have let them play because I felt bad when I saw them that night and they weren't included. It just didn't feel right, because the estrangement, on some level, was beyond their control and beyond John's control, and they shouldn't have blamed each other for what happened.

WAYNE KRAMER We were not only *not* asked to play the rally but were also refused permission to play. I'd been calling [John Sinclair's brother] David Sinclair for maybe four weeks before the concert happened. I knew it was coming. I said, "Hey, Dave, the band's available, and we want to play the rally." He wouldn't return my calls. It hit me the day of the gig, when I made the last call, that we weren't going to be allowed to perform. That made me angry, and I said, "We've been there for John from the beginning. I don't know about all you White Panthers, but we were there for John. And this might be the thing that does it for him, this level of attention."

I think Dave Sinclair was just rankled that we had sports cars. Ultimately, it was a great show. I was there. But the band was conspicuous by its absence. Everybody who gave a shit knew that it wasn't right.

We were being ostracized in Detroit, but suddenly there was interest in us overseas. Ronan O'Rahilly wanted us to come back to Europe and had been working to get us a new contract with Philips Records in Holland. He had the deal 99 percent in his pocket, but the label wanted to see the band live, so we went over to do it. It was a festival that went on for like twenty-eight hours. It was band after band after band. Our set time got pushed back, and we didn't get onstage until the sun was coming up.

We'd been taking Quaaludes *all* night, so by the time we hit the stage nobody could do anything. Tyner tried to leap off the stage to these platforms that were set up on the side and missed. Splat. We just couldn't do anything right. Of course, that queered the record deal.

Meanwhile, Michael had been making more money dealing drugs in Detroit than he was playing in the band, and he started showing up when he felt like it. He had missed his plane to England, and we had to find a replacement for our first two shows there until he arrived. Then, when he arrived, he wasn't playing well. That's when we had a big meeting and decided that he should not be in the band. He obviously didn't want to be, and it wasn't fair to the rest of us. He couldn't think of any reason to convince us otherwise, so he went back to America.

MICHAEL DAVIS At the end, there was such pressure and tension. And everything seemed so phony to me. Everything seemed so forced and contrived. We were still having to talk about "the revolution" and all this stuff we didn't really believe in anymore. I started medicating myself to just avoid the whole situation. After I left the band in February 1972, it was like this huge weight was off me. For quite a while I had felt like I was a prisoner of the MC5, and when it ended it was like, I don't have to be *that* anymore. It had been a totally ecstatic experience in the early days, but it became an absolute nightmare.

WAYNE KRAMER When Michael didn't make his flight to the U.K., we didn't have a bass player. Fortunately, Fred had a boyhood pen pal in England, Steve Moorhouse, who played bass in a band. Steve was at our show the first night, just coming to the gig as a friend. We were desperate, so we said, "Steve! Play the bass." He did and, thank God, he played really well.

Despite the problems with Michael, working with Ronan in England opened the band to a lot of new possibilities. Having a manager again was big for us, and he provided a house for us to live in.

Everything started seeming controllable again. But at the same time, I also knew that the band was basically self-destructing. At this point Dennis had a serious habit. I mean, his life revolved around going downtown and copping every day, but I couldn't point fingers because I was using a fair amount myself. Even Rob was having issues with his Quaaludes and weirdness . . .

Ronan wanted to help us get back on track and had a good idea. He had us take this course called "Ourselves." It was basically for actors, to help put them in touch with their feelings: if they needed to conjure up how they felt about something, they got a tool to get right at it. It had to do with the Stanislavski method of acting kind of thing. You're not really acting a part; someone else is just being you under different circumstances. We did exercises in concentration. Ronan's idea was that this was going to help us control the audience and really connect with people. Which it would have done if the band had been able to stay together long enough to apply it.

But perhaps the most memorable time in the U.K. was a gig at Wembley Stadium, where we were invited to play a rock-'n'-roll revival show and revealed a new look, yeah. We had been talking and scheming and planning with Ronan about how we could bring the band into the new generation, and one of the ideas we had was about our appearance. We were originally known for our flashy clothes, but we had slowly drifted down to a basic Levi's-and-black-leather-jacket kind of thing. We had none of the glamour and flamboyance we used to have, and we wanted to recapture that energy.

I started by cutting all my hair off. In my new way of thinking, I decided that hair had lost its meaning. It didn't symbolize what it used to in the '60s. Then I painted myself gold. I wore a black suit, a pair of sunglasses, and gold skin.

Tyner had on a gold lamé jacket, had poofed his hair out way bigger than usual, and filled his afro up with glitter. Our new bassist, Derek Hughes, wore Indian war paint—that's the best we could come up with for him. I forget what Dennis did. And Fred painted himself silver and put on the superhero outfit that he wore when we played the rock-'n'-roll revival show in Michigan. On the same bill was going to be all our favorite classic-rock bands: Jerry Lee Lewis, Little Richard, Bill Haley & His Comets, Chuck Berry, Bo Diddley, and Gary Glitter.

We had to share the dressing room with them. We were looking over at their glittery stuff, they looked at ours. But when the audience saw us, they just started booing. The crowd was all dressed in black leather jackets, pointed-toe shoes, creepers and drapes and sideburns, and motorcycle jackets. They looked like we looked on the street. If we had walked up with our street gear on, we would have destroyed the place. But we walked out with our spaced-out regalia, and they didn't want to hear it. At one point, they started throwing beer cans at us.

One beer can almost hit Tyner's head and he made the mistake of throwing it back. When he did that, it *rained* beer cans. It was wild. I said, "Jesus, Rob, you've done it again." Just the *wrong* thing to do. Chuck Berry liked us, though. We knew him; we'd played with him before in Michigan on little farm-community jobs. He was right there on the stage, videotaping us with his own camera. He said he liked my gold paint—he said I looked like "a golden boy." But the show was a total disaster. We didn't run away, but we sure didn't win the audience over!

BECKY TYNER I think drugs had a lot to do with what went wrong with the MC5, and the lack of management. They went to Europe and hooked up with Ronan O'Rahilly, who later claimed he almost saved the band—and he almost did. But it wasn't enough. Michael had left the band because of his severe addiction. Dennis was really, really in trouble. Ronan couldn't overcome that.

Rob so passionately believed in the MC5, and he would always try to see the positive side of things. His attitude was always *We can do this!* The music he made after the MC5 was always uplifting. But even for Rob, being in the MC5 was becoming difficult.

There was a plan to return to England, but Dennis came over to our house and flat-out said, "I'm not going. I cannot go back and do this again. There's no money in it, and nothing is working out. It's all horrible." And Rob said, "You know what? I'm not going either." It's always been rumored that Rob was the first person to quit the band, but it was really Dennis.

A few days later Fred and Sigrid came over to convince Rob to go back to the band. But after dinner Rob said, "I'm not going." Fred then stood up and punched him. Then all four of us started fighting. I yelled, "Sigrid, get Fred the fuck out of my house now!" Then Wayne started threatening us. He was hanging out with a bunch of gangsters on the East Side, and we literally had to move out of our house because we were in fear for our lives.

ROB TYNER Our last album, *High Time*, was all about the band taking control. Had we stayed together, it would've been a good beginning. The main thing that caused our breakup was that the frustration finally just got to everybody. You can only bang your head against the wall for so long. You either wear a hole in the wall or your head, and our heads started to wear out. There were money problems, personal problems, chemical problems, and all kinds of different problems, but the one underlying cause was probably the frustration. We had been blasting away for so long, we just ran out of time. Like on the cover of *High Times*, our clock was smashed, busted, done . . .

WAYNE KRAMER Ronan had booked us for what promised to be a world-class six-week tour of Europe. When Rob quit, I started thinking, Who can I call to sing for us? What about Bob Seger? He could sing our songs! Scott Morgan of the Rationals? For some reason, neither were available. To make matters worse, the day before we were about to leave, Dennis said, "I'm not going to go either." I said, "C'mon, man." He said, "No, my doctor says that if I stop my methadone, I'll have withdrawal sickness." I said, "So go back on dope for the tour. Go back and use dope, just finish this. Six weeks long. The best money. Ten days in Scandinavia, two weeks in Italy, French, German TV, college dates in England, British TV." All we had to do was show up with our clothes. All interior transportation was paid for, meals were paid for. It was a sweet tour. It was what we had been working to achieve.

DENNIS THOMPSON I had made up my mind I wasn't going. I talked to my parents, and they were willing to pop for me to go to a clinic. I finally came to my senses, and told myself, "I got to stop doing this. If I keep it up, I'll be dead in a year." Wayne and Fred didn't hit it up; they snorted it, so they weren't as in bad shape as I was. Michael and I would mainline. The two of us saved Iggy Stooge's life one night. Iggy was at Michaels's house; Michael was dealing. Saving Iggy was one of the turning points for me.

My dad and I had a heart-to-heart after that, and he said, "What the hell has happened to you? My brilliant son, you've turned yourself into a pincushion. Is this what you had in mind?" That got me thinking and—even more than Iggy—turned me around. Someone had to slap me in the face and wake me up. My family rescued me. I had a case of hepatitis from a bad needle, and they forced me to go to the hospital. The doctor told them I was about two days from dying because I had jaundice. After the hospital, I made plans and arrangements to go to the clinic. My mind was set: I decided I wasn't going to Europe! I couldn't go because if I did, I'd be back in London scoring.

After I told the guys, we had a big fight—a blowout. I asked them if they could put the tour on hold. "Give me a month to clean up, and then I think I'll be able to handle it." All they cared about was the money. Here I was dying, and they wanted to make money. So, I quit.

That's how the band stopped. If everyone had looked at the situation more intelligently instead of emotionally and given me the month I needed, I think I could've handled it and it might have worked.

WAYNE KRAMER So neither of them went. We had to call Ronan and tell him to find us a drummer, and Fred would work on singing the songs. We met the drummer in the dressing room the first night of the tour in London. You know, it was like, "Hey, are you any good?" "I don't know, you'll see." "You know Chuck Berry music?" "Sure." "Okay, well this one's kind of like Chuck Berry." "You know Bo Diddley?" "Yeah." "Okay, this one's kind of like Bo Diddley."

Naturally, we went out and it wasn't anything like the MC5. It was two guitar players struggling to get through songs they'd never sung, backed by a drummer they had never played with. The rooms emptied out real quick. The tour went on and people were complaining, and booking agents wanted to sue us. "Where's Rob Tyner?" they'd ask. "I don't know. I'm here. If you want to sue Rob, you can find him in Detroit. I'm here to perform." It was really like the Fear and Loathing tour of all time. Everything was going bad.

We hit Scandinavia, where it was fucking freezing in the winter, and we had no money. We'd arrive at the show and meet the promoter and his wife and his kids and his cousins and his uncles, and there'd be food and whiskey. Everyone wanted to meet you. Then we'd go out and play, and it was so horrible; and when we came back to the dressing room, there was no food, no booze, no friends . . . and still no money.

This happened night after night after night. We could barely sing any of those songs. They weren't in the right key for either of us. Honestly, Fred and I didn't even know what a key was. We just played everything on the guitar in E because it had a big sound. From the beginning, Rob was forced to sing in E and got used to it, but it was an impossible key for me and Fred to sing in. In the end, when the Italian promoters found out Rob wasn't going to be there, they canceled our two weeks in Italy. Then the Scandinavians began to cancel dates because the word started getting around that we were terrible.

We did the German leg of the tour, and the Germans were really disappointed. "*Scheissen!*" one promoter said. "You know the meaning of this word *Scheissen*? It was *Scheissen* what you do!" Fred and I worked out pretty quick that it meant "shit."

All our plans were falling apart. It was like being in a bunker at the end of World War II. One night, just before Fred and I came back, neither one of us could sleep. We were just kind of staring at the walls, saying, "What do you think we should do next?"

The best idea we came up with at the time was to start a new band and have Michael Davis be the singer, because Michael could sing. We figured that could work, which was ridiculous. We thought we'll use Dennis, too, but we'll just call it something new. We also considered getting some additional musicians in the band, just switch things around a little bit. But when we got back to Detroit, I don't know, I started to meet other players and had second thoughts. I could see other things were happening. Fred was so heavy and serious about everything. He wanted to call the band Ascension, after the John Coltrane album. It was just too heavy for me. Too deep. I was done with deep for a while. Everything had to be scholarly with Fred. I think I just finally got to the point where I couldn't do it, and told him, "I don't know, I think I'll step off of this and do what I want to do."

We played one farewell job on New Year's Eve—with the original band at the Grande. I remember it being so bad that I left in the middle of the set. I went over to Fred and said, "Fred, I can't do this anymore." I unplugged and walked out, copped, went home, and got loaded. We were unbelievably bad. Michael was so out of it that the tempos were gone. There was no energy. I remember "Looking at You" just disintegrated on us.

DENNIS THOMPSON New Year's Eve, 1972, at the Grande Ballroom—a very tragic night. That's where Wayne walked off the stage, and that was it. The whole night was even more depressing because only a smattering of people had attended. There was a time when we played the Grande and there was 1,500 people butt to butt, and at our last show, there were maybe 300 people. And we sucked.

BECKY TYNER If someone had just taken the MC5 by the hand and said, "All right, this is what's going to happen," they would've been more successful. But that's part of a tragedy that their whole career seemed to embody. Think about Aristotle's theory of the tragedy. It's that tragic flaw that always doomed them.

WAYNE KRAMER I can narrow what broke the MC5 down to three or four things. The first was when Elektra rushed the first album out. The second was when we lost John Sinclair as a manager, and the third was when we couldn't get Landau to manage us. Then dope. We discovered heroin, and that proved to be our greatest downfall.

BECKY TYNER At the end, they could barely get arrested... even in Detroit, which was ironic considering how many times they got busted.

MICHAEL DAVIS What happened to us? We lost that sense of fun. Yeah, we lost the fun. To hell with the other stuff. Fucking Panthers and the Republican Party and Weathermen or anybody that's trying to take your attention away from what you love. Did the politics hurt us? Maybe so. It was all connected to what we wanted to do. I think we just got overwhelmed by too much information and too much responsibility. And we weren't very responsible characters anyway.

DENNIS THOMPSON We got beat up by so many different forces. First was drug usage. The second was improper timing with the band's music and the audience. We were definitely ahead of our time. The third was poor management. We didn't have a real manager. John Sinclair should've been our spiritual adviser, period. Being dropped from the record label. Harassment by police from the local city level to the county level to the state level to the federal level to the CIA. Being dropped from Atlantic. No promotion, no tour support. The list goes on. And you throw all that together, you can't say it was all because we did drugs.

WAYNE KRAMER At the time I didn't much care for John's liner notes on *Kick Out the Jams*. But as more and more time went on, they're more and more right-on. There was really this "groupthink" about everything. We were about as close as you can be on all levels, which made things doubly weird when we all quit playing together and working together. Not only did I lose my way of making money, I also lost all my friends. Without that I was adrift.

ROB TYNER The music was more powerful than any of the politics. The music has outlived the band and the politics of the day. Without the MC5's influence, things would be different. I'm proud to be able to say that. I don't think that's taking on too much to say that.

WAYNE KRAMER What's the legacy of the MC5? I think it's the big bang—the MC5 was the spark that ignited a sense of responsibility and a political consciousness in contemporary artists. Now musicians can take a stand on political issues, and on issues that are bigger than their careers, and somehow be connected to their brothers and their fellow man. They can have an influence and make things better.

BECKY TYNER Rob believed in the Great Spirit—the creator of all things. And he really embraced and took that in his heart. I think he did live a good spiritual life, aware of so many things beyond that day-to-day scamming for money or whatever. What was the reason he thought we were here? To see if we could fly. I think the MC5 could've done a lot more. And I go back to the kinds of music that Rob wrote after MC5. What if they were still together in the time after that? Not today, but in the immediate years afterwards—who knows what they could've done. But they lost their flame. They lost their soul. But thinking about them, I just sit back from a place of awe.

EPILOGUE

When the MC5 came to their bittersweet conclusion at the Grande Ballroom, the band members were still in their early twenties. Even their mentor and sage, John Sinclair, was only thirty-one. So, what happened to the group and their associates after their time together came to an end? Below is a brief synopsis of their post-band exploits, and in many cases, tragic demise.

WAYNE KRAMER

After the band split, Wayne Kramer became, by his own admission, a "small-time Detroit criminal." In 1975, he was convicted of selling drugs to undercover federal agents and sentenced to four years in federal prison, of which he served two. During his two years behind bars, he developed a friendship with fellow prisoner Red Rodney, who had played bebop trumpet with jazz legend Charlie Parker in the early '50s. Together, they performed in a prison band and studied music via a correspondence course from the Berklee College of Music.

Following his release Wayne relocated to Manhattan, where he co-founded Gang War with Johnny Thunders of the New York Dolls. In the '80s, he returned to Detroit and joined Don and David Was in the experimental funk collective Was (Not Was), until he moved to Key West, Florida, and began making a living doing commercial carpentry.

Kramer returned to music in 1994 and moved to Los Angeles, where he signed to Epitaph Records and recorded three eclectic albums, *The Hard Stuff* (1995), *Dangerous Madness* (1996), and *Citizen Wayne* (1997). He reunited with John Sinclair in 1998 and co-wrote and co-produced *Full Circle* for Sinclair and his band, Blues Scholars. In 2001, Kramer applied for and received a small-business loan from the federal government and started his own label, Muscle Tone Records, along with his second wife, Margaret Saadi.

From 2004 onward, Wayne performed with his former MC5 cohorts Michael Davis and Dennis Thompson as DKT/MC5. He also composed film scores and wrote his autobiography, *The Hard Stuff: Dope, Crime, the MC5, and My Life of Impossibilities*.

In 2009, Kramer along with Billy Bragg and his wife, Margaret, founded the nonprofit Jail Guitar Doors USA inspired after the Clash song that references the guitarist's drug-related incarceration. Together, they facilitated the distribution of guitars to more than 250 American correctional facilities across the United States, as well as initiating songwriting workshops within the prison system.

In the spring of 2018, Kramer unveiled plans for a MC50 Tour to celebrate the fiftieth anniversary of *Kick Out the Jams*. Subsequently, in 2023, he achieved a significant milestone by spearheading the recording of the first MC5 album in over five decades. Titled *Heavy Liftin'*, and produced by Bob Ezrin, it featured collaborations with musicians such as Slash, Tom Morello, William DuVall, Vernon Reid, and Brad Brooks. Notably, original drummer Dennis Thompson performed on two tracks.

Tragically, Kramer did not live to witness the release of the album, nor the tour he planned. On February 2, 2024, he passed away after battling pancreatic cancer.

FRED "SONIC" SMITH

After the MC5, Smith assembled Ascension with Dennis Thompson, Michael Davis, and John Hefti. The project was short-lived, and Smith left to form the Sonic Rendezvous Band with Detroit vocalist Scott Morgan, former Stooges drummer Scott Asheton, and Up bassist Gary Rasmussen. They released one single, "City Slang," now considered a garage-rock classic.

Smith met singer/poet Patti Smith in 1977 at a press event for the release of her now-classic debut album, *Horses*. At the time he was married to Sigrid Dobat, whom he left for Smith. Fred and Patti married three years later and had two children. After a period of semiretirement, they collaborated on Patti's 1988 album *Dream of Life*. The couple had been working together on several other projects when Fred suffered a heart attack and died on November 4, 1994.

ROB TYNER

Rob Tyner became a writer and journalist, working as a contributing editor for Detroit's *CREEM* magazine and a frequent contributor to *Phonograph Record* magazine. In 1977 the British music magazine *New Musical Express* (*NME*) commissioned Tyner to report on the new English punk scene. The story appeared complete with photos of Tyner with members of Dr. Feelgood, the Clash, and the Sex Pistols.

Tyner's U.K. trip also resulted in the first major-label release by any of the former MC5: a one-off single with Tyner fronting Eddie and the Hot Rods: "Till the Night Is Gone (Let's Rock)" b/w "Flipside Rock" on Island Records. Back in Detroit, he headed an outfit he called MC5 until his former bandmates complained. He changed the name to the Robin Tyner Band, which was followed by Rob Tyner & the National Rock Group.

The singer also helped start the Community Concert Series at St. Andrews in Detroit, an Episcopalian church on Wayne State University's campus. In 1985, he recorded and donated a song for a benefit LP for Vietnam veterans, then recorded a solo album, *Blood Brothers*, with the Weapons in 1990. He was planning a series of live dates with Blackfoot drummer Jackson Spires when he died suddenly of a heart attack on September 17, 1991.

MICHAEL DAVIS

Bassist Michael Davis joined his former MC5 bandmates Fred Smith and Dennis Thompson as vocalist in the short-lived band Ascension. His musical career was cut short in January 1975 after several drug arrests resulted in his being sent to the same federal prison in Lexington, Kentucky, where Kramer was incarcerated. While doing time, Davis was commissioned to do a series of paintings for the facility. His work ethic and a sympathetic judge led to his early release.

In 1977 he returned to Ann Arbor and was invited to join Destroy All Monsters, an arty, experimental band featuring his friend and former Stooges guitarist Ron Asheton. He left the band in 1984 to work as a silk screener, then moved to Tucson, Arizona, where he worked in an automobile body repair shop. In the early 2000s he joined Rich Hopkins & Luminarios, who released three gritty "desert rock" albums for Germany's Blue Rose label, and from 2004 onward, Davis performed with Wayne Kramer and Dennis Thompson as DKT/MC5. He succumbed to liver failure on February 17, 2012. His wife, Angela, released his autobiography *I Brought Down the MC5* six years later.

DENNIS THOMPSON

Not long after the MC5 came to an end, Dennis Thompson formed Ascension with Fred Smith. Subsequent bands included Sirius Trixon and the Motor City Bad Boys, and Dodge Main. In 1975 he played percussion in the Los Angeles–based New Order with Ron Asheton (not to be confused with the U.K.-based New Order). In 1981 he and Asheton joined New Race, which featured three former members of the Australia-based punk band Radio Birdman. In 2003, Thompson joined Kramer and Davis in an MC5 revival band that featured a rotating cast of lead singers. Thompson died on May 8, 2024, after a series of medical issues. He was seventy-five.

JOHN SINCLAIR

John Sinclair was relieved of his managerial duties with the MC5 on July 25, 1969, when he began serving a ten-year sentence for marijuana possession. During his incarceration, Sinclair wrote *Guitar Army*, a memoir/history of his time managing the MC5. After he was granted an early release from prison, he co-produced the Ann Arbor Blues and Jazz Festival in 1972, and in 1974 he formed Rainbow Productions with his wife, Leni Sinclair, which specialized in advertising, public relations, and club management.

Sinclair briefly served as the editor in chief of the *Detroit Sun* newspaper. After it folded in 1976, he was named state coordinator of the National Organization for the Reform of Marijuana Legislation (NORML). In 1991, he moved to New Orleans, where he hosted a weekly blues show on Public Radio WWOZ-FM and began performing spoken-word gigs backed by a group of musicians he called the Blues Scholars. In 1995, he launched a small record label called Total Energy and released a solo album, *Full Moon Night*, along with vintage recordings by the MC5, the Rationals, and Mitch Ryder. On December 1, 2019, Sinclair became the first person in Michigan to legally purchase recreational cannabis. He died of heart failure at the Detroit Receiving Hospital on April 2, 2024, at the age of eighty-two.

DANNY FIELDS

After leaving Atlantic Records, Fields served as a columnist for the *Soho Weekly News* and became a music manager, looking after Iggy Pop's career. In 1975 he discovered the Ramones at CBGB and helped them get signed by Sire Records; he also co-managed the band with Linda Stein for five years. During this period, the Ramones recorded their classic punk trilogy, *Ramones*, *Leave Home*, and *Rocket to Russia*. Their 1980 record, *End of the Century*, included the song "Danny Says," which was about Fields.

After leaving the front lines of the record industry, Fields co-wrote *Dream On*, a biography of music scenester and former wife of Aerosmith lead singer Steven Tyler, Cyrinda Foxe. He followed that with *Linda McCartney: A Portrait*, which was turned into a television miniseries by

CBS. He was the subject of a 2015 documentary entitled *Danny Says*; and *My Ramones*, his book of photographs of the band, was published in 2016.

RON ASHETON

After releasing two albums with the Stooges—1969's *Stooges* and 1970's *Fun House*—guitarist Ron Asheton left the band. He rejoined the Stooges a year later, playing bass on 1973's *Raw Power*, which was produced by David Bowie. The band imploded again a year later.

Asheton was unabashed in his admiration for the MC5 and played with Michael Davis and Dennis Thompson in several post-Stooges bands (as previously noted). In 2003, Iggy Pop invited Ron and his brother, Scott, to record four songs for 2003's *Skull Ring* album, then reunited the Stooges officially, touring extensively with ex-Minuteman Mike Watt on bass from 2003 until 2008. Together, they recorded *The Weirdness* in 2007. Ron suffered a fatal heart attack at his Ann Arbor home on January 6, 2009.

JON LANDAU

Jon Landau rose to prominence in the 1960s as a writer and critic for counterculture magazines like *Rolling Stone* and *Crawdaddy*. After producing *Back in the USA* for the MC5, he returned to *Rolling Stone* as the magazine's album-review editor.

In 1974, after seeing the performance of a little-known rocker at the Harvard Square Theater in Boston, Landau wrote: "I saw rock and roll's future, and its name is Bruce Springsteen." He struck up a friendship with Springsteen, who asked him to co-produce his third record, *Born to Run*, which became his breakout success. Jackson Browne subsequently asked Landau to produce his next album, the iconic *The Pretender*.

Eventually, Landau became Springsteen's manager and producer, and he subsequently made management deals with Livingston Taylor, Jackson Browne, Train, Shania Twain, Alejandro Escovedo, and Natalie Merchant.

RUSS GIBB

Schoolteacher, DJ, Grande Ballroom impresario, and cultural visionary Russ Gibb is perhaps best remembered these days as the primary instigator of the "Paul is dead" hoax. Gibb fueled rumors of McCartney's death with a special two-hour program on the subject, *The Beatle Plot*, which aired on Detroit's WKNR radio station on October 19, 1969. The show brought him worldwide notoriety.

In 1970, Gibb traveled to England and spent some time with Rolling Stones singer Mick Jagger. He was impressed with Jagger's home video system, which led to his interest in cable TV. Gibb bought several key Michigan cable licenses in the late '70s, and when he sold them in the '80s he made millions. He passed away on April 30, 2019, at the age of eighty-seven.

GARY GRIMSHAW

Gary Grimshaw was the main poster artist and the first light-show operator for the Grande Ballroom in Detroit, and one of the few poster artists to gain notoriety and national status outside San Francisco. In 1972, Grimshaw became the art director for the Ann Arbor Blues and Jazz Festival, as well as *CREEM* magazine's associate art director from 1976 to 1984. In 1987, Iggy Pop hired Grimshaw to create the cover for his *Instinct* album on A&M Records, and the latter continued to create poster art for contemporary musicians like Beck and the White Stripes. In 1999, the *Detroit Free Press* honored Grimshaw by placing him on their list of Michigan's 100 greatest artists and entertainers of the twentieth century. In 2012, he and MC5 photographer Leni Sinclair published *Detroit Rocks! A Pictorial History of Motor City Rock and Roll, 1965 to 1975*. After a series of strokes, he died January 13, 2014, at the age of sixty-seven.

BECKY TYNER

The first of the commune-living residents to enter the "straight" world, Rob Tyner's wife, Becky, became an analyst for a Detroit bank. She remained there for the next thirty-two years, rising through the ranks of upper management. She and Rob moved from Detroit to the suburbs, where they raised their three children: Robin, Amy, and Elizabeth Leslie, who was named after music writer Lester Bangs, whose given name was also Leslie. She founded a vegetarian kitchen catering company called Queen of Cups and then returned to Detroit and is currently a community activist living in the Motor City's historic Woodbridge neighborhood.

LENI SINCLAIR

Photographer, activist, and wife of John Sinclair, Leni Sinclair documented all the important events of the late-'60s counterculture explosion with her camera (several of her shots are featured in this book). She was a moving force in the Free John benefit in Ann Arbor on December 10, 1971, going to New York to meet with John Lennon and Yoko Ono to convince them to appear on the bill. Five years after John Sinclair's release from prison, the couple divorced. They remained close, and when John moved to New Orleans, Leni and her daughter and granddaughter moved there for several years. In 1998, Sinclair held the first retrospective of her work at the Museum Boijmans Van Beuningen in Rotterdam. Leni wrote two books on her own: *The Detroit Jazz Who's Who* and *Participant Observer*, as well as *Detroit Rocks! A Pictorial History of Motor City Rock and Roll, 1965 to 1975* with artist Gary Grimshaw.

In 2013, Sinclair received a grant from the John S. and James L. Knight Foundation to a create a public archive of her photos of the Detroit music scene. In January 2016, she was recognized for her work by the Kresge Foundation as that year's Kresge Eminent Artist. In 2021, the Museum of Contemporary Art Detroit dedicated a show to her photography and published a 408-page monograph titled *Motor City Underground: Leni Sinclair Photographs, 1963–1978*, edited by Lorraine Wild and Destroy All Monsters founder Cary Loren.

CHRIS HOVNANIAN

After four years together, Chris Hovnanian and Wayne Kramer went their separate ways in 1970. Hovnanian, an actor, attended Wayne State University's theater program, then dropped out to continue her studies in New York. Currently, she lives in Long Island, New York, with her two children, enjoying a considerably quieter lifestyle than when she was known as "Li'l Chick."

BOB RUDNICK

Underground DJ, writer, poet, and cultural lightning rod Bob Rudnick (known as "Righteous Bob Rudnick") and his DJ cohort, Dennis Frawley, were responsible for helping spread the word about the MC5 in New York City, with weekly references in their "East Village Other" column, and frequent spins of the band's first single, "Looking at You," on their *Kokaine Karma* show on WFMU. He retired from radio in 1975 and moved back to Detroit in 1987. He died of pancreatic cancer in July 1995.

PUN PLAMONDON

During the 1970s Plamondon found work driving equipment trucks for rock bands, including KISS and Foreigner, and for Bob Seger. During this period Plamondon was drinking heavily. After several lost years, Pun, a Native American, changed his life by rediscovering his roots and becoming a respected Odawa tribal elder. In the early 1980s, he became involved with the Circle Pines Center in Delton, Michigan, a nonprofit education and recreation center, where he organized summer-camp programs for youth. Plamondon published a memoir in 2004, *Lost from the Ottawa: The Story of the Journey Back*. He died on March 5, 2023, at age seventy-seven, in Barry County, Michigan.

ACKNOWLEDGMENTS

In completing this book, the authors are indebted to the individuals who bore witness to the remarkable times surrounding the MC5 and generously shared their memories, imbued with audacity and drama, which almost defy belief.

Foremost, we express our profound gratitude to the late Ben Edmonds, coauthor of *MC5: An Oral Biography of Rock's Most Revolutionary Band*. The book would've been inconceivable without his extensive notes and interviews. Ben fearlessly posed the tough questions, leaving no stone unturned in his quest to understand why a band brimming with so much talent and unyielding determination ultimately fell short of its potential.

Our heartfelt appreciation extends to Mary Cobra, partner of Edmonds and exceptional guitarist with the legendary Detroit Cobras, for granting us access to these invaluable documents. Mary's dedication knew no bounds as she meticulously scanned Ben's handwritten transcripts to over 150 interviews, ensuring we had full access to every piece of paper and memento in his remarkable collection.

Becky Tyner, the wise and delightfully witty wife of the late MC5 singer Robin Tyner, played an invaluable role in filling in many gaps and offering guidance when we encountered obstacles in our research. Beyond that, she provided essential insight into the incendiary times and generously shared personal letters from her husband, Rob.

Acknowledgments

The late Brother Wayne Kramer, along with his wife, Margaret Saadi Kramer, paved the way for this project with their sharp commentary and generosity. Their contributions shed light on why the legacy of the MC5 continues to resonate deeply decades later.

We also pay tribute to the memory of the band members Rob Tyner, Fred Smith, Michael Davis, Dennis Thompson, and their indomitable leader, John Sinclair, who have left an indelible mark on rock-'n'-roll history.

Integral to the narrative are the supporting figures who played pivotal roles in shaping the band's journey. We express our appreciation to the band's always-captivating A&R person, Danny Fields, and the insightful producer of *Back in the USA*, Jon Landau, whose contributions enriched the band's legacy.

We also extend our gratitude to others who have departed yet whose influence continues to resonate. Among them, we acknowledge Stooges guitarist Ron Asheton, promoter Russ Gibb, poster artist Gary Grimshaw, writer and media personality Bob Rudnick, and photographer Emil Bacilla.

We also express our thanks to the artists, photographers, curators, and partners who gave us permission to use their work, enriching our understanding of the band and the era. Special mention to Leni Sinclair, Charles Auringer, Laura Grimshaw, Sari Bacilla Flowers, and Angela Davis.

Lastly, our appreciation goes to the City of Detroit, the backdrop against which this saga unfolded, for its enduring significance in shaping the MC5's story.

INDEX

Adderley, Cannonball, 13
Alexander, Dave, 155
Allman Brothers, 208
Alpert, Richard, 65
Amboy Dukes, 100
"American Revolution '69" (*Rolling Stone* issue), 179
Anderson, Ian, 184–185
Andrews, Pete, 48, 248
Andrews, Punch, 3, 100
"Angel Baby" (song), 3
angel dust, 230
Ann Arbor Sun (newspaper), 142
Anthony, Dee, 230–233, 239–240
anti-Vietnam War movement, 161
Apple, 122
Are You Experienced (album), 79
Arndt, Magdalene "Leni," 37–38
Artists' Workshop Press, 38
Ascension, 260, 262
Asheton, Ron, 83, 121, 262, 264
  on commune, 190
  on Davis, Michael, 208
  on Hamburg house, 212
  on Landau, 210–212
  playing with MC5, 209
  on recording *Kick Out the Jams*, 133–134
  on White Panthers, 155
Asheton, Scott, 49
  later career, 264
  Stooges formation and, 155

Atlantic Records, 12, 187–190, 195, 206
  High Time production and, 242
  London press party and, 238–239
  MC5 dropped by, 236, 244
"Attica State" (song), 224
avant-rock, 25, 33

Bach, Frank, 41, 67
Bacilla, Emil, 47, 183
Back in the USA (album), xiv, 88, 174, 201, 232, 241–242
  recording of, 88, 188–189, 203–207, 210–211, 214–217
  release of, 235
  reviews of, 235–236
Baker, Ginger, 77, 95
Bangs, Lester, 162, 168, 179–180, 195, 203, 229
Barsalona, Frank, 231
Battle of the Bands, x
Beacon Street Union, 78, 81–82
the Beatles, 23, 122
beatniks, 4, 37, 40–41, 100
Belle Isle Love-In, 61–64
Bennett, Tony, 230–231
Berkeley, 181–182
Berkeley Barb (newspaper), 163, 183
Berkeley Poetry Conference, 38, 43
Berry, Chuck, 196, 237, 252, 255
Big Brother & the Holding Company, 80–81

Bikel, Theodore, 163, 173
Billboard charts, 179, 235
Black Lives Matter, 142
Black Mask, 161
Black Panther Party, xi, 142–143, 146–147, 161, 181, 210
"Black People" (Jones, L.), 161
"Black to Comm" (song), 25, 29, 81, 90, 97
   creation of, 42–43
   Kick Out the Jams recording and, 137
Blondie, xii
Blood, Sweat & Tears, 82
Blue Cheer, 98, 146
"Borderline" (song), 87–88, 123
Boston Tea Party, 161, 164
Botnick, Bruce, 132, 174
Bounty Hunters, 3–5, 31
Bragg, Billy, 260
British Invasion, 89
Brown, H. Rap, 218
Brown, James, 237
Browne, Jackson, xiv
Brownsville Station, 246
Bruce, Jack, 78
Buckley, Tim, 69–70
Burnish, Bruce, 21
Burroughs, William, 38, 238
Burrows, Pat, 3, 15–16, 32
the Byrds, 124

"Call Me Animal" (song), 237
"Can I Get a Witness" (song), 204
cannabis legalization, ix
Carson, David A., 62
Cass Corridor area, 35
Change (magazine), 38
Chicago Police Department, 114, 116–118
Chosen Few, 48–49
Church of Zenta, 145, 153–154
CIA office bombing, 225–226
CKLW radio station, 6
Clapton, Eric, 76–78, 80
Cleaver, Eldridge, 146

Cocker, Joe, 230–231
Cohen, Kip, 166
Collins, Carter, 69–71
Collins, Judy, 163
Coltrane, John, 13–14, 78
Cooper, Alice, 101, 109
Craig, Roger, 98
Crawford, Jesse, 107, 210
   glue sniffing and, 156
   as hype man, 126, 145
   White Panthers and, 148–149, 153–155, 182
   Zenta and, 145, 153
Cream, x, 76–78, 95, 97, 123, 146
Crystal Bar, 30–31, 34–35

Daley, Richard, 113–114
Dallas, Danny, 88
D'Ambrosio, Antonio, xiii
the Damned, xiii
"Dance to the Music" (song), 89
Datebook (magazine), 124
Dave Clark Five, 21–22
Davis, Michael, ix, 6, 203
   Asheton, R., on, 208
   on Atlantic record deal, 188
   Back in the USA recording and, 204–205, 210
   bass playing, 214
   drug dealing by, 250
   on end of MC5, 257
   heroin and, 245–246
   High Time and, 243
   joining MC5, 24–29
   after MC5, 262
Davis, Miles, 146
Davis, Rennie, 248
DAW. *See* Detroit Artists' Workshop
death system, 36
Dellinger, David, 248
Democratic National Convention of 1968, xi, 113–117, 120
Derminer, Ricky, 4
Destroy All Monsters, 83, 195, 262

Index

Detroit, 1–2
    competitiveness of music scene in, 21
    Lincoln Park border with, 5
Detroit Artists' Workshop (DAW), 37–40, 46, 60–61, 75
Detroit Free Press (newspaper), 64
Detroit Police Department, 62
    Grande Ballroom and, 54
    Sinclair, J., and, 37
    Special Investigative Bureau, 59
the Dictators, xii
Dixon, Dave, 88–89
Dixon, Larry, 12
DKT/MC5, 260
Dobat, Sigrid, 261
Donahue, Tom, 46
Donovan, 61
the Doors, 124–125, 163, 177
double-tracking, 211
Downbeat (magazine), 38
Dunbar, Jim, 43–44
Dylan, Bob, 79, 245

East Village Other (newspaper), 123–124
Edmonds, Ben, xi–xii
Ehrmann, Eric, 170–171, 179
"Eight Miles High" (song), 124
E. J. Korvette (department store), 172
Elektra Records, xi, 121, 123–125, 128
    album censoring incident, 178–179
    criticism of, 172
    Fields and management of, 177–178
    Fillmore East show and, 160–162, 165
    Hudson's and, 163, 173, 177
    MC5 contract cancelled by, 163, 188
Emerson, Lake & Palmer, 187, 208
Ertegun, Ahmet, 189, 239–240

Family Dog, 46
Farren, Mick, 238–239
FBI, ix, 225
feedback, 29
Festival of Life, 113–121
Festival of People, 38

Fields, Danny, 111, 121, 123–124, 195, 213, 263
    Atlantic Records and, 188
    Elektra management and, 177–178
    on MC5 and Atlantic, 208
    on MC5 contract cancellation, 163
    MC5 drifting from, 207
    MC5 signing to Elektra and, 127–130
    on Sinclair, J., politics, 150
Fifth Estate (newspaper), 39, 41, 46–47, 98–99, 164
Fillmore East, 160–162, 165–166, 169–170
"Fingertips" (song), 9
Finnish Kaleva Hall, 181–182
First Amendment, 177
Flack, Roberta, 237
"Fly Translove Airlines" (song), 61
Forrest, Jack, 225–226
Fourth Amendment, 225
Frantic Ernie, 12
Frawley, Dennis, 123–124, 178, 181
free speech, 176
the Fugs, 89, 113, 115

Gang War, 259
Gardner, Brother Dave, 154
Garrison, Jimmy, 14
Gasper, Bob, 3, 16, 29–30, 33
Gavin Report, 139
Gibb, Russ, 3, 82, 96, 196, 264–265
    Cream and, 78
    Guerrilla Love Fair and, 63
    meeting Sinclair, J., 45
    Sinclair, J., relationship with, 98–99
Ginsberg, Allen, 38, 100, 112, 119, 248
Glantz, Gabe, 44, 96
"Gloria" (song), 55–56
Goodwin, Jerry, 56
Graham, Bill, 44, 160–161, 165–168, 170
Grande Ballroom, x–xi, 11, 40, 42, 44–45, 176
    acoustics of, 49–50, 89
    Cream at, 76–77, 95
    drugs in, 54–55

Grande Ballroom (*continued*)
   ghost in, 53–54
   Grateful Dead at, 75
   Guerrilla Love Fair and, 63
   Holland booking of, 89–90
   lights and decorations, 47–48
   MC5 final performance at, 236, 256, 259
   opening night, 46
   stage in, 51
   Stooges at, 83
   12th Street Riot and, 70–71
Grand Funk Railroad, 196
Grateful Dead, 75
Grimshaw, Gary, 41, 47, 60–61, 237, 265
Guerrilla Love Fair, 60, 63
Guitar Army (Sinclair, J.), 60, 227–228, 263
Gurley, James, 80

hambone, 7
Harnadek, Steve, "the Hawk," 96–97, 104, 141
Harper's (magazine), 115, 119
Harris, Larry, 178
Haslam, Geoffrey, 242
Have a Marijuana (album), 124
Hayden, Tom, 112, 181
Heider, Wally, 132
Helms, Chet, 46
Hendrix, Jimi, 79
Herman, Woody, 8
heroin, 245–246, 257
High Time (album), 253
   recording of, 242–243
   release of, 236
Hill House commune, 91, 94–95, 127, 129, 191–193
   MC5 moving out of, 188
Hoffman, Abbie, 112–114, 116–117, 161, 247–248
Holland, Jeep, 76, 89–90
Holzman, Jac, 126, 139, 165, 175, 185
   "Kick Out the Jams" single release and, 173–174
   MC5 signing and, 128–129
   recording *Kick Out the Jams* and, 132–133, 135, 137–138
Hooker, John Lee, 76
Hoover, J. Edgar, ix
hot-rod culture, 11–12
Hovnanian, Chris, 26, 266–267
   Back in the USA recording and, 216
   on cars, 241
   clothes made by, 106–107
   on commune, 193
   on Hamburg house, 209–210
Hudson's, 163, 172–173, 177
"Human Being Lawnmower" (song), 202–204, 206, 233, 237

"I Can Only Give You Everything" (song), 55
Iggy Pop, 82–83, 220, 263–264
   Elektra and, 121, 127–128
   overdose, 254
   Tyner, B., making clothes for, 108
   White Panthers and, 155
I Need More (Iggy Pop), 220
"I Want You Right Now" (song), 103

Jackson, Al, 204
Jagger, Mick, 239, 265
Jail Guitar Doors USA, 260
James, Brian, xiii
jazz, 4–6, 12–13
   "Kick Out the Jams" name origin and, 175–176
   Sinclair, J., and, 39–41
Jefferson Airplane, 95
Jethro Tull, 184–185, 231
Jimi Hendrix Experience, 121
John Birch Society, 92
"John Sinclair" (song), 224
John Sinclair Freedom Rally, 248–249
Johnson, Lyndon B., 62
Jones, Brian, 80
Jones, Elvin, 14
Jones, LeRoi, 100, 161
Joplin, Janis, x, 76, 80–81, 121, 150, 185

Kalitta, Conrad "Connie," 3
Kennedy, John F., 150
Kick Out the Jams (album), 50, 122, 187, 194
   backlash against, 162–163, 172
   Bangs review of, 162, 168, 179–180, 195, 203, 229
   recording, 131–138
   release of, 138–140, 162
"Kick Out the Jams" (song), xiii, 31, 102
   origin of name, 175–176
   radio version, 138, 160, 162
   single release, 165, 173–175
Kilmister, Lemmy, xiii
King, Martin Luther, Jr., 91, 114
K-Mart, 172
Koda, Cub, 246
Kokaine Karma (radio show), 123
Kovachovich, John, 123
Kramer, Wayne, ix, x, xiii
   Back in the USA recording and, 203–206, 210, 216
   on Black music, 6
   on cars, 241
   choosing name, 16
   on end of MC5, 257
   on heroin, 245–246
   after MC5, 259–260
   on MC5 legacy, 258
   meeting Smith, F., 2–3
   meeting Tyner, R., 4, 14
   on reputation with bookers, 244
Krassner, Paul, 113

Landau, Jon, xiv, 85, 104, 229, 264
   album planning by, 188–189, 201–203
   Anthony and, 230–232
   Asheton, R., on, 210–212
   Back in the USA recording and, 88, 174, 203–207, 213–217, 235
   hiring, 194–195, 199
   Kramer and, 210
   MC5 management and, 230–231
   Sinclair, J., on, 215

Thompson and, 203–206
   on Tyner, B., 213
Law, Don, 162, 164, 168
Led Zeppelin, 233
LEMAR, 60
Lennon, John, 224, 248–249
Levine, Ron, 104
Levise, Billy, 21
Lincoln Park, 56
   Detroit border with, 5
   MC5 members growing up in, 1–2, 9
the Loft, 101
"Looking at You" (song), 30–31, 87–88, 123
Loving Awareness, 244
LSD, 32, 48, 54–55, 61, 63
   Chicago Democratic Convention and, 114, 116
   recording *Kick Out the Jams* and, 133–134
"The Luck of the Irish" (song), 224

Mailer, Norman, 115, 119
Malcolm X, 150
Maoism, 227
Marcus, Greil, 182–183
marijuana, 37, 54, 129, 223, 230
   Michigan court ruling about, 224, 248
Masonic Auditorium, 79
Maxwell, Bob, 9–10
MC5
   Ann Arbor changes in, 192–193
   Anthony management of, 230–233, 239–240
   Asheton, R., playing with, 209
   Atlantic Records dropping, 236, 244
   Atlantic Records signing, 188–190
   Bangs review of, 179–180
   buying equipment, 21
   choosing name, 15–16
   Crawford introductions for, 145
   Detroit influence on, 1–2
   driving to shows, 247
   early supporters of, 104

MC5 (continued)
   Elektra album censoring incident, 178–179
   Elektra cancelling contract with, 163, 188
   Elektra signing, 127–130
   end of, 253–259
   in England, 236, 238–239, 250–252
   factionalism in, 216
   at Festival of Life, 113–115
   Festival of Life performance, 114–121
   Fillmore East show, 160–162, 165–166, 169–170
   finances of, 198–200
   Hamburg house, 188–189, 200–202, 206, 209–210, 212
   heroin and, 245
   influences on, 5–6
   John Sinclair Freedom Rally and, 249
   Landau and management of, 230–231
   landscaping budget, 178
   leadership in, 85
   Led Zeppelin show with, 233
   legacy of, 258
   in Los Angeles, 178
   management of money, 130–131
   Motherfuckers and, 161–162
   moving out of commune, 188
   moving to Ann Arbor, 92–95
   planning second album, 201–202
   power dynamics in, 84–85
   press releases, 123
   propaganda of, 124–125
   reactions to, 52
   recording first album, 131–138
   releasing first album, 138–140
   reputation, 90
   Rock 'n' Roll Revival show, 196–197
   Rock & Roll Hall of Fame induction, xiv
   Sinclair, J., fired by, 219–220
   Sinclair, J., managing, 75–76
   Sinclair, J., meeting, 38–39, 41–42
   Sinclair, J., mentorship of, 74
   stage costumes, 105–109
   West Coast shows, 180–182, 184–186
   White Panthers rift with, 227–228
   White Panthers supported by, 197–198, 227
   Yippies and, 113
McCartney, Paul, 122
McDonald, Country Joe, 120, 150
methadone, 254
Metzner, Ralph, 65
Miller, Dave, 77
Miller, Jimmy, 232
Miller, Larry, 46
Minor Key (club), 13
Mitch Ryder & the Detroit Wheels, 21
Moby Grape, 75
Moore, Charles, 243
Moorhouse, Steve, 250–251
Morgan, Scott, 86
Morrison, Jim, 163, 182
Morrison, Van, 55
Motherfuckers, 161–162, 164–170
Mother's, 48
"Motor City's Burning" (song), 165
Motörhead, xiii
Motown, 10, 20, 76
Mouse, Stanley, 11
Muhammad, Elijah, 150
Muscle Tone Records, 260
"My Favorite Things" (song), 13

Naked Lunch (Burroughs), 38
National Guard, 67–68, 114
Newman, David, 104, 199, 213
Newton, Huey P., 142
New York Times (newspaper), 159
Nugent, Ted, 100–101

Oakland County Sheriff, 102
Ochs, Phil, 248
"One of the Guys" (song), 56
Ono, Yoko, 224, 248–249
O'Rahilly, Ronan, 236, 244, 249–253, 255
"Ourselves" (course), 251

Peel, David, 124, 248
penny caps, 245
Philips Records, 250
Phun City festival, 236, 238–239, 244
Pink Pussycat Club, 10, 44
Plamondon, Pun, 66, 152, 210
    CIA office bombing and, 225–226
    later career, 267
    light show and, 47
    White Panthers and, 142, 144–146, 149
police reform, ix
Premiere Talent, 90
Procol Harum, 108
Public Enemy, 207

Quaaludes, 180, 246–247, 250–251
Quatro, Mike, 182

Radio Caroline, 236, 244
Rage Against the Machine, xiii
Rainbow People's Party, 249
"Ramblin' Gamblin' Man" (song), 202
the Ramones, xii, 167, 263
the Rationals, 89–90, 100
redlining laws, 5
Richards, Keith, 80
Robinson, Smokey, 20
rocket reducer, 156
Rock 'n' Roll Revival show, 196–197
Rock & Roll Hall of Fame, xiv
Rodney, Red, 259
Rolling Stone (magazine), 159, 173, 188
    Back in the USA review in, 235–236
    Ehrmann story in, 170–171, 179
    Kick Out the Jams review in, 162, 168, 179–180, 195, 203
    as rock culture arbiter, 180
Rolling Stones, 19, 23, 204
Romney, George, 62
Rosie and the Originals, 3
Rowe, Bill, 241
Rubin, Jerry, 112–114, 116–117, 248
Rudd, Roswell, 248

Rudnick, Bob, 123–124, 199, 219, 267
Ryder, Mitch, 101, 246

Saadi, Margaret, 260
Sanders, Ed, 113, 115–116
San Francisco, 43, 46, 48, 180, 182–183
Santana, Carlos, 206
the Satellites, 20
"Satisfaction" (song), 55
Saugatuck Pop Festival, 100
Saunders, Ed, 38
Scully, Rock, 75
SDS. *See* Students for a Democratic Society
Seale, Bobby, 248
the Seeds, 162, 179
Seeger, Pete, 248
Seger, Bob, 53, 86, 100–101, 202, 224
segregation, 5
Shadows of Knight, 55
"Shakin' Street" (song), xiii, 242
Shepp, Archie, 224, 248
Silver, Jimmy, 128
Simon, Audrey, 93
Simul-Sync, 211
Sinclair, David, 249
Sinclair, John, ix–xi, 17, 36–39, 73, 257
    arrests of, 38, 60–61, 102–103, 147–148, 223
    Atlantic Records and, 188–190
    on *Back in the USA*, 237
    becoming MC5 manager, 75–76
    CIA office bombing and, 225–226
    on communes, 61
    Detroit Police Department and, 59–60
    Gibb relationship with, 98–99
    house rules of, 193
    imprisonment of, 207–208, 224–226, 229, 247
    Kramer reuniting with, 260
    on Landau, 215
    later career, 266
    Lennon and Ono benefit concert for, 224

Sinclair, John *(continued)*
  after MC5, 262–263
  MC5 drifting from, 207, 227
  on MC5 finances, 198–200
  MC5 firing, 219–220
  MC5 mentored by, 74
  MC5 signing to Elektra and, 127–130
  moving to Ann Arbor, 91, 94–95
  radicalization of, 146–148
  record production by, 88
  release from prison, 248
  second album planning by, 194–195
  Stooges and, 155–156
  Thompson and, 217–219
  trials, 207–208, 223
  White Panther Party launch and, 141–147
  YIP and, 112–113, 115, 121
Sinclair, Leni, 60–61, 93, 125, 127
  on commune, 191
  on freedom rally, 249
  later career, 266
  on MC5 finances, 199
  on MC5 split with Sinclair, J., 219
  White Panther Party and, 142
"Sisters, O Sisters" (song), 224
"Skunk" (song), 243
Slick, Grace, 95
Sly and the Family Stone, 89
Smith, Fred, "Sonic," ix, xiii
  Back in the USA recording and, 205, 215–216
  after MC5, 260–261
  meeting Kramer, 2–3
  Rock 'n' Roll Revival show costume, 196–197
  songwriting by, 241–242
  Tyner, R., fight with, 14–15
Smith, Jackson, xiii
Smith, Patti, xii, 261
Solanas, Valerie, 161
Sommers, Robin, 47
Sonic Rendezvous Band, 261

Soundgarden, xiii
Special Investigative Bureau, 59
Springsteen, Bruce, xiii, xiv, 215, 264
Stanislavski acting method, 251
"Starship" (song), 50, 120
Staudenmaier, Eugene, 91–93
Stevens, Gary, 10–11
the Stooges, 53, 82–83, 94, 97, 209, 264
  drug use, 156
  Elektra signing, 121, 127–130
  Fields and, 208
  White Panthers and, 155
Straight Theatre (Chicago), 118
Straight Theatre (San Francisco), 180, 183
Strummer, Joe, xiii
Student Non-Violent Coordinating Committee, 23
Students for a Democratic Society (SDS), 112, 142, 152, 218
Summer of Love, 64–65, 124
Sun Ra, 196–197

Taube, Skip, 145–146, 152
Taylor, Cecil, 41, 100
"Teenage Lust" (song), 237
teen clubs, 10, 35
television, 193
Thayil, Kim, xiii
Thompson, Dennis, ix, 6
  Back in the USA recording and, 203–206, 213–217
  choosing name, 16
  drug habit, 251
  on end of MC5, 257
  on Hamburg house, 209
  hepatitis case, 254
  on heroin, 245–246
  on *High Time*, 243–244
  joining MC5, 31–34
  Landau and, 203–206
  after MC5, 262
  quitting MC5, 253–254
  Sinclair, J., and, 217–219

"Thunder Express" (song), 241
Thunders, Johnny, 259
TLE. *See* Trans-Love Energies Unlimited
"Tonight" (song), 242
Trans-Love Energies Unlimited (TLE), 75, 112. *See also* Hill House commune
   Belle Isle Love-In and, 63–64
   DAW becoming, 61
   MC5 supporting, 73–74
   moving to Ann Arbor, 91
   Plamondon and, 144, 146
   Stooges and, 155
   Zenta and, 145
Twain, Shania, xiv
12th Street Riot, 62, 64–71
Tyner, Becky, 22–25
   Back in the USA recording and, 216–217
   clothes made by, 105–106, 108
   on commune, 191–193
   on end of MC5, 257
   on Landau, 213
   after MC5, 265–266
   on MC5 finances, 200
   on MC5 legacy, 258
Tyner, McCoy, 16
Tyner, Rob, ix, xvii, 1–3, 5
   Back in the USA recording and, 211
   band picking on, 85–86
   choosing name, 16
   hair, 79–80
   on harmonica, 9
   High Time and, 242
   on Lincoln Park, 7
   after MC5, 261
   meeting Kramer, 4, 14
   motivations of, 87
   politics and, 150–151
   quitting MC5, 253
   on screaming, 42–43
   Sinclair, J., and, 41
   on Sinclair, J., memoir, 227–228
   Smith, F., fight with, 14–15

the Up, 116
Up Against the Wall Motherfucker, 161–170

Vanilla Fudge, 81
Velvet Underground, xiv, 126, 161, 187, 208
"Venus Rising" (song), 89
Village Voice (newspaper), 232
Vox Super Beatle amp, 21, 50

WABX radio station, 88, 123
Warhol, Andy, 126, 161
Was (Not Was), 259
Watts, Charlie, 204, 239
Wayne State University, 22–24, 36–37
WBBC radio station, 12
WCHB radio station, 6, 12
WCHD radio station, 13
Weather Underground, 146
"We Gotta Get Out of This Place" (song), 55
Wembley Stadium, 251–252
Wexler, Jerry, 188–189, 195, 206, 210, 236
WFMU radio station, 123–124
White, David, "Panther," 145–146, 149, 153
White, Meg, xiii
White Panther Party, xi, 148–154, 184, 210, 218, 220
   Berkeley and, 181–182
   "Kick Out the Jams" and, 175–176
   launch of, 139, 141–147, 161
   manifesto of, 143
   MC5 distanced from, 191, 225
   MC5 rift with, 227–228
   MC5 supporting, 197–198, 227
   Yippies inspiring, 121
White Stripes, xiii
the Who, 53, 76, 81, 247
Wilson, Wes, 43
WKNR radio station, 6
WNEW radio station, 166

Wonder, Stevie, 9, 224, 248
Woodstock Music and Art Festival, 161, 217, 247
Work (magazine), 38
Wyman, Bill, 214

YIP. *See* Youth International Party
Yippies, 112–113, 115–116, 120, 142
Younkins, Jerry, 145
Youth International Party (YIP), 113, 121
    White Panther Party and, 139